God and Government

Volume 2

God and Government

Issues in Biblical Perspective

Gary DeMar

AMERICAN VISION, INC.

Atlanta, Georgia

First Published 1984
Printed in the United States of America.
04 03 02 01 00 99 98   10 9 8 7 6 5 4

Unless otherwise noted, all Scripture quotations are from the *New American Standard Bible*, © 1960, 1963, 1971, 1972, 1973, 1975, 1977, by the Lockman Foundation and are used by permission.

God and Government: Issues in Biblical Perspective is produced by American Vision, a Christian educational and communications organization. American Vision publishes a monthly magazine, *The Biblical Worldview*. For more information about American Vision and how to obtain a subscription to *The Biblical Worldview* and receive a catalog of materials, write: American Vision, P.O. Box 724088, Atlanta, Georgia 31139 or call 1–800–628–9460.

E-mail: avision1@aol.com
World-Wide Web: www.avision1.com

ISBN (volume 2): 0–915815–13–3
ISBN (3 volume series): 9–915815–15–X

Photo acquisition by Gary DeMar
Art Direction by Diane Hosch
Series design by Erin Sherman

Dedication and Acknowledgments

This second volume of the *God and Government* series is dedicated to Robert M. Metcalf, Jr., whose tireless efforts and dedicated service to the cause of Christ inspired a generation of young Christians to explore the Bible for what it has to say about every area of life. Through the Christian Studies Center in Memphis, Tennessee, he published a significant number of books that have been instrumental in the development of a comprehensive biblical world view. This is especially true in the area of economics. Since this second volume of *God and Government* deals with the economic sphere, it is a fitting tribute to him that much of his work will be carried on through its pages.

No author can claim the credit for the final production of his work, though he must claim all the responsibility for the content and conclusions. I would like to thank all my teachers for their lectures, books, and personal conversations that in some manner have found their way into this volume. My wife, Carol, and my son, David, were very supportive during the year that this book was researched. Many evenings were taken up with long hours of research, writing, and sifting though hundreds of photos, engravings, and prints. As always, the American Vision staff was most helpful, reading over a number of manuscript drafts and making valuable suggestions to the overall project. Archie Jones read the entire manuscript and made innumerable helpful suggestions. In fact, he made so many suggestions for this volume that I had to begin a third, *God and Government: The Restoration of the Republic*. Charlotte Hale did a masterful job in editing the manuscript.

George Whitefield (1714-1770): *It is a great mistake that some run into, to suppose that religion consists only in saying our prayers. I think . . . he only will adorn the Gospel of our Lord Jesus Christ in all things, who is careful to perform all the civil offices of life . . . with a single eye to God's glory. . . . This is the morality I preach.*

Contents

The development of the printing press by Johann Gutenberg in 1438 set the stage for the Reformation of the 16th century. The printing press made Bibles, printed sermons, Bible commentaries, and theological works available to a wider audience. These printed works led to the development of a biblical world view that swept across Europe and settled on the shores of America. *Religious truth is captive in a small number of little manuscripts, which guard the common treasures instead of expanding them. Let us break the seal which binds these holy things; let us give wings to truth that it may fly with the Word, no longer prepared at vast expense, but multitudes everlastingly by a machine which never wearies — to every soul which enters life* (Johann Gutenberg)

Foreword

Goethe, the famous German literatus, once aptly observed that the only subject in all of history worthy of consideration was the struggle between faith and unbelief. That struggle is now entering its climacteric in the United States of America. Christian theism and secularist unbelief are locked in a life and death struggle for the soul of this nation.

Through the rewriting of history and the use of humanist doublespeak, the proponents of disbelief have almost written God out of the history of America and the functioning of its government. This is why the volume by Gary DeMar entitled *God and Government: Issues in Biblical Perspective* is so crucial at this time. Never has there been a greater need for Americans to understand the Biblical and Christian foundations of our nation. Indeed, the statement made by the Supreme Court in 1892 after a careful perusal of all of the founding documents of this country that "This is a religious people, this is a Christian nation" sounds almost alien to most Americans today. So thorough has been the indoctrination that this is supposed to be a secularist nation.

This volume provides a refreshing and welcome clarification of a most basic issue of our time.

D. James Kennedy, PhD.
December, 1983
Fort Lauderdale, Florida

Preface

I charge you, citizens of the United States, afloat on your wild sea of politics, there is another king, one Jesus: The safety of the state can be secured only in the way of humble and whole-souled loyalty to his person and of obedience to his law.

−A. A. Hodge

The problems we face today seem hopelessly complicated and beyond our ability to solve. The Bible, however, tells a different story. Conditions are hopeless when God's people fail to recognize that the solution to our problems do not reside in man. "Stop regarding man, whose breath of life is in his nostrils; for why should he be esteemed?" (Isaiah 2:22). The prophet Isaiah goes on to inform us that there is only one Savior (43:11). Too often Christians limit the effects of the saving work of Jesus Christ. We are willing to turn to Jesus Christ and entrust Him with our eternal destiny but we are often unwilling to submit to His instructions concerning the affairs of this world.

Our unwillingness to bring every thought captive to the obedience of Christ (2 Corinthians 10:5) has left a cultural vacuum that has been filled by those who repudiate the claims of Christ. Christian influence is now limited to Church structures, Christian schools, and para-church organizations. Even these traditionally sacrosanct institutions are under attack by those who want to remove every vestige of Christianity from our nation.

Christians no longer can hesitate between two opinions (1 Kings 18:21). We must take the claims of Christ everywhere. There is not one neutral atom in the universe. The world and all that is in it is under the Lordship of Jesus Christ. Politics will not save us. The gold standard will not save us. A strong defense system will not save us. Only Jesus Christ saves (Acts 4:12). While politics is an area that must come under the Lordship of Jesus Christ, politics is not the solution to our nation's problems. "Righteousness exalts a nation, but sin is a disgrace to any people" (Proverbs 14:34).

Nearly a century ago A. A. Hodge, professor in Systematic Theology at Princeton Seminary (1877-1886), taught that even the state must acknowledge the Lordship of Jesus Christ. The state must govern its affairs according to the commandments set forth in Scripture and the people must cease from a false security, a security often found in wealth, peace, affluence, liberty, and politics.

> In the name of your own interests I plead with you; in the name of your treasure-houses and barns, of your rich farms and cities, of your accumulations in the past and your hopes in the future — I charge you, you never will be secure if you do not faithfully maintain all the crown rights of Jesus, the King of men. In the name of your children and their inheritance of the precious Christian civilization you in turn have received from your sires; in the name of the Christian Church — I charge you, that its sacred franchise, religious liberty, cannot be retained by men who in civil matters deny their allegiance to the King. In the name of your own soul and its salvation; in the name of the adorable Victim of that bloody and agonizing sacrifice whence you draw all your hopes of salvation; by Gethsemane and Calvary — I charge you, citizens of the United States, afloat on your wild sea of politics, THERE IS ANOTHER KING, ONE JESUS: THE SAFETY OF THE STATE CAN BE SECURED ONLY IN THE WAY OF HUMBLE AND WHOLE-SOULED LOYALTY TO HIS PERSON AND OF OBEDIENCE TO HIS LAW (*Evangelical Theology*, p. 247f.).

Jesus Christ is our hope. He came into the world to save us from sin. No political system or ideology can match such a claim. The answers we seek to solve the complex problems of our day are found in the saving work of Jesus Christ and obedience to His commandments. Submission to Him will come either through obedience or judgment. "God highly exalted Him, and bestowed on Him the name which is above every name, that at the name of Jesus every knee should bow, of those who are in heaven, and on earth, and under the earth, and that every tongue should confess that Jesus Christ is Lord, to the glory of God the Father" (Philippians 2:9-11).

Special Features

The *God and Government* textbook series is designed for individual, church, school, seminar, and group Bible study. The question and answer format requires you to pause and to consider the issues under study in the light of biblical revelation before moving to another question. This educational device is necessary for a faithful application of Scripture to all of life. More often than not books are designed for reading, not reflection and meditation. The following special features are included to make the *God and Government* textbook series a true student's handbook:

1. Each lesson begins with an introduction to provide a frame of reference for the questions that follow.

2. The questions are designed to deal with each topic from a number of vantage points. This is why a number of the questions have a substantial list of Bible passages.

3. Scripture passages are included to encourage you to begin your study from a biblical perspective, always asking the question, "What does God's Word say about this issue?" Keep in mind that the interpretation of any one passage must be interpreted in its larger context. Consider the paragraph, chapter, book, author, Testament (Old or New), period of biblical history, audience, circumstances surrounding the writing, and other interpretive factors when formulating your answer.

4. Each lesson ends with a summary designed to focus your attention on each lesson's main theme. I've chosen quotations from respected Christian authors to summarize each chapter.

5. The unique feature of this textbook series is the answers supplied to each of the questions. The answers are comprehensive in most cases. Try to formulate your own answer before turning to the supplied answers.

6. Volume 2 of *God and Government* shows that there are two competing world views — one Christian and the other Humanistic. In addition, these two world views manifest themselves in every area of life. The Christian world view must be revived if America nd the world are to survive. In order to enhance your understanding and appreciation of America's rich Christian history, American Vision has produced *America's Christian History: The Untold Story*. This award-winning audio presentation uses original source documents, sound effects, music, and drama to portray the true history of America's founding. You can order a copy from American Vision, P.O. Box 724088, Atlanta, Georgia 31139.

Our forefathers used the Word of God as the standard for the development of a biblical world view.

How to Use this Textbook

You will gain maximum benefit from this textbook by following these suggestions:

1. Pray for wisdom and insight from the Holy Spirit as you study each lesson. You are dealing with the Word of God when you are searching the Scriptures for answers to the questions, thus, only the Spirit of God can bring out a text's true meaning.

2. Read the introduction to each lesson. They are designed to establish the context for the topic being studied.

3. Answer the questions using the Scripture passages as the foundation for your answer. Do not expect to develop as complete an answer as is found in the workbook. You should, however, be able to summarize an answer in the space provided under each question. An extra lined answer sheet is included in the back of this volume for longer answers. This answer sheet can be copied and passed out to students who are using this textbook as a workbook or supplement to a course in government or history.

4. For group study, each student should answer the questions before the group meets for discussion. This will allow more time for evaluation and informed exchange of ideas. A leader who is familiar with the topics presented in this volume should be chosen for each lesson to guide the discussion.

5. Each lesson is designed for a series of forty-five minute to one-hour sessions to be taught over a period of ten to twelve weeks. The study should not go on for a long period of time. It is best for students to want more than for them to say that they have had enough. The aim is to *introduce* Christians to the topics in such a way that they will want to study on their own.

6. Evaluate current events in the light of the biblical principles under discussion. Daily newspapers, magazines, radio and television news programs, talk shows, and issues that arise during local and national elections are helpful sources of information to help you think through the issues as they arise through your study.

7. Based on your study, construct biblical solutions that can replace humanistic policies and programs. Develop strategies to implement these biblical solutions to correct current problems. This might mean establishing additional study groups so these biblical principles can be shared. As more people learn what the solutions are they will be better equipped to implement them. Pray that we do not hear this lament for our nation: "My people are destroyed for lack of knowledge" (Hosea 4:6).

In 1820, at the bicentennial celebration of the landing at Plymouth Rock, Daniel Webster (1782-1852), delivered a classic speech on the significance of the Pilgrims: *Our ancestors established their system of government on morality and religious sentiment. Moral habits, they believed, cannot safely be trusted on any other foundation than religious principle, nor any government be secure which is not supported by moral habits . . . Whatever makes men good Christians, makes them good citizens* (Daniel Webster).

Timothy Dwight, president and professor of divinity of Yale College from 1795 to his death in 1817. Taken from his sermon of July 4, 1798, titled *The Duty of Americans at the Present Crisis, Illustrated in a Discourse, Preached on the Fourth of July.*

Religion and liberty are the meat and drink of the body politic. Withdraw one
of them and it languishes, consumes, and dies. If indifference to either, at
any time, becomes the prevailing character of a people, one half of their motives to
vigorous defense is lost, and the hopes of their enemies are proportionally
increased. Here, eminently, they are inseparable.

Without religion we may possibly retain the freedom of savages, bears, and
wolves, but not the freedom of New England. If our religion were gone, our state
of society would perish with it and nothing would be left which would be worth
defending. Our children, of course, if not ourselves, would be prepared, as the ox
for slaughter to become the victims of conquest, tyranny, and atheism. . . .

Another duty to which we are also eminently called is an entire separation
from our enemies. Among the moral duties of man none hold a higher rank than
political ones, and among our own political duties none is more plain, or more
absolute, than that which I have now mentioned. . . .

The two great reasons for the command are subjoined to it by the Savior —
"that ye be not partakers of her sins; and that ye receive not of her plagues"; and
each is a reason of incomprehensible magnitude.

— Timothy Dwight

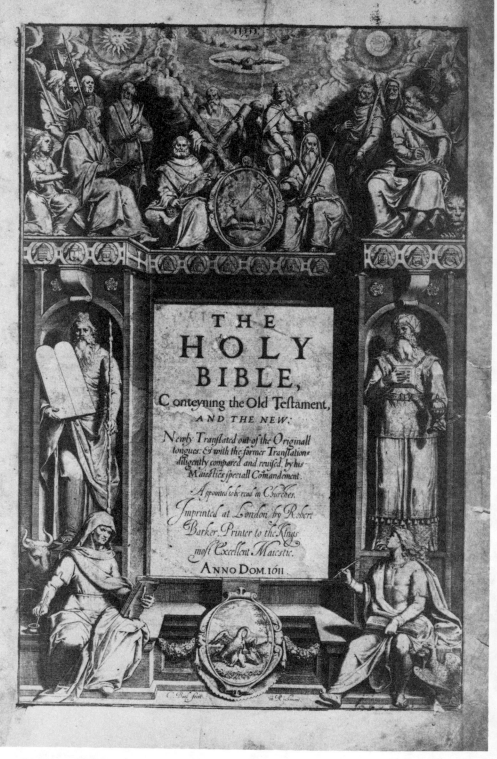

THE HOLY BIBLE,

Conteyning the Old Testament,

AND THE NEW:

Newly Translated out of the Originall tongues: & with the former Translations diligently compared and reuised, by his Maiesties speciall Comandement.

Appointed to be read in Churches.

Imprinted at London by Robert Barker, Printer to the Kings most Excellent Maiestie.

ANNO DOM. 1611.

All Scripture is inspired by God and profitable for teaching, for reproof, for correction, for training in righteousness; that the man of God may be adequate, equipped for every good work (2 Timothy 3:16, 17).

Lesson 1

Developing a Biblical World View

Ideas have consequences. What you *think* about God, yourself, and your world will determine how you will *live* in relation to God, yourself, and your world; therefore, ideas form the basis of your *world view*. Your world view is made up of a set of presuppositions, first principles of belief that give meaning to the world in which you live. Many times, however, you are not aware what these first principles are or how you came to believe them. But they are there nonetheless. There is no way to escape them. Of course, they can change as new evidence arrives to challenge them. A world view is either shaped by presuppositions that find their meaning in the all-knowing and holy God of the Bible or presuppositions that attempt to find their meaning in man.

The idea of a world view is not new. God interpreted the world for Adam and Eve. Adam and Eve, as submissive creatures made in God's image, were to view all creation within God's evaluation and interpretation. God's word was (and is) the starting point in the construction of a world view. Though Adam and Eve were morally perfect, they lacked total knowledge of God, themselves, and their world. They had to depend continually upon God as the source of knowledge and understanding: "The fear of the LORD is the beginning of knowledge; fools despise wisdom and instruction" (Proverbs 1:7).

God's understanding of Himself and His creation is *independent* and *complete*. God created the world out of nothing; therefore, God is not dependent upon anything outside Himself for knowledge. Man's knowledge, however, is *dependent* and *incomplete*. Without God as our source of knowledge and interpreter of reality man would know nothing. It is only in God's light that we see light (Psalm 36:9). The Apostle Paul, affirming God's *independent* and *complete* knowledge, writes that in Christ "are hidden *all* the treasures of wisdom and knowledge" (Colossians 2:3). If man truly wants to know, he must understand that God "teaches man knowledge" (Psalm 94:10).

Men may be induced to abandon their old religion and to adopt a new one; but they never can remain long free from all religion. Take away one object of worship and they will soon attach themselves to another. If unhappily they lose the knowledge of the true God, they will set up gods of their own invention or receive them from others.

–Archibald Alexander

Satan intended to overturn God's moral order by convincing Adam and Eve that God's view of His world was only one view among many. By persuading Eve to eat of the tree of the knowledge of good and evil, Satan was leading her to develop an *independent* world view that would compete with God's: "You will be like God, knowing good and evil" (Genesis 3:5). The temptation involved more than a piece of fruit. It began a struggle over who would interpret all reality. "Men may be induced to abandon their old religion and to adopt a new one; but they never can remain long free from all religion. Take away one object of worship and they will soon attach themselves to another. If unhappily they lose the knowledge of the true God, they will set up gods of their own invention or receive them from others" (Archibald Alexander, *Evidences of the Authenticity, Inspiration and Canonical Authority of the Holy Scriptures*, p. 18f.).

The world view of humanism sees man as the center of all reality — an idol created by man for man. Humanism declares that a man can determine good and evil for himself, independent of God's view of reality. This was and is Satan's lie. By contrast, the Christian world view declares that God gives meaning to all of life; thus, no fact in the universe can be *adequately* explained unless evaluated in terms of God's word. By rejecting God's interpretation of reality, man believes he can interpret reality *independently*, not realizing the consequences of distortion due to his own inherent limitations. Adam and Eve failed to recognize their very existence and ability to think depended on God. Their humility and submission before God were replaced by human pride — a pride that infected God's entire created order. The creature assumed the role of Creator.

What was to be fed was [Eve's] pride, and what would grow was her appetite for self-worship.

The same human propensity for self-worship is behind the incessant biblical injunctions against pride. Tyre was struck down " 'Because your heart is proud, and you have said, "I am a god." ' " (Ezek. 28:2). Habakkuk wrote of "guilty men, whose own might is their god!" (Hab. 1:11). The judgment of the Tower of Babel was evidently of the same order; those who wished to "make a name for ourselves" built their tower having "its top in the heavens" as a declaration of independence from God (Gen. 11:4). Surveying civilizations across the whole span of history [Arnold] Toynbee concluded that self-worship was the paramount religion of mankind, although its guises are numerous and diverse (Herbert Schlossberg, *Idols for Destruction*, pp. 39-40).

Of course, if man's dependence on God for knowledge is considered optional, then God's view of the world is also considered optional. By rejecting God's view of the world, Adam and Eve became "free" to construct their own world view. Any attempt, however, to form a world view independent of God's view of His world makes man an idol worshipper. New gods with independent knowledge seek to rule in their own way.

Pride has blinded our eyes (cf. 2 Corinthians 4:4; 1 Timothy 3:6; 1 John 2:16). The world view each of us possesses is now distorted. Since it is created in our own image and motivated by pride against God, we no longer "see" the world clearly. We are not aware of the "bent" character of our world (cf. Genesis 3:16-19; Romans 8:20-25). When we attempt to construct our world view independent of God, the standard we use (ourselves and our limited knowledge distorted by sin) is not reliable. Because we sin, we must constantly return to God's view of the world as He sets it forth in Scripture. We must see things as God does. Our biblical world view, therefore, means simply to think God's thoughts after Him.

The Christian should evaluate *all* of life in terms of God's word, not just those certain aspects of reality he considers important. Since the effects of man's fall permeated every aspect of God's created order, the Christian must evaluate and restore all aspects of God's creation using Scripture as a corrective lens. In fact, the Bible directs our attention to the effects of the fall and our responsibility to restore all things in Christ:

> The first twelve chapters of the book of Genesis recount the development of human culture from the resources of creation, and tell of God's concern about man's perverted use of things. Mosaic legislation concerned matters of bodily health as well as morality, the artistry of the tabernacle as well as its religious functions, a civil justice that protects the underprivileged and falsely accused, and an economic structure that would not perpetuate abject poverty. The psalmist saw all of nature and history as God's doing. Job struggled, as the blows fell, to understand his sufferings; he forsook every other point of reference in his thinking except the sovereign providence of God. The writer of Ecclesiastes wrestled with the value of wealth, family, learning, and leisure, and found such things vacuous apart from the fact that they are of God's good gifts to men. The prophets brought the life of the nation under the judgment of God's law — its political ups and downs, its social and economic injustices, and its religious practices. In all of this, the outline of a theistic world-view becomes apparent. The truth about every area is interrelated as a coherent whole in God's wisdom, so that for man "the fear of the Lord is the beginning of wisdom." That is to say, the believer has a starting point which gives perspective on life both in its parts and as a whole (Arthur F. Holmes, *All Truth is God's Truth*, pp. 9-10).

We cannot construct a reliable and comprehensive biblical world view without God at the foundation (Matthew 7:24-27). False conceptions of reality must be "put off" while a biblical perception of reality is "put on": "This I say, therefore, and affirm together with the Lord, that you walk no longer just as the Gentiles also walk, in the *futility of their mind*, being *darkened in their understanding*, excluded from the life of God, *because of the ignorance that is in them*, because of the hardness of their heart" (Ephesians 4:17, 18).

The belief that man himself is the center of life, capable of interpreting all the facts at his disposal, must be repudiated. Each of us must choose his God. Joshua's exhortation to Israel is an exhortation to all nations: "And if it is disagreeable in your sight to serve the LORD, choose for yourselves today whom you will serve: whether the gods which your fathers served which were beyond the River, or the gods of the Amorites in whose land you are living; but as for me and my house, we will serve the LORD" (Joshua 24:15).

Augustine (354-430), author of *The Confessions* and *The City of God*, maintained that man's limited reason must submit to God's infinite wisdom as set forth in Scripture: *But we must bend our necks to the authority of the Holy Scriptures, in order that we may arrive at knowledge and understanding through faith.*

Questions For Discussion

1. What is a world view? (Proverbs 23:7a; Matthew 6:22-24)

2. What first principle governs your world view? (Romans 1:18-32; Genesis 1:1; Hebrews 11:6)

3. How does the doctrine of salvation affect the development of your biblical world view? (John 1:29; 4:42; 8:12; 2 Corinthians 5:19; Revelation 11:15; Psalm 36:9; 1 Corinthians 2:12-16; Colossians 2:8)

4. What often distorts an individual's world view?

a. Job 38-41; Psalm 146:3, 4; Isaiah 2:22; 55:8, 9; Jeremiah 17:5; cf. Job 7:16; Psalm 147:5; Isaiah 43:13; 1 John 3:20

_____

_____

_____

_____

_____

_____

_____

_____

b. Matthew 15:14; Romans 1:21; 1 Corinthians 2:8

_____

_____

_____

_____

_____

_____

_____

c. Jeremiah 8:9; 17:9; Matthew 7:17, 18; Mark 7:20-23; Romans 1:18-32; 8:7; Ephesians 4:17, 18

_____

_____

_____

_____

_____

_____

_____

5. How is a biblical world view developed?

a. Ezekiel 36:26; John 3:3, 5; cf. Jeremiah 17:9 and Ephesians 2:1

_____

_____

_____

_____

_____

_____

b. Romans 12:2; 1 Corinthians 2:14; 2 Corinthians 5:17; Ephesians 4:17-24

_____

_____

_____

_____

_____

_____

c. Psalm 19:7, 8; Proverbs 30:6; Isaiah 55:8-11; Jeremiah 23:29; 2 Timothy 3:16, 17; Hebrews 4:12, 13

_____

_____

_____

_____

_____

_____

_____

6. How comprehensive should your world view be? (Acts 20:27)

_____

_____

_____

_____

_____

_____

10

7. Can Christians hope to implement a biblical world view even though we live in a hostile world? (Romans 8:26-29; 2 Corinthians 2:14; 2 Timothy 3:8, 9; cf. Acts 4:1-22; 5:17-42; 7:54-60; 12:1, 2)

_____

_____

_____

_____

_____

_____

_____

_____

_____

Summary

"When seeking to persuade men to accept the truth of the system of doctrine revealed in Scripture, we speak of our Christian view of Life. And we subdivide this Christian view of life into three main sections, the Christian theology of being, the Christian theory of knowledge and the Christian theory of ethics or behavior. We must set off the Christian view of life sharply from the non-Christian view of life. Basic to all the differences between the Christian and the non-Christian views of life is the fact that Christians worship and serve the Creator, while non-Christians worship and serve the creature. Through the fall of mankind in Adam, the first man, the representative of all men, all become creature worshippers. But through the redemption wrought by Christ and applied to his people by the Holy Spirit, the chosen ones have learned, be it only in principle, to worship and serve the Creator more than the creature. They now believe the theory of reality offered in Scripture. They now believe in God as self-sufficient, in the creation of all things in the universe of God, in the fall of man at the beginning of history and in the 'regeneration of all things' through Christ" (Cornelius Van Til, The _Defense of the Faith_, p. 48f.).

Answers to Questions for Discussion

1. A world view is simply the way you look at yourself and the world around you. It includes your beliefs about God, yourself, your neighbors, your family, civil government, art, music, economics, history, morality, education, business, and all other areas of life. When you ask a person's opinion about himself or something he does, you learn his views on these subjects. This type of examination could continue until every conceivable aspect of his life was examined providing you with a substantial portion of that person's world view.

World views include far more than what you can observe with your eyes or hear with your ears. Numerous intangibles labeled as religious, philosophical, or theoretical first principles, serve as the starting place in developing each person's world view: "For example: What is the nature of the external world? Who is in charge of this world — God, or man, or man and God, or no one at all? Is man determined or is he free? How can we know and how can we know that we know? Is man alone the maker of values? Is God really good? Is God personal or impersonal? Or does he exist at all?" (James W. Sire, *The Universe Next Door*, p. 18)

Some people's world view is more developed than others, but everybody has a world view, no matter how limited in scope. Some of us never formulate detailed opinions about international economic matters; the dimensions of the universe; differences between opposing philosophical ideologies; the essence of change; the relationship between faith and reason; plus a host of other mind-expanding questions. No matter how limited or inconsistent your world view may be, however, the Bible assures you that the meaning you give to yourself and your world, seen and unseen, originates within your own mind: "For as [a man] thinks within himself, so he is" (Proverbs 23:7).

If you believe you are a *created* being, responsible to your Creator for all things, then your world view is dependent upon God for a proper understanding of the world. If you believe you are an independent, highly evolved animal, dependent upon no one, your world view will reflect this self-centeredness. Such world views reflect man's glory instead of God's. Your world view invariably reflects whatever first principles you choose.

2. World views are governed by your *assumptions* about the world in which you live. These assumptions or *presuppositions* are first-principles of interpretation that give meaning to every fact or idea that enters your mind. Presuppositions are religious in nature. For example, the atheist *believes* there is no God, despite clear evidence of God's observable attributes displayed throughout creation: "For since the creation of the world His invisible attributes, His eternal power and divine nature, have been clearly seen, being understood through what has been made, so that they are without excuse" (Romans 1:20; cf. Psalm 19:1-6; Acts 14:15-17; 17:22-31).

A Christian must analyze the unbeliever's basic assumptions before attempting to counter his man-centered world view. The unbeliever's rejection of God is an anti-faith, but a faith nevertheless. He rejects faith in God and instead trusts himself. His world view builds on his basic assumption of God's non-existence, or his reinterpretation of God. He concludes that certain facts are valid and others are not, based upon his own definition of who or what God is. Confronted with facts which support the thesis that the God of the Bible exists, his atheistic presuppositions force him to conclude that such facts must be "invalid." He turns to a "naturalistic" interpretation to accommodate his own preconceived assumptions.

Of course, not many individuals actually deny the existence of God. Rather, numbers of people who believe in "God" actually define Him in their own terms. This is idolatry. Many forms of idolatry wear such otherwise innocent labels as science, progress, pluralism, humanitarianism, social consciousness, open-mindedness, objectivity, and the like. "Idolatry in its larger meaning is properly understood as any substitution of what is created for the creator. People may worship nature, money, mankind, power, history, or social and political principles instead of the God who made them all" (Herbert Schlossberg, *Idols for Destruction*; p. 6). Scripture, therefore, must be not only our standard for belief in God, it also must be our standard for describing and defining the God in whom we believe. An atheist, in the broad definition of the term, creates a god in his own image.

Satan gains when he persuades the "objective" and "modern" person not to believe in the God of the Bible, but to substitute some creaturely principle or idea. The serpent did not confront Eve with the question of God's existence. Rather, he acknowledged God's existence, then attempted to place man on the same level as God thereby making Adam and Eve rival gods: "For

God knows that in the day you eat from it your eyes will be opened, and you will be like God, knowing good and evil" (Genesis 3:5). The deception can lead even Christians to believe they are following the God of Scripture, because the words of Scripture are used, when in fact they are making idols for their own destruction (Hosea 8:4). God is never denied, He is only redefined.

The Christian *believes* God exists. He does not "suppress the truth in unrighteousness" (Romans 1:18) or create a god in his own image (Psalm 115:2-8; Isaiah 44:9-20). The Christian's faith rests upon God's word as the first principle for developing a clear view of the world. Genesis 1:1 is his starting point for it assumes, *presupposes*, God's existence: "In the beginning God created the heavens and the earth." God does not seek to prove His existence. Rather, God requires our belief, for "without faith it is impossible to please Him, for he who comes to God must believe that He is, and that He is a rewarder of those who seek Him" (Hebrews 11:6).

As you begin to develop your world view, the presuppositions that God exists and reveals Himself to us in the Bible become the foundational principles that give meaning to your entire world view. When the world is "viewed," you will evaluate everything in terms of revelation, the word of God.

Ein Volk, ein Reich, ein Führer!

An official German poster (1938), which says, "A People, A Nation, A Leader." *In Germany there was Nazi truth, a Nazi political truth, a Nazi economic truth, a Nazi social truth, a Nazi religious truth, to which all institutions had to subscribe or be banned.*

3. Developing a biblical world view can never be separated from Jesus' saving work. If men and women do not turn to Jesus Christ as Savior and Lord, they will turn to themselves, to another individual, an idea, an ideological movement, or the state. Our choice of "savior" determines the basis of our trust and reason for living. For example, during Hitler's reign of terror, the state assumed the role of God and savior of the people. Life was evaluated solely in terms of the state: "[I]n Germany there was Nazi truth, a Nazi political truth, a Nazi economic truth, a Nazi social truth, a Nazi religious truth, to which all institutions had to subscribe or be banished" (C. Gregg Singer, *From Rationalism to Irrationality*, p. 28). We, and the institutions we build, reflect the image of our savior.

For many, the Bible merely imparts "spiritual" truth with little to say about "secular" matters (things pertaining to this age). It is important to understand that the Bible does not divide life between sacred and secular, or spiritual and material levels of reality in an ethical way. Jesus said, "Thy kingdom come. Thy will be done, on *earth* as it is in *heaven*" (Matthew 6:10) and "All authority has been given to Me in *heaven* and on *earth*" (28:18). The Apostle Paul tells us that material things are not evil, and those who despise material things because material things are of this world, misunderstand the nature of evil: "If you have died with Christ to the elementary principles of the world, why, as if you were living in the world, do you submit yourself to decrees such as, 'Do not handle, do not taste, do not touch!' (which all refer to things destined to perish with the using) — in accordance with the commandments and teachings of men? These are matters which have, to be sure, the appearance of wisdom in self-made religion and self-abasement and severe treatment of the body, but are of no value against indulgence" (Colossians 2:20-23).

A real division exists between good and evil (Hebrews 5:14), obedience and disobedience (2 Corinthians 10:5, 6), faith and faithlessness (Matthew 21:21). Viewing the world dualistically forces the Christian to abandon society and its institutions (because they are material and earthly), thus the effects of the gospel message are internalized and made irrelevant to the society in which the saved person lives. A biblical world view takes the things of this world and uses them for God's glory. Music, art, gold, silver, land, factories, homes, schools, and every other *material* thing can be used for good or evil. The word of God shows us *how* they are to be used.

15

The message that God "so loved the world" (John 3:16), shows that salvation includes far more than isolated individuals or a single aspect of the individual (e.g., the soul or body). God's view of salvation includes man in all his relationships, i.e. man and the *world*. Salvation affects family affairs (Ephesians 5:22-6:4), personal economic matters (Romans 13:8), personal relationships (Galatians 5:18-24), sinful habits (Ephesians 5:25-32), judicial decisions (1 Corinthians 6:1-11), eating and drinking (1 Corinthians 10:31), business dealings (1 Thessalonians 4:6), church discipline (Matthew 18:15-20), education (Ephesians 6:4), civil affairs (Romans 13:1-7; 1 Peter 2:13-17), etc. "God was in Christ reconciling the world to Himself" (2 Corinthians 5:19); Jesus is "the light of the world" (John 8:12), "the Savior of the *world*" (4:42), and "the Lamb of God who takes away the sins of the *world!*" (1:29); and finally, "the kingdom of the *world* has become the kingdom of our Lord, and of His Christ; and He will reign forever and forever" (Revelation 11:15).

The world needs restoring (Genesis 3:18, 19 and Romans 8:20) but the world's standard must not be applied in carrying out the restoration process: "We do speak wisdom among those who are mature; a wisdom, however, not of this age, nor of the rulers of this age, who are passing away; but we speak God's wisdom in a mystery, the hidden wisdom, which God predestined before the ages to our glory; the wisdom which none of the rulers of this age has understood; for if they had understood it, they would not have crucified the Lord of glory" (1 Corinthians 2:6-8). We are not to "love the world, nor the things of the world" (1 John 2:15) and we are no longer to walk "according to the course of this world" (Ephesians 2:2). Rather, we are to *change* the course of this world.

A biblical world view, therefore, sees all of life through the "corrective lens" of Scripture, recognizing that "a natural man does not accept the things of the Spirit of God; for they are foolishness to him, and he cannot understand them, because they are spiritually appraised" (1 Corinthians 2:14). The only true world view is God's view of the world. Fallen man, therefore, must think God's thoughts *after* Him: "But he who is spiritual appraises all things, yet he himself is appraised by no man. For who has known the mind of the Lord, that he should instruct Him? But we have the mind of Christ" (vv. 15, 16). The Bible is God's blueprint to us for righteous living.

16

I waste away; I will not live forever. Leave me alone, for my days are but a breath (Job 7:16).

17

4. Man's finiteness, fallibility, and fallenness contribute to distort an individual's world view.

a. *Finiteness* (Job 38-41; Psalm 146:3, 4; Isaiah 2:22; 55:8, 9; Jeremiah 17:5; cf. Job 7:16; Psalm 147:5; Isaiah 43:13; 1 John 3:20): Every creature has a beginning and an ending: "I waste away; I will not live forever. Leave me alone, for my days are but a breath" (Job 7:16). God, unlike His creatures, has no limits: "Even from eternity I am He" (Isaiah 43:13); "God is greater than our heart, and knows all things" (1 John 3:20); and "His understanding is infinite" (Psalm 147:5). Because God's nature is boundless, He knows all things comprehensively. He interprets and gives meaning to all the facts in the universe (because He created and knows all things). Finite (limited) men and women who attempt to interpret reality *independent* of God cannot make absolute statements concerning ultimate reality: unlike God, they do not have all the facts at their disposal. They can *speculate* and *opinionate* about ultimate reality but cannot be definite in their conclusions since they abandon God as the starting point for interpretation.

When Job sought to question the works of God, God reminded him of his own finiteness: "Who is this that darkens counsel by words without knowledge? Now gird up your loins like a man, and I will ask you, and you instruct Me! Where were you when I laid the foundation of the earth! Tell Me if you have understanding, who set its measurements, since you know? Or who stretched the line on it? On what were its bases sunk? Or who laid its cornerstone when the morning stars sang together . . .?" (Job 38:2-7; cf. Psalm 139:6, 12, 17, 18; Isaiah 55:8, 9).

The unbeliever who develops a world view from his own finite nature possesses an extremely limited view of life. Even the independent thinker who gathers facts from the experts will be left with facts far too insufficient to construct a complete world view. He will have to depend upon the experts' limited interpretation of the facts also. By contrast, though the Christian also is finite, by trusting God's word, he can come to correct conclusions about ultimate reality: God's evaluation of creation is true, and His knowledge is comprehensive. This does not imply that with the Bible an individual can know everything. What he knows from Scripture he knows truly: "The secret things belong to the LORD our God, but the things revealed belong to us and to our sons forever, that we may observe all the words of this law" (Deuteronomy 29:29).

18

Those who trust in man's standards for interpreting the world submit to a creature limited by the nature of his origin: "Stop regarding man, whose breath of life is in his nostrils; for why should he be esteemed" (Isaiah 2:22). God breathed into man so he became a *living* being (Genesis 2:7) and He continues to sustain man by giving "to all life and breath and all things" (Acts 17:25). When we reject God as our standard for interpretation, man immediately must turn to other creatures or gods of his own making. God reminds us that trusting in man or the things of man is to trust in a fragile, transient being. Moreover, all those who trust in man must contend with the judgment of God: "Cursed is the man who trusts in mankind and makes flesh his strength, and whose heart turns away from the LORD" (Jeremiah 17:5). Trusting man or corporate man (e.g., the state) is to worship the "creature rather than the Creator" (Romans 1:25).

b. *Fallibility* (Matthew 15:14; Romans 1:21; 1 Corinthians 2:8): By denying God, finite man attempts to create a universe after his own image. While he may worship God, he does so in a distorted and mistaken way: "For even though they knew God, they did not honor Him as God, or give thanks; but they became futile in their speculations, and their foolish heart was darkened. Professing to be wise, they became fools, and exchanged the glory of the incorruptible God for an image in the form of corruptible man and of birds and four-footed animals and crawling creatures" (Romans 1:21). When lost men and women trust other lost men and women to help them find God, both groups are led to the pit of destruction: "And if a blind man guides a blind man, both will fall into a pit" (Matthew 15:14). Without God's special revelation about Himself, finite creatures become mistaken about God's character, law, creation, and man's need for reconciliation to God through the shed blood of Jesus Christ.

Truth about finite man's attempt to know God is also true of knowledge in general. What was established scientific fact ten years ago, in many cases, by now has been declared outdated theory. The supposed age of the universe exemplifies man's fallibility. Not too long ago, scientists at the University of Chicago announced that the universe is 20 billion years old, based on the radioactive isotope rhenium 187 (See "20-billion-year Universe," in *Science News*, 111:14 [April 2, 1977], p. 215). But new discoveries bring a different conclusion: "Today many scientists agree the universe goes back as far as 20 billion years, when it was created by an explosion . . . referred to as the Big

Bang. Last week a team of astronomers . . . detonated something of a minibang. Using new data obtained by observing the movements of a family of galaxies in the vicinity of the Virgo cluster, they assigned a new age to the universe. The universe, it now seems, is closer to 10 billion years old" (*TIME*, "Fickle Universe," January 25, 1982). Thus, with one stroke of the pen the age of the universe is now only *10 billion years* old! The question of the age of the universe was summed up with these words: "Everyone in this game is in disagreement." Who will we believe?

What's true of science also holds true for other disciplines. Economic and political theories instituted decades ago were then accepted as absolute. But now such theories have been updated to rectify the effects of policies which engendered inflation, recession, unemployment, bank defaults, and high taxes. Will man's fallible nature influence the future consequences of these new policies? How does man's fallibility affect theology, medicine, psychology, education, music, and law?

While a Christian is just as finite and fallible as an unbeliever, he does not begin with his own nature's limitations in developing his world view. Rather, he starts with the light of Scripture: "For with Thee is the fountain of life; in Thy light we see light" (Psalm 36:9). Since the word of God is inerrant, infallible, and authoritative, the Christian has a sure starting point. This does not mean, however, that the Christian's world view necessarily will be without error. Remnants of sin and observation of the fallen created order can distort a Christian's world view. As long as Christians evaluate their world view in the light of Scripture they will encounter less distortion by creaturely and sinful limitations.

c. *Fallenness* (Jeremiah 8:9; 17:9; Matthew 7:17, 18; Mark 7:20-23; Romans 1:18-32; 8:7; Ephesians 4:17, 18): The mind, influenced by the condition of the heart, is the standard by which all reality is evaluated. There is a problem, however: "The heart is more deceitful than all else and is desperately sick; who can understand it?" (Jeremiah 17:9). Jesus' assessment of the human heart is even more telling: "Out of the heart of men proceed the evil thoughts and fornications, thefts, murders, adulteries, deeds of coveting and wickedness, as well as deceit, sensuality, envy, slander, pride and foolishness. All these evil things proceed from within and defile the man" (Mark 7:21-23; cf. Romans 8:7; 1 Corinthians 2:14-16). An individual's words and deeds lead you to the basis of his world view. Jesus explained that we can know an individual's basic faith commitment (world view) by the fruit he bears: "Every good tree bears good fruit; but the rotten tree bears bad fruit. A good tree cannot produce bad fruit, nor can a rotten tree produce good fruit" (Matthew 7:17, 18).

The fall of mankind was Satan's *purposed* attempt to overthrow God's moral order. "When man fell it was . . . his attempt to do without God in every respect. Man sought his ideals of truth, goodness, and beauty somewhere beyond God [Genesis 3:6], either directly within himself or in the universe about him. God had interpreted the universe for him, or we may say man had interpreted the universe under the direction of God, but now he sought to interpret the universe without reference to God . . . The result for man was that he made for himself a false ideal of knowledge [Genesis 3:5]" (Cornelius Van Til, *The Defense of the Faith*, p. 31).

Stop regarding man, whose breath of life is in his nostrils; for why should he be esteemed (Isaiah 2:22).

21

Man's fallenness caused him to desire to interpret all reality. That is the essence of sin. Man decides for himself what is good and evil without reference to God (Genesis 3:5, 6). Because of sin, facts pertinent to a particular issue are often ignored, no matter how convincing those facts might be. For example, the evidence for God's existence is overwhelming, yet there are those who "suppress the truth" (Romans 1:18). It is "in *unrighteousness*" that they suppress the truth, not because the facts do not apply. Construction of a world view based upon man's rebellious nature can only result in distortion and opposition to the world view based upon the infinite, infallible, and holy character of God.

5. A biblical world view is developed by learning how God views the world. In order for this to take place at least three things must happen:

a. A New Heart (Ezekiel 36:26; John 3:3, 5; cf. Jeremiah 17:9 and Ephesians 2:1): There must be a new heart before the eyes of the spiritually blind can be opened to "see" God's view of the world. The "desperately wicked" heart (Jeremiah 17:9) must be removed and a new heart implanted: "I will give you a new heart and put a new spirit within you; and I will remove the heart of stone from your flesh and give you a heart of flesh" (Ezekiel 36:26). The new heart gives life to an otherwise dead person (Ephesians 2:1). The life imparted through this new birth makes the spiritually blind man able to see the things of God (John 3:3).

John Calvin, the great 16th century reformer, described the effects of the new birth on the sinner's ability to perceive God's view of the world: "Just as old and bleary-eyed men and those with weak vision, if you thrust before them a most beautiful volume, even if they recognize it to be some sort of writing, yet can scarcely construe two words, but with the aid of spectacles will begin to read distinctly; so Scripture, gathering up the otherwise confused knowledge of God in our minds, having dispersed our dullness, clearly shows us the true God" (*Institutes of the Christian Religion*, ed. John T. McNeill, Vol. I, p. 70). Prior to the new birth "the god of this world has blinded the minds of the unbelieving, that they might not see the light of the gospel of the glory of Christ, who is the image of God" (2 Corinthians 4:4; cf. John 3:3).

b. A New Mind (Romans 12:2; 1 Corinthians 2:14; 2 Corinthians 5:17; Ephesians 4:17-24): The mind must be renewed because "the natural man does not accept the things of the Spirit of God; for they are foolishness to him and he cannot understand them, because they are spiritually appraised" (1 Corinthians 2:14). Regeneration within an individual affects every aspect of his being. The mind changes radically and must be renewed continually by not being conformed to the world's way of thinking (Romans 12:2). This means we "put off" old ways of thinking (man-centered ways of thinking) and "put on" new ways of thinking (God-centered ways of thinking) (Ephesians 4:17-24). We must train the mind in biblical thinking so we can "discern good and evil" (Hebrews 5:14). Unless the Christian begins with God in his thinking process, he surely will not come to God's conclusions about the way he should act.

Seal of Columbia University, New York, first adopted in 1755. Over the head of the seated woman is the (Hebrew) Tetragrammaton, YHVH (*Jehovah*); the Latin motto around her head means *In Thy light we see light* (Psalm 36:10); the Hebrew phrase on the ribbon is *Uri El* (*God is my light*), an allusion to Psalm 27:1; and at the feet of the woman the New Testament passage commanding Christians to desire the pure milk of God's word. Our early educational institutions presupposed a biblical world order.

23

c. A New Standard (Psalm 19:7, 8; Proverbs 30:6; Isaiah 55:8-11; Jeremiah 23:29; 2 Timothy 3:16, 17; Hebrews 4:12, 13): The word of God must serve as the standard for equipping every Christian with all he or she ever will need to evaluate life: "All Scripture is inspired by God and profitable for teaching, for reproof, for correction, for training in righteousness; that the man of God may be adequate, equipped *for every good work*" (2 Timothy 3:16, 17). The word of God projects a standard before which all other standards must bow. Experience, majority consensus, tradition, circumstances, or autonomous reason never can be used as standards of authority for developing a consistently biblical world view. God's word, however, is "perfect" (Psalm 19:7), "forever" (Isaiah 40:8), "trustworthy" (Psalm 93:5), a "light" (Psalm 19:8), "fire" (Jeremiah 23:29), a "crushing hammer" (Jeremiah 23:29), "living" (Hebrews 4:12), and never fails to accomplish its stated purpose (Isaiah 55:8-11). The word of man is feeble and fallible, and cannot be trusted to evaluate his life and world.

John Knox is preaching at St. Andrews on June 11, 1559 with the Duchess of Argyll and Catholic prelates present. Both Church and State are required to submit to a biblical world view. This was the occasion on which it was threatened that Knox would be shot in the pulpit.

6. Your world view should be as comprehensive as the Bible. When the Bible "speaks," it is your duty to study and act upon the Bible's commands. Paul declares that he did not shrink from declaring the "whole purpose of God" to the Ephesians (Acts 20:27). A quick survey of the Bible will reveal its comprehensive subject matter: The Bible speaks about history (Matthew 24; Hebrews 13:8), economics (Leviticus 25:35-38; Deuteronomy 8:18), education (Deuteronomy 6:4-9), political science (Romans 13:1-7), administration (Exodus 18:13-27), the military (Deuteronomy 20), leadership (Proverbs 28:2; 29:8), social relationships (Luke 10:30-37; 1 Corinthians 13; Colossians 3:14), social problems (Isaiah 1:1-23; Ezekiel 16:49, 50; James 2:15, 16), marriage (Genesis 2:23, 24; Matthew 19:5), family relationships (Ephesians 5:22-6:4), property (Exodus 20:15), jurisprudence (Exodus 20-23;9).

When the Bible instructs us directly or indirectly, the Christian must *act* in obedience: "But prove yourselves doers of the word, and not merely hearers who delude themselves. For if any one is a hearer of the word and not a doer, he is like a man who looks at his natural face in a mirror; for once he has looked at himself and gone away, he has immediately forgotten what kind of person he was. But one who looks intently at the perfect law, the law of liberty, and abides by it, not having become a forgetful hearer but an effectual doer, this man shall be blessed in what he does" (James 1:22-25).

7. Christians must optimistically expect to implement the biblical world view. The early church saw itself surrounded by hostile religious and civil authorities. Peter and John were arrested by the temple guard, put in jail, and commanded not to speak or teach in the name of Jesus (Acts 4:1-22). The apostles later were put "in a public jail" at the insistence of religious leaders (5:17-41). The disciples experienced the death of two church leaders; Stephen (7:54-60) and James (12:1, 2). In each case God's people remained optimistic: "And every day, in the temple and from house to house, they kept right on teaching and preaching Jesus as the Christ" (5:42). Even after the death of Stephen "those who had been scattered went about preaching the word" (8:4). "The apostle who suffered innumerable hardships, including beatings and imprisonment, wrote: 'But thanks be to God, who in Christ always leads us in triumph' (2 Cor. 2:14). Hope is what enabled him to see the essence of the situation — triumph — beyond the accident of disaster" (Herbert Schlossberg, *Idols for Destruction*, p. 333).

The Apostle Paul would not allow imprisonment, beatings, stonings, shipwrecks, being lost at sea, robberies, sleepless nights, hunger and thirst, cold and exposure, and the daily pressure of his concern for all the churches to deter him from implementing the biblical view of the world with which he was entrusted. Despite all obstacles thrown in the path of Christians, "we overwhelmingly conquer through Him who loved us" (Romans 8:37). The Christian need never fear intimidation by enemies of a biblical world view: "We think we are too weak, too unorganized, to achieve victory in social, political, and economic affairs. But look around us. What does the enemy have? He has inflation one year and recession the next. In some years he has both at once. He has a culture filled with people who have lost faith in everything: God, law, the political system, the sanctity of marriage, and even physical survival. Men without faith have difficulty in building anything permanent. People today have begun to lose faith in the future. Two generations ago, Americans were optimistic about the future . . . *Men without hope are ripe for defeat by men who have hope.* People are aborting their children, perhaps the ultimate rejection of the future" (Gary North, "Why Fight to Lose," *Biblical Economics Today*, Vol. VI, No. 1, 1982/3).

The Apostle Paul would not allow imprisonment, beatings, stonings, shipwrecks, being lost at sea, robberies, sleepless nights, hunger and thirst, cold and exposure, and the daily pressure of his concern for all the churches to deter him from implementing the biblical world view with which he was entrusted.

And those who had seized Jesus led Him away to Caiaphas, the high priest, where the scribes and the elders were gathered together (Matthew 26:57).

Lesson 2

World Views
in Conflict

The Bible is filled with conflict and reconciliation. The conflict results from man's ethical rebellion against God — the transgression of God's holy law. The way of reconciliation must satisfy divine justice. Adam and Eve's rebellion set the conflict in motion. Because of sin, enmity was placed between the seed of the woman, the Messiah and His people, and the seed of the serpent, Satan and his followers (Genesis 3:15). Yet in the midst of conflict a note of victory is sounded: the head of the serpent will be "crushed" by the seed of the woman, Jesus Christ. Jesus would die on the cross and thus make "peace with God" (Romans 5:1), taking upon Himself the "curse of the Law" (Galatians 3:13).

Just before the Messiah was born, Satan, aware of the prophecy concerning his own inevitable demise (Genesis 3:15b; cf. Matthew 8:28, 29), attempted to nullify the prophecy's implications by eliminating the promised Savior. Satan appealed to Herod's sinful lust for pride and power: "When Herod saw that he had been tricked by the magi, he became very enraged, and sent and slew all the male children who were in Bethlehem, and in all its environs, from two years old and under, according to the time which he had ascertained from the magi" (Matthew 2:16; cf. Revelation 12:1-6). The conflict between the Messiah's mission and the devil's forces had begun, but God holds the ultimate victory. Even Satan derives his limited power and authority from God (Job 1-2).

The conflict continued to rage when Satan tempted Jesus with the kingdoms of the world. But what was the nature of the kingdoms Satan claimed to possess? They were counterfeit kingdoms made up of lawlessness and perpetual strife. Jesus, because He understood the nature of God's kingdom, refused to succumb to Satan's perverted means of resolving the conflict. Satan was asking Jesus to join him in the battle so there no longer would be any need for conflict. Jesus' answer silenced Satan: "Begone, Satan! For it is written, 'You shall worship the Lord your God, and serve Him only' " (Matthew 4:10). Jesus would not resolve the conflict by compromise and capitulation, but by obedience to God's commandments.

Even Jesus' disciples failed to understand the nature of the conflict and God's way of reconciliation. As Jesus told His disciples He must go to the cross to resolve the conflict, Peter took Jesus aside to rebuke Him: "God forbid it, Lord! This shall never happen to you" (Matthew 16:22). Jesus quickly called Peter to realize the conflict was real: He alone could resolve it through reconciliation with God the Father by means of His own shed blood. Peter wanted compromise, but compromise was out of accord with the plan of God: "But He turned and said to Peter, 'Get behind Me, Satan! You are a stumbling block to Me; for you are not setting your mind on God's interests, but man's' " (v. 23). Peter saw the *effects* of the conflict, but he did not understand what energized those who manifested the deeds of darkness.

Satan continued his attempt to overthrow the purposes of God through the agency of Judas (Luke 22:3-6). Even here the tables were turned on Satan. The cross became the crushing instrument that for all time curtailed any possible victory of the devil.

The conflict continues to rage even today: The Apostle Paul tells us "our struggle is not against flesh and blood, but against the rulers, against the powers, against the world forces of this darkness, against the spiritual forces of wickedness in the heavenly places" (Ephesians 6:12). He reassured the soon-to-be-persecuted Roman Christians with an allusion to the victory promise given to Adam and Eve centuries before: "The God of peace will soon crush Satan under your feet" (Romans 16:20).

Paul encourages us to confront the battle head-on, with weaponry God has supplied to defeat the enemy: "Therefore, take up the full armor of God, that you may be able to resist in the evil day . . ." (v. 13). Notice that Paul does not instruct us to remain passive as the battle rages around us. Christians are to "put on the full armor," "stand firm" in the midst of the battle, and "take up" the spiritual weaponry (vv. 13-17). In another place Paul tells Christians "not to sleep as others do, but let us be alert and sober" (1 Thessalonians 5:7). The forces of darkness have no choice but to retreat as

Christians advance in the name of Jesus Christ. "It is not only unwise, but it is wicked to be disheartened because of the external feebleness of the Church, compared with the work she has to do, and the enemies she has encountered. God is her strength, her glory and her hope, and to despair of her is to deny God" (Thomas V. Moore, *A Commentary on Zechariah*, p. 77).

It is not only unwise, but it is wicked to be disheartened because of the external feebleness of the Church, compared with the work she has to do, and the enemies she has encountered. God is her strength, her glory and her hope, and to despair of her is to deny God.
    –Thomas V. Moore

God assures believers He will "abolish all rule and all authority and power" in opposition to His kingdom (1 Corinthians 15:24). While Satan rails against the church, God promises "the gates of Hades shall not overpower" it (Matthew 16:18). Jesus describes the church as a marching army, ready and able to move against the stationary gates of Hades. Satan and his minions are on the defensive as the church makes a frontal attack. The outcome is certain. The gates of Hades cannot stand against the power of God's people. Once the territory of Satan and his forces are "swept clean," Christians still must remain vigilant or the devil will take seven other spirits more evil than himself and again occupy the once secured territory (Luke 11:17-26).

The manifestation of evil today is real. The conflict is expressed by differing world views, energized by contrary principles. There is no neutral ground in the conflict between world views. Jesus says, "He who is not with Me is against Me; and he who does not gather with Me, scatters" (Luke 11:23). There is no place for the Christian to hide, claiming the conflict does not concern or affect him. Every aspect of reality is interpreted from the perspective of *man* and his *fallible* word, or from that of *God* and His *infallible* word. If Christians attempt to be neutral (an impossibility) they allow man's world view (humanism) to prevail. The myth of neutrality must be eliminated from the Christian's mind: "In the last analysis we shall have to choose between two theories of knowledge. According to one theory God is the final court of appeal; according to another theory man is the final court of appeal" (Cornelius Van Til, *The Defense of the Faith*, p. 51).

A new political order cannot resolve the battle, nor can reconciliation come by military strength and power (Zechariah 1:18-21; 4:6). Before man can be reconciled with his fellow-man, he first must be reconciled to God. In our battle with contrary world views we must never lose sight of the ethical conflict that creates differing opinions. The Christian does not fight the battle solely with intellectual weaponry; rather he wields the sword of the Spirit that is able to create life-changing effects within the rebellious sinner: "For the word of God is living and active and sharper than any two-edged sword, and piercing as far as the division of soul and spirit, of both joints and marrow, and able to judge the thoughts and intentions of the heart. And there is no creature hidden from His sight, but all things are open and laid bare to the eyes of Him with whom we have to do" (Hebrews 4:12, 13).

The first prayer in Congress testifies that our Founding Fathers did not adopt a neutral stance regarding religion in general and Christianity in particular. Rev. Duche concluded his prayer with these words: *All this we ask in the name and through the merits of Jesus Christ, Thy Son and our Saviour.*

32

Questions For Discussion

1. Compare and contrast the biblical world view with the humanistic world view.

a. Romans 11:36:_____

b. Romans 1:17:_____

c. Exodus 20:1-17:_____

d. John 8:36; Psalm 119:97-106:____

e. Romans 13:1-4:_____

f. Genesis 1:26-28:_____

g. Ephesians 1:11:_____

h. Philippians 2:10:_____

i. Psalm 36:9:_____

j. Romans 3:23:_____

a. Daniel 4:30:_____

b. Genesis 11:4:_____

c. Judges 17:6:_____

d. Psalm 2:1-3:_____

e. 1 Samuel 8 and 12:_____

f. Jeremiah 2:26-28:_____

g. Revelation 13:11-18:_____

h. Isaiah 44:9-17:_____

i. 1 Corinthians 1:22:_____

j. Genesis 3:8-13:_____

2. Why do people claiming the same world view often differ over similar issues? (1 Corinthians 13:12). Why can the individual who does not have a biblical world view still function in the world and add to the betterment of mankind with his discoveries? (Genesis 1:26, 27; Romans 2:15)

_____

_____

_____

_____

_____

_____

_____

_____

_____

_____

3. What is the history of humanism and how does it express itself today? (This question can be answered by studying some of the books listed under "Humanism" in the section _Books For Further Reading and Study_)

_____

_____

_____

_____

_____

_____

_____

_____

_____

4. What is a "synthetic" world view? (Genesis 4:2-8; Exodus 32:1-10; Judges 8:33; 1 Kings 13:28-31; Revelation 3:16)

_____

_____

_____

_____

_____

_____

_____

5. What happens when Christians fail to develop a consistently Christian and comprehensive world view? (Hebrews 5:11-14)

_____

_____

_____

_____

_____

_____

_____

_____

_____

6. Is neutrality an option for the Christian in developing and implementing a biblical world view? (Matthew 12:30; cf. Joshua 24:15; 1 Kings 18:21)

_____

_____

_____

_____

_____

_____

_____

_____

7. Who defines what is moral? Should law be _legislated_ or _administered?_ Explain. (Isaiah 5:20; Romans 13:1-7)

_____

_____

_____

_____

_____

_____

_____

_____

_____

Summary

"Most importantly, man's most basic presuppositions are always ultimately religious where religion is defined as: the ultimate court of appeal in any system of thought. The humanist cannot live with this definition, of course. He's spent vast sums of money, time, and effort, on convincing the world that he alone is non-religious, and therefore unbiased the way Christians are supposed to be. He alone is neutral in the ultimate category of religion. Yet, if we examine the efforts of humanists in every area of life, from a presuppositional base, we can easily see that in all things, they have an ultimate court of appeal in the autonomy of human reason which manifests its own system of law, doctrine, and Bible (*Humanist Manifesto I and II*) . . .Christians insist that salvation comes through Jesus Christ. Humanists insist that man must save himself. In his heart of hearts, humanists know the need for salvation just as the Christian does, and he knows of this need because God has placed it in the ground of his being. He cannot escape the knowledge of it. Christian and humanist may both use the same word (salvation), but, by virtue of their different religious starting points or presuppositions, they mean two entirely different things which have two entirely different sets of consequences" (John H. Saunders, III, "Christian Based Communications," *The Journal of Christian Reconstruction*, Symposium on the Media and the Arts, ed. Douglas F. Kelly, Vol. X., No. 1 [1983], p. 47f.)

Answers to Questions for Discussion

1. The following is a comparative study contrasting the basic presuppositions that make up the biblical and humanistic world views. The study is not exhaustive.

Biblical World View

"In the Judeo-Christian world view, final reality is the infinite-personal God who truly is there objectively whether we think He is there or not. He is the Creator of everything else. We must never forget that one of the distinguishing marks of the Judeo-Christian God is that not everything is the same to Him. He has a character, and some things agree with His character and some things conflict with that character. Therefore, there are absolutes, right and wrong, in the world."

Humanistic World View

"In contrast is the humanistic world view. As we look at the final reality of humanism taught in our schools and which provides much of the framework of the thinking and writing of our day — we find that it is thought of as material or energy. It is impersonal, totally neutral to any value system or any interest in man as man. It has existed in some form forever and has its present configuration by pure chance. This view of final reality offers no absolute value system, no fixed basis for law, and no basis for viewing man as unique and important in the eyes of a loving Creator."

(Francis Schaeffer, "The Secular Humanist World View versus The Christian World View and The Biblical Perspective on Military Preparedness." A speech given at the Mayflower Hotel, Washington, D.C., June, 1982).

a. God alone is sovereign (Romans 11:36).	**a.** Man is sovereign (Daniel 4:30)
b. Faith in God (Romans 1:17).	**b.** Faith in man (Genesis 11:4).

c. Law originates with God. Absolutes based upon the character of God (Exodus 20:1-17).

d. Man's freedom comes from redemption in Christ and obedience to His law (John 8:36; Psalm 119:97-106).

e. All power and authority are ordained by God. Rulers are "ministers of God" (Romans 13:1-4)

f. Man is created in the image of God, and therefore, is accountable to Him for all his actions (Genesis 1:26-28).

g. Man's end is predestined by God (Ephesians 1:11).

h. Man bows in subjection to Christ (Philippians 2:10).

i. Man learns by thinking God's thoughts after Him. Truth is revelational (Psalm 36:9).

j. Man's problem is sin. Man must be recreated by God (Romans 3:23).

c. Law originates with man. No absolutes. Law is what man says it is (Judges 17:6).

d. Man's goals of liberty and freedom come about by denying the need for God's law (Psalm 2:1-3).

e. Government is of, by, and for the people. Elected officials are servants of the majority (1 Samuel 8 and 12).

f. Man has evolved from impersonal matter over a long period of time. He is accountable to no one (Jeremiah 2:26-28).

g. Man or the state is the predestinator of all things (Revelation 13:11-18).

h. Man bows the knee to a god of his own making (Isaiah 44:9-17).

i. Man learns by reason alone. If it is not reasonable, it cannot be true (Acts 17:22-34; 1 Corinthians 1:22).

j. The blame for society's ills is shifted to others and ultimately to God (Genesis 3:8-13).

(Adapted from Norman De Jong, *Christianity and Democracy*, p. 159 and R. J. Rushdoony, *The Philosophy of the Christian Curriculum*, pp. 172-173).

The world view of humanism leads to destruction: *A blind man cannot guide a blind man, can he? Will they not both fall into a pit?* (Luke 6:39)

2. There are basically only two world views — the Christian (biblical) world view and the humanistic (man-centered) world view. There are, however, world views within world views because none of us is totally consistent. Even so, the world views within world views rest upon the basic presuppositions of a biblical or humanistic world view. Thus Christians may disagree with one another on theological, scientific, philosophical, and political issues even as non-Christians disagree.

The rise of "denominationalism" further shows that no Christian group has a pure world view. Since all are limited in knowledge and suffer sin's effects, there remains disagreement about life's most basic issues. Though Peter and Paul had a biblical world view, Peter was inconsistent with it at one point and Paul had to rebuke him for his error: "When Cephas [Peter] came to Antioch, I opposed him to his face, because he stood condemned" (Galatians 2:11).

We should expect to find flaws in what *we* might consider the most comprehensive and consistent world view, since each of us reflects the same finiteness, fallibilities, and fallenness as do other children of God. No Christian will ever be fully aware of his world in this present state of existence.

39

Only in the hereafter will self-consciousness be fully realized. "For now we see in a mirror dimly, but then face to face; now I know in part, but then I shall know fully just as I also have been fully known" (1 Corinthians 13:12). Even so, we must acknowledge that God holds a perfectly comprehensive and consistent world view to which we must conform our thinking. Duty requires us to study God's word diligently, bringing every thought captive in obedience to Jesus Christ (2 Corinthians 10:5).

Our problem, then, does not include the consistent biblical world view as presented in Scripture, but man's distortions of truth as he seeks to accommodate it to his sinful inclinations. The Berean Christians are commended because they did not take Paul's view of things at face value: "Now these [Bereans] were more noble-minded than those in Thessalonica, for they received the word with great eagerness, examining the Scriptures daily, to see whether these things were so" (Acts 17:11).

A question concerning the unbeliever often arises at this point. Obviously traces of a biblical world view may be sprinkled through his man-centered world view. Just as Christians are not consistent with the *biblical* world view they espouse due to their finiteness, fallibility, and fallenness, non-Christians are not totally consistent with their man-centered world view, since they are created in God's image. Nor can they altogether deny God's government of the universe, no matter how much they protest. Unbelievers must work within the universe created by God and with the laws He established for its government (e.g., gravity).

Scripture informs us that unbelievers "show the work of the Law written in their hearts" (Romans 2:15). For example, the non-Christian, despite his effort to suppress the knowledge of God, acknowledges such ideals as love, compassion, hope, justice, and joy. However, unless such character traits are defined biblically, they soon become perverted and twisted. For example, the pro-abortion movement would have us believe that denying women the "right" to abort their unborn babies somehow lacks compassion: "A righteous man has regard for the life of his beast, but the compassion of the wicked is cruel" (Proverbs 12:10).

Christians often can learn from non-Christians, since non-Christians also are created in God's image and thus are able to discover truth in the created order when they operate with unacknowledged biblical presuppositions. "The success of modern science has been due to its 'borrowed capital,' because modern science is like the prodigal son. He left his father's house and is rich, but the substance he expends is his father's wealth" (R. J. Rushdoony, *The Mythology of Science*, p. 87). When the unbeliever is pressed as to the foundation that allows his discipline (e.g., science) to make progress, we often find his foundation is borrowed. Theoretically, the unbeliever has a foundation of sand, but practically his foundation may be biblical.

Even as he believes we live in a chance-directed universe, he may operate as if he lives in a law-determined universe. Were the unbeliever consistent in practice with what he believes in theory, he would end up with a philosophical structure incapable of giving him knowledge. But the unbeliever is rarely totally consistent, and for this we can be thankful. For example, non-Christians who develop new surgical techniques operate in a universe created and ordered by God. A scientist must depend on certain absolutes if his experiments are to be reliable. He must be able to repeat the experiment; therefore, he believes in order and absolutes, something a humanistic world view cannot offer.

See, I have set before you today life and prosperity, and death and adversity; in that I command you today to love the LORD your God, to walk in His ways and to keep His commandments and His statutes and His judgments . . . (Deuteronomy 30:15, 16).

41

3. Historically, humanism has meant "concern for what is human." However, as cultures rejected the concern for man created in the image of God, humanism became a religious movement where men decided for themselves what is best for man, independent of God's evaluation of man. Even human-itarianism, usually thought simply to mean the practice of doing good for people who need help, has its roots in subjective religious thought. "Human-itarianism was the term originally applied to the followers of eighteenth-century theologians who affirmed the humanity but denied the deity of Christ. It was later used when speaking of the Religion of Humanity, and it carries the subsidiary meaning of the worship of the human race. It is only recently that humanitarianism has come to imply almost exclusively the doing of good deeds that help people. That recent usage should not be allowed to obscure the origins and motivations of humanitarianism. It is above all a religious term" (Herbert Schlossberg, *Idols for Destruction*, p. 51).

Obviously God was and is concerned about man and the world He created for him: "God created man in His own image, in the image of God He created him; male and female He created them" (Genesis 1:27). The Psalmist meditates on God's consideration of man compared to the excellency of creation: "When I consider Thy heavens, the work of Thy fingers, the moon and the stars, which Thou hast ordained; what is man, that Thou dost take thought of him? And the son of man, that Thou dost care for him. Yet Thou hast made him a little lower than God, and dost crown him with glory and majesty! Thou dost make him to rule over the works of Thy hands; Thou hast put all things under his feet" (Psalm 8:3-6).

The New Testament's concern for our humanness shows even more clearly as we consider that God became man for the redemption of His people: "The Word [Jesus Christ] became *flesh*, and dwelt among us, and we beheld His glory, glory as of the only begotten from the Father, full of grace and truth" (John 1:14; cf. 1 John 1:1-3). God showed His love for His people by becoming human, by taking the "form of a bond-servant, and being made in the likeness of men" (Philippians 2:7). To deny the human side of God's creative acts and His concern for that which is human in His redemptive acts is to deny God and the created order. Too often, however, Christians, in their battle with humanism, deny man's basic humanness and despise the human and material aspects of creation. Art, music, literature, and science can be mistakenly ignored as not worthy of biblical study. "We must be . . . careful not to confuse humanism with the Humanities, which refers to the study of human activity. These studies include 'classical' learning, but they extend to the whole field of human creativity. Christians above everyone should be interested in the Humanities" (Francis Schaeffer, "The Secular Humanist World View Versus the Christian World View and Biblical Perspectives on Military Preparedness," in *Who Is For Peace?*, p. 13). God has endowed His creatures with gifts, which properly used, show not only man's humanity but God's glory and majesty as well.

Christian concern for man's humanity expressed itself early, especially as abortion and infanticide were practiced in pagan cultures. When the Romans discarded unwanted children through abortion and desertion (the results of their pagan world view), first century Christians denounced such actions as evil and showed their concern for unwanted children in a positive and action-oriented way. Moreover, widows and orphans could find shelter with these early Christians: "In the *Didache* ('Teaching'), a document that some scholars date as early as A.D. 50, Christians were told not to 'murder a child by abortion.' Aristides described Christians in his *Apology* by saying, 'They love one another and from widows they do not turn away their esteem; and they deliver the orphan from him who treats him harshly.' The dignity in which Christians held human life stood in sharp contrast to the average pagan indifference to human life" (Robert E. Webber, *Secular Humanism: Threat and Challenge*, p. 25).

The *School of Athens* typifies man's love for knowledge independent of God and His word. Plato (l) and Aristotle (r) exemplify man's desire to know apart from God where "man is the measure of all things."

43

Christianity reacted to a crumbling pagan humanism that evaluated man in terms of the Greek Philosopher of the fifth century B.C., Protagoras: "Man is the measure of all things." Ethical dilemmas were evaluated in terms of man and man alone. The supernatural was often denied or explained in mystical terms. All of life was deemed naturalistic. The material world was the only concern for these early humanists. "The humanists reject revelational values and search for values *within the created order*, preferably from human experience" (Robert E. Webber, *Secular Humanism: Threat and Challenge*, p. 30). This brand of humanism is hostile to the Christian religion. The Christian is concerned about man in his humanness, man created in the image of God, not man as the measure of all things.

Humanism is both "secular" and "religious." The adjective "secular" comes from the Latin *saeculum*, which means "time" or "age." "To call someone secular means he is completely time-bound, totally a child of his age, a creature of history, with no vision of eternity. Unable to see anything in the perspective of eternity, he cannot believe that God exists or acts in human affairs" (James Hitchcock, *What is Secular Humanism*, p. 10f.). Secular humanism is an attempt to define man and his many relationships solely from naturalistic presuppositions. Only that which can be seen with the eyes and heard with the ears are valid for evaluating life.

Calling humanism religious denotes that the basic tenets of humanism are based on faith. Evidence is not offered to support the creed espoused by the movement. A reading of the *Humanist Manifesto*, drafted in 1933 by the American Humanist Association, will show the religious intent of the authors: "Religious humanists regard the universe as self-existing and not created . . . Religious humanism considers the complete realization of human personality to be the end of man's life and seeks its development and fulfillment in the here and now" (*Humanist Manifesto I and II*, pp. 7-11). The self-centered religious character of *Humanist Manifesto II* (1973) is evident with phrases like "we can discover," "we affirm," "we must save ourselves," and "we believe."

The humanistic world view of today begins and ends with man. All of life is interpreted by and for man. Since the humanist believes God probably does not exist, he holds an evolutionary explanation for the existence of the universe. All of life is explained through the accidents of impersonal matter, plus time, plus chance. As "chance" would have it, man has become the greatest effect of evolution. Since God is discounted, man now rules independent of any higher being and is responsible to no one. Man results from nature's "laws," but laws can change at any time since all things are in flux, a process of change. Independent human reason becomes the standard for authority: ". . . traditional dogmatic or authoritarian religions that place revelation, God, ritual, or creed above human need or experience do a disservice to the human species. . . . we can discover no divine purpose or providence for the human species. While there is much that we do not know, humans are responsible for what we are or will become. No deity will save us; we must save ourselves. We affirm that moral values derive their source from human experience. Ethics is *autonomous* and *situational*, needing no theological or ideological sanction. In the area of sexuality, we believe that intolerant attitudes, often cultivated by orthodox religions and puritanical cultures, unduly repress sexual conduct. The right to birth control, abortion, and divorce should be recognized" (*Humanist Manifesto I and II*, pp. 13-31).

Where God says, "Come now, and let us reason together" (Isaiah 1:18), the humanist says, "My ability to reason determines right from wrong without aid from God's revealed word." Moreover, for the humanist, there is no external (divine) plan to the universe. Meaning and purpose are whatever men say they are. Man, at the center of the world, gives meaning to life from his limited perspective.

4. A synthetic world view attempts to mix the Christian world view with some elements of the humanistic view. The word of God and unaided, independent human reason are seen as equal standards of authority for evaluating reality. The synthetic world view must eventually collide with God's word. For example: Cain offered sacrifices, as commanded by God, but he offered them according to his standards: "So it came about in the course of time that Cain brought an offering to the LORD of the fruit of the ground . . . but for Cain and his offering [God] had no regard" (Genesis 4:3, 5).

The Israelite nation wanted to worship God, but in their own way: "Now when the people saw that Moses delayed to come down from the mountain, the people assembled about Aaron, and said to him, 'Come, make us a god who will go before us' " (Exodus 32:1). King Jeroboam attempted to unify the nation by changing the place of worship and accommodating the people's religious desires: "So the king consulted, and made two golden calves, and he said to them, 'It is too much for you to go up to Jerusalem; behold your gods, O Israel, that brought you up from the land of Egypt.' And he set one in Bethel, and the other he put in Dan. Now this thing became a sin, for the people went to worship before the one in Dan. And he made houses on high places, and made priests from among all the people who were not of the sons of Levi" (1 Kings 13:28-31).

A synthetic world view attempts to mix the Christian world view with elements of the humanistic world view. King Jeroboam is being rebuked for making golden calves objects of worship. It was his desire to unify the nation by accommodating the people's desires for pagan religious practices.

During the period of the Judges, the Israelites "did what was right in their own eyes" (Judges 17:6). While they still worshipped God, they worshipped according to their own standards. They no longer worshipped Jehovah, but instead worshipped Baal-Berith. Baal-Berith is a combination word — Baal is the name for the Canaanite god and *berith* is the Hebrew word for "covenant." At this point in Israel's history, the Canaanite religion was mixed (synthesized) with God's covenant promises. The people wanted not only the covenant promises of Jehovah, but also the "benefit" of Canaanite (humanistic) ways. They wanted to be in *and* of the world (cf. John 17:14-18).

A synthetic world view espouses the religion of the Bible, but implements the religion of Baal (humanism). Israel combined the rituals associated with the worship of Jehovah with what it learned from the surrounding culture of Canaan. This is made clear when God brought revival to Israel under King Josiah (2 Kings 23). The priesthood was intact and the Temple continued to function, but the people's worship was synthetic: "Then the king commanded Hilkiah the high priest and the priests of the second order and doorkeepers, to bring out of the temple of the LORD all the vessels that were made for Baal, for Asherah, and for all the host of heaven . . . (2 Kings 23:4).

Jesus constantly disputed with the Pharisees and their synthetic view of God's word. In their attempt to be "law abiding," they added to Scripture. While such additions might have the "appearance of wisdom" (Colossians 2:23), they had the effect of setting "aside the commandments of God" (Mark 7:9). The early church faced the same dilemma when confronted by those who wanted to synthesize the gospel message — believing that a sinner is justified "through faith in Jesus" and "the works of the law" (Galatians 2:16). Such a perverted gospel actually nullifies the work of Christ and is anathema to the Christian religion: "I do not nullify the grace of God; for if righteousness comes through the Law, then Christ died needlessly" (v. 21).

The Christian must be aware of compromise, of making the gospel message palatable to those outside of Christ and hostile to His commandments. In our eagerness to get a hearing before unbelievers, we often add non-Christian elements to our message in order to gain their favor: "For the time will come when they will not endure sound doctrine; but wanting to have their ears tickled, they will accumulate for themselves teachers in accordance to their own desires" (2 Timothy 4:3). For example, some political leaders who claim the name of Jesus Christ frequently say, "While I am personally opposed to abortion, I cannot in good conscience impose my religious values on those who favor abortion; therefore, I cannot vote for anti-abortion legislation." This is the synthetic world view in action. This type of individual takes the biblical mandate against abortion and attempts to wed the humanistic premise that every individual can do what he or she wants as long as it does not infringe upon the rights of others. A synthetic world view makes God sick: "I know your deeds, that you are neither cold nor hot; I would that you were cold or hot. So because you are lukewarm, and neither hot nor cold, I will spit you out of My mouth" (Revelation 3:15, 16).

5. The book of Hebrews was written to a group of Christians who had forgotten the basic tenets of the Christian faith. The author begins a discussion about the priesthood of Melchizedek but stops short of developing the full implications of his priestly ministry with these words: "Concerning him we have much to say, and it is hard to explain, since you have become dull of hearing. For though by this time you ought to be teachers you have need again for some one to teach you the elementary principles of the oracles of God, and you have come to need milk and not solid food. For every one who partakes only of milk is not accustomed to the word of righteousness, for he is a babe. But solid food is for the mature, who because of practice have their senses trained to discern good and evil" (Hebrews 5:11-14).

The first-principles of the Christian faith could not be evaluated by these relatively new Christians because their biblical world view had fallen into disuse. The distinction between good and evil was a blur to them (v. 14). How can the modern Christian ever hope to evaluate the complicated issues of our day with an unexercised, inconsistent, and incomplete biblical world view? As the humanist's world view begins to crumble, what do Christians have to offer in its place? Can Christians present solutions to problems that occur in economics, civil government, medicine, science, education, law, the arts, ethics, and every other area of life? The Christian cannot call these areas outside Scripture since the Bible instructs us to take "every thought captive to the obedience Christ" (2 Corinthians 10:5). Only our *implemented* biblical world view can save our culture from decay and judgment.

6. The world views of humanism and biblical Christianity directly conflict. There is no neutral zone. Neither world view will rest until one displaces the other. Jesus said you cannot serve two masters. The Christian cannot serve man, the master of humanism, and God, the Master of man: "He who is not with Me is against Me; and he who does not gather with Me scatters" (Matthew 12:30; cf. Joshua 24:15; 1 Kings 18:21).

Christians are often accused of interpreting reality with certain "religious" presuppositions (first principles) while non-Christians maintain that they are being neutral (objective) when interpreting the facts. Neutrality is a myth: "Every human being has faith in something which affects his understanding of everything . . . The premise that facts may be objectively known, absolutely uninfluenced by the faith of the knower, is simply untrue" (Norman Harper, *Making Disciples*, p. 1).

Darwinism flourished because it allowed men and women to adopt an alternative to biblical Christianity. In time, through the mechanism of evolution, "sinful" practices would decline and eventually would be eliminated. Darwin's theory allows man to be his own god.

49

Effectiveness of the biblical world view is neutralized when Christians abandon their religious foundation in dealing with such issues as economics, government, or morality. For example, those who favor abortion stipulate that no religious values must apply to the abortion question by those opposed to abortion. In effect, those who are pro-life (anti-abortion) are expected to be neutral. How does one remain neutral? By being silent? In the story of the Good Samaritan, were the priest and Levite neutral when they did not concern themselves with the condition of the wounded Samaritan (Luke 10:30-37)? Are we "neutral" when we act as the priest and Levite did, ignoring the plight of the helpless? Silence allows the supposedly "neutral" humanist to pass legislation which allows women to abort babies at will. The humanist is not neutral. He or she injects his or her world view into the ethical discussion of abortion based on man's religion. A decision is made about the status of the fetus. Is the fetus a human being that should be protected by law? Is the fetus a *potential* human being that can be legally controlled by the *potential* mother and her doctor until the time of the fetus' birth? Or is the fetus a human being in the fullest sense of the term? These questions cannot be answered in the context of neutrality. The determination of what constitutes life and what one does with it are moral considerations.

7. All law deals with morality. There are laws against theft and murder. There is no possible way to implement laws without encountering people's perceptions of good and evil. Obviously, those who oppose murder say it is good to sustain life and evil to kill. Good and evil are moral terms; therefore, laws express our morality. The question, then, is what standard determines good (moral) and evil (immoral)? Will autonomous (humanistic) man determine good and evil or will good and evil be determined by God?

Our age seems preoccupied with morality. But morality that does not rest on absolute standards eventually destroys society. People feel comfortable about programs deemed "moral," but few ask, "Whose morality?" All kinds of atrocities are done in the name of "morality": "An invasion is called an act of love; destroying a village is an act of salvation; reducing a poor man to perpetual dependence or killing an infant an act of compassion. There are few miserable little despots who do not use this language. No matter how vicious the action, the justification will be the promotion of equality, the helping of the poor, the protection against unfair competition, the extension of compassion, the defense against wicked imperialism or communism" (Herbert Schlossberg, *Idols for Destruction*, p. 267f.). "Woe to those who call evil good, and good evil; who substitute darkness for light and light for darkness; who substitute bitter for sweet, and sweet for bitter" (Isaiah 5:20).

When man approaches law, his function cannot be legislative. He cannot *create* law. His function is *ministerial*, acting in behalf of a master: "For Christ, the function of man in relationship to God's law is *ministerial, not legislative*; i.e., man must administer that law, not alter, add to, or revise it" (R.J. Rushdoony, *Revolt Against Maturity*, p. 151). Those who represent the citizenry in the halls of justice must administer laws that are in conformity with the word of God. Those in authority are ministers of God "for good" (Romans 13:4). Man's society, state, and legal structure reflect his religion. When a legislator enacts a law, he implements either God's law or his own. There is no other option. God governs every domain, including morality.

Every word written and book printed reflects a world view that either has God or man at the center.

51

William Carey (1761-1834), missionary to India. For Carey, the mission field was the way to extend God's kingdom. Carey believed the dominion mandate and established schools and medical work in obedience to God's command. By 1798 he had learned Sanskrit and had translated into Bengali the whole Bible except Joshua to Job. To print it he set up his own press. *Expect great things from God; attempt great things for God* (William Carey).

Lesson 3

Sovereignty
and
Dominion

Christians are experiencing the effects of a new Sovereign. Because our courts, for the most part, reject the sovereign rule of the Lord Jesus Christ, attacks on traditional Christian freedoms abound. Doors to Christian schools are locked by state officials and Christian groups are denied opportunity to gather for religious purposes before and after school hours on public school property. The people of God realize the battle is not new. For centuries Christians were seen as a threat by those who claim the state as the only true sovereign: "These men who have upset the world have come here also; and Jason has welcomed them, and they all act contrary to the decrees of Caesar, saying that there is another king, Jesus" (Acts 17:6, 7).

Whoever claims sovereignty expects his subjects to govern his realm in terms of his law and name. Sovereignty, therefore, brings with it the inevitability of dominion, the power of governing and controlling all things. Noah Webster, in his *American Dictionary of the English Language* (1828), defines sovereignty this way: "Supreme power; supremacy; the possession of the highest power, or of uncontrollable power. Absolute *sovereignty* belongs to God alone." The beast of Revelation 13 claims absolute sovereignty by requiring his subjects to operate in terms of his law and name. Those who do not conform eventually will be destroyed: "And he causes all, the small and the great, and the rich and the poor, and the free men and the slaves, to be given a mark on their right hand, or on their forehead, and he provides that no one should be able to buy or sell, except the one who has the mark, either the name of the beast or the number of his name" (vv. 16, 17). The Lamb, the only true Sovereign, expects dominion to be exercised in His name (14:1-5).

The denial of one sovereign assumes the sovereignty of another. If God is denied as the only truly independent sovereign, man will claim this attribute for himself. To deny God as sovereign does not destroy the reality of sovereignty. Sovereignty is only transferred. For example, when Jerusalem was plundered by Nebuchadnezzar and his army, certain young men were brought to Babylon "to enter the king's personal service" (Daniel 1:5). Nebuchadnezzar showed his denial of the absolute and independent sovereign rule of God by besieging Jerusalem and taking some of the holy vessels of the house of God and bringing them to the house of his god (vv. 1, 2). This action by Nebuchadnezzar was symbolic. It was to show the sons of Judah that there is now a new sovereign who claims absolute control and expects them "to enter the king's personal service" (v. 5). Dominion would continue, but it would be on Babylonian terms.

That whatever the world now enjoys of civil and religious liberty, it owes to the Bible and Christianity; and that the progress of the principles of true liberty depends upon the progress of Christianity. Both the past history and the present state of the world justify this conclusion.

–N. L. Rice

To symbolize the change in sovereignty, new names were given to the sons of Judah. The names of Daniel, Hananiah, Mishael, and Azariah reflect the majesty and sovereignty of the God of Israel. The suffixes to these names either use the general name for God, *el*, or God's personal name, *yah*. For example, Daniel means "God is my judge"; Hananiah, "Jehovah has favored me"; Mishael, "Who is what God is?"; and Azariah, "Jehovah has helped." In each case the new Babylonian names reflected the attributes of the Babylonian gods, Marduk and Nebo. The formal change in sovereignty had taken place.

Nebuchadnezzar, however, learned the true nature of sovereignty the hard way. The greatness and splendor of Babylon was known throughout the world. When the king surveyed his kingdom, he made the following claim: "Is this not Babylon the great, which I myself have built as a royal residence by the might of my power and for the glory of my majesty?" (Daniel 4:30). God's response to Nebuchadnezzar's words brought realization of the true nature and source of sovereignty: "While the word was in the king's mouth, a voice came from heaven, saying, 'King Nebuchadnezzar, to you it is declared: sovereignty has been removed from you, and you will be driven away from mankind, and your dwelling place will be with the beasts of the field . . . until you recognize that the Most High is ruler over the realm of mankind, and bestows it on whomever He wishes" (vv. 31, 32).

Only when men recognize the sovereign rule of God can true liberty be secured. Biblical Christianity, because it alone acknowledges the one and only Sovereign, has brought liberty in abundance. "That whatever the world now enjoys of civil and religious liberty, it owes to the Bible and Christianity; and that the progress of the principles of true liberty depends upon the progress of Christianity. Both the past history and the present state of the world justify this conclusion" (N. L. Rice, "The Moral Effects of Christianity," *Lectures on the Evidences of Christianity*, ed. William S. Plumer, p. 601). Those who wish to rule must do so in terms of the Absolute Sovereign, God. Nebuchadnezzar saw himself as an *independent* sovereign who was responsible to no one. He thought of himself as a divine king in a divine State (Daniel 3). His claim to sovereignty destroyed the liberties of the people and similar actions by his posterity brought judgment upon the nation (Daniel 5).

All derived sovereignties are limited. No one man or institution can claim absolute sovereignty. To claim absolute sovereignty is to claim to be God. For example, Pharaoh's refusal to permit the sons of Israel to worship God in the wilderness was a declaration that he was the only absolute and unlimited sovereign. He claimed to be a rival god with jurisdiction over his subjects, the sons of Israel. Man's claims to absolute sovereignty become foolish in light of the fact that God laughs at the schemes of the nations to overturn His sovereign rule (Psalm 2).

But how comprehensive is the sovereignty of God? Does it include all of life? Is the sphere of civil government included? Arthur W. Pink (1886-1952) describes God's sovereignty in these terms:

We mean the supremacy of God, the kingship of God, the godhood of God. To say that God is sovereign is to declare that God *is* God. To say that God is sovereign is to declare that He is the Most High, doing according to His will in the army of heaven, and among the inhabitants of the earth, so that none can stay His hand or say unto Him what doest Thou? (Dan. 4:35). To say that God is sovereign is to declare that He is the Almighty, the Possessor of all power in heaven and earth, so that none defeat His counsels, thwart His purpose, or resist His will (Ps. 115:3). To say that God is sovereign is to declare that He is "The Governor among the nations" (Ps. 22:28), setting up kingdoms, overthrowing empires, and determining the course of dynasties as pleaseth Him best. To say that God is sovereign is to declare that He is the "Only Potentate, the King of Kings, the Lord of lords" (1 Tim. 6:15). Such is the God of the Bible (*The Sovereignty of God*, p. 20).

A careful study of biblical history shows all attempts to oppose God's absolute authority met with judgment. Pharaoh (Exodus 14), Nebuchadnezzar (Daniel 4:28-37), Belshazzar (5:25-31), the king of Tyre (Ezekiel 28:1-10), Herod (Acts 12:20-23), and the whore Babylon (Revelation 18:1-3) have undergone judgment and offer testimony that no earthly ruler can claim for itself what belongs to God.

Claims of absolute political sovereignty have grave implications for nations today. God's laws still operate. The principles of judgment as they were applied to tyrannical governments of the past still apply. When a modern state claims absolute and independent authority, it has deified itself. Our forefathers who operated within the context of biblical Christianity understood the limits of derived sovereignty. The framers of the United States Constitution made no mention of the word "sovereignty" for some very good reasons. The Constitution follows the Puritan tradition where absolute sovereignty is reserved for God alone. Moreover, the colonies' earlier experience with King George III made them wary of granting sovereignty to any one political entity.

Many in our day have turned from God as absolute Sovereign and look to the state as the new sovereign: "As a People and as a nation, we have made the state our sovereign. The word 'sovereignty' was deliberately left out of the U.S. Constitution; the writers felt that the term could only be applied to

God, not to a civil government. But the federal government and all the states now routinely assert their sovereignty, that is, their deity and lordship over man. The lawmaker in any system is always the actual god of that social system" (R. J. Rushdoony, "Modern Morality: Tampering With God's Law," *New Wine Magazine*, [October, 1981], p. 23).

The Bible makes it clear that God has called His people to go forth in His name, under His authority, to exercise dominion for the extension of Christ's kingdom. If Christians fail to recognize that they have been sent by the Absolute Sovereign of the universe to fulfill a dominion task in His name, a usurper of God's sovereignty will compel us to exercise dominion in his name. The choice is before us: "And if it is disagreeable in your sight to serve the LORD, choose for yourselves today whom you will serve: whether the gods which your fathers served which were beyond the River, or the gods of the Amorites in whose land you are living; but as for me and my house, we will serve the LORD" (Joshua 24:15). There is no room for compromise.

John Wesley preaching at Bristol, England, before the Mayor and Corporation of the city.

Questions For Discussion

1. What is the nature of God's sovereignty and how does it express itself in the area of dominion?

a. 1 Chronicles 29:10-15; Psalm 103:19; 115:3

_____

_____

_____

_____

_____

_____

_____

b. Matthew 20:15; Romans 11:36

_____

_____

_____

_____

_____

_____

c. Psalm 103:19; Isaiah 45:12; Genesis 7-8; Exodus 7:14-11:8; 14:13-31; Numbers 11:31; 22:22-30; Jonah 1:17; 2:10; Matthew 17:27

_____

_____

_____

_____

_____

_____

_____

2. What is man's dominion task? (Genesis 1:24-30; 9:7; Psalm 8: Matthew 28:18-20; 2 Corinthians 10:4-6)

_____

_____

_____

_____

_____

_____

_____

_____

3. In what ways can the mandate for dominion be abused? (Leviticus 25:4; 2 Chronicles 36:21; Jeremiah 50:34; 1 John 3:4)

_____

_____

_____

_____

_____

_____

_____

4. What is the relationship between evangelism and dominion? (Genesis 1:26-28 and Matthew 28:18-20)

_____

_____

_____

_____

_____

_____

_____

_____

5. How does the division of labor principle, as it is taught in Romans 12:3-8, 1 Corinthians 12, and Ephesians 4:11-16, affect the Christian's dominion task?

_____

_____

_____

_____

_____

_____

_____

_____

6. How will the Christian's dominion task be met with opposition? (Jeremiah 23:11; Ezekiel 22:26; 2 Corinthians 10:3-5; Ephesians 6:10-20)

_____

_____

_____

_____

_____

_____

7. How does absolute governmental sovereignty manifest itself when God is not recognized as the true Sovereign, either by citizens or rulers? What happens to the Christian's task of dominion when the nation is under judgment? (1 Samuel 8:14; 1 Kings 21:1-16; Jeremiah 25:1-12; 29:10; Daniel 1:1; 9:1, 2)

_____

_____

_____

_____

_____

_____

_____

_____

Summary

"Almighty God wants us to recapture the dominion man held in the beginning. He has gone on to great lengths to make that possible, sending His own Son as the second Adam to restore what was lost in Eden.

"Remember, at the time of creation man exercised authority, under God's sovereignty, over everything. He was God's surrogate, His steward or regent.

"The Genesis account uses two colorful words to describe this. One, *radah*, we translate 'dominion.' Man was to have dominion. The word means to 'rule over' or 'tread down,' as with grapes. It comes from a Hebrew root meaning 'spread out' or 'prostrate.' The picture we get from it is one of all the creation spread out before man, whose dominion would extend wherever his feet trod.

"The other word, *kabash*, is translated 'subdue.' Man was told to subdue the earth. The root means 'to trample under foot,' as one would do when washing dirty clothes. Therefore, in *kabash* we have in part the concept of separating good from evil by force.

"With the first word, *radah*, God gives man the authority to govern all that is willing to be governed. With the second, *kabash*, He grants man authority over the untamed and the rebellious. In both instances, God gave man a sweeping and total mandate of dominion over this planet and everything in it.

"But stewardship requires responsibility. And implicit in the grant was a requirement that man order the planet according to God's will and for God's purposes. This was a grant of freedom, not of license. As subsequent history proved, God's intention was that His world be governed and subdued by those who themselves were governed by God. But man, as we know, did not want to remain under God's sovereignty. He wanted to be *like God* without having anyone to tell him what to do" (Pat Robertson, *The Secret Kingdom*, p. 199f.)

61

Answers to Questions for Discussion

1. a. (1 Chronicles 29:10-15; Psalm 103:19; 115:3): God's sovereignty is universal. It extends over all His creatures, from the highest to the lowest: "Thine, O LORD, is the greatness and the power and the glory and the victory and the majesty, indeed everything that is in the heavens and the earth; Thine is the dominion, O LORD, and Thou dost exalt Thyself as head over all" (1 Chronicles 29:11). David, king of Israel, acknowledged God's sovereign dominion over all creation even though he was ruler in Israel.

b. (Matthew 20:15; Romans 11:36): God's sovereignty is absolute: "For from Him and through Him and to Him are *all* things. To Him be the glory forever. Amen" (Romans 11:36). God is controlled by no citizen, king, or nation. He is the "ruler over the realm of mankind, and He bestows it on whom He wishes, and sets over it the lowliest of men" (Daniel 4:17). God does what He wishes with what is His: "Is it not lawful for me to do what I wish with what is my own?" (Matthew 20:15). Though God's sovereign dominion is absolute, it is not tyrannical. Wisdom, righteousness, and goodness rule His most perfect counsel: "Oh, the depth of the riches both of the wisdom and knowledge of God! How unsearchable are His judgments and unfathomable His ways!" (Romans 11:33).

c. (Psalm 103:19; Isaiah 45:12; Genesis 7-8; Exodus 7:14-11:8; 14:13-31; Numbers 11:31; 22:22-30; Jonah 1:17; 2:10; Matthew 17:27): God's sovereignty includes dominion of the created order: "The Lord has established His throne in the heavens; and His sovereignty rules over all" (Psalm 103:19). The inanimate creation is governed by God and operates according to His sovereignly ordained laws: "It is I who made the earth, and created man upon it. I stretched out the heavens with My hands, and I ordained all their host" (Isaiah 45:12). When it serves God's purpose, "natural" laws are "overturned" (Genesis 7-8; Exodus 7:14-11:8; 14:13-31). The animate creation is ruled by God through the built-in control systems that direct animal behavior. When God desires His creatures to do His bidding, they immediately comply (Numbers 11:31; 22:22-30; Jonah 1:17; 2:10; Matthew 17:27). God providentially governs the universe in a sovereign way by orchestrating all things to suit His purpose: "And we know that God causes all things to work together for good to those who love God, to those who are called according to His purpose" (Romans 8:28). God's creatures must work and exercise dominion in terms of God's sovereignly administered created order. Any attempt to ignore God's laws, whether they are creational (related to the created order) or moral, will be met with judgment.

2. God gave Adam a creation mandate (sometimes called the *Dominion Covenant* or *Cultural Mandate*), commanding him and his posterity to subdue and rule the created order (Genesis 1:26-28). The specifics of this initial commandment were repeated to Noah after the flood (9:1-3, 7) and commented on by David (Psalm 8:5-8). Jesus Christ, in effect, reiterated the original creation mandate and gave His blood-bought people throughout history the power to accomplish the task of subduing the earth to the glory of God, through the instrument of His word (2 Timothy 3:16, 17), and the power of the Holy Spirit in the preaching of the gospel (Matthew 28:18-20).

The people of God are to rule or dominate the entire universe using the law of God as their blueprint. The Hebrew word for "rule" (Genesis 1:26, 28) means to assert one's authority over something by treading upon it. Since man is to extend his rule over the created order under God, the "treading" must be done in accordance with God's commandments. The Dominion Covenant, therefore, is ethical or moral. The creature, as God's image-bearer, must rule himself in self-government (motivation to serve God from the heart without external force, Ephesians 6:5, 6) before he can rule or have dominion over other aspects of creation (cf. 1 Timothy 3:1-7). If man will not curb the lusts of his own heart, he will use the created order to feed his ungoverned desires for pleasure and power to the detriment of all around him (Daniel 4:28-37). Adam's dominion task, and all those who are in Adam (cf. Romans 5:12-21), was made more difficult because of his *ethical* rebellion against God. In sinning against God, Adam maintained that dominion would occur, but it would be on new terms. God showed Himself to be the true and only Sovereign by expelling Adam and Eve from the garden (Genesis 3:22-24).

The Dominion Covenant includes all creational endeavors. The created order is to be studied and cultivated to bring forth its God-ordained potentialities, all for the glory of God and the advancement of His kingdom. This includes agriculture, astronomy, engineering, architecture, navigation, medicine, biology, science, aviation, physics, music, aesthetics, industry, education, horticulture, athletics, economics, politics, health, law, and every conceivable creational endeavor. For example, atmospheric laws had to be understood and obeyed before Wilbur and Orville Wright could gain dominion over the sky. Mechanical, mathematical, and aerodynamic laws had to be studied to invent an apparatus that could overcome the effects of gravity. Those who wish to work with God's creation must do so with His laws, both ethical and creational. (It is interesting to note the Wright Brothers would never demonstrate their "flying machine" on the Lord's Day, no matter what the reason. See Harry Combs, *Kill Devil Hill: Discovering the Secret of the Wright Brothers*, p. 281).

The first powered flight by Orville Wright, December 17, 1903 at Kill Devil Hill, near the village of Kitty Hawk, North Carolina. Without an understanding and strict adherence to God's creational laws (mechanical, mathematical, and aerodynamic), the Wright brothers would have failed to conquer the demands of flight.

George Washington Carver's study of chemical and agricultural laws allowed him to develop the potential of the created order that brought economic prosperity to the world. The results of his studies, in the use of God's creational laws, led to the development of innumerable products from the peanut. Carver based his scientific study of the created order on Genesis 1:29: "Behold, I have given you every plant yielding seed that is on the surface of all the earth, and every tree which has fruit yielding seed; it shall be food for you." George Washington Carver "devoutly believed that a personal relationship with the Creator of all things was the only foundation for the abundant life" (Rackham Holt, *George Washington Carver: An American Biography*, p. 226). The abundant life for Carver included more than "spiritual" things. Carver took seriously the Dominion Mandate in all its fulness: "I carried the peanuts into my laboratory and the Creator told me to take them apart and resolve them into their elements. With such knowledge as I had of chemistry and physics I set to work to take them apart. I separated the water, the fats, the oils, the gums, the resins, sugars, starches, pectoses, pentosans, amino acids. There! I had the parts of the peanuts all spread out before me" (Rackham Holt, *George Washington Carver: An American Biography*, pp. 226-227). From this seemingly insignificant legume he made cheese, milk, flour, ink, dyes, wood stains, and soap, to list but a few of his nearly 300 derivative products.

3. The mandate for dominion can be abused in at least two ways. *First*, the dominion mandate can be abused by denying that Christians are obligated to keep it. Jesus identifies the faithful steward who shows a profit on kingdom activity. He "does business" until Jesus returns (Luke 19:13). Some teach that sin has made the dominion mandate impossible to fulfill; therefore, it is no longer in effect. Of course, there is no evidence for this. If sin abrogates our responsibility to fulfill the dominion mandate then we could say, for example, sin abrogates our responsibility to love God. Both are commands that are affected by sin. Sin makes both tasks more difficult, but this in no way relieves Christians of their duties. Adam and Eve were to show their love toward God by keeping His commandments, and this included the fulfilling of the Dominion Covenant (This is implied in Genesis 2:15-17). The New Testament emphasizes the same standard (John 14:15). The Dominion Mandate cannot be brushed aside simply because sin has made the task more difficult.

As shown, dominion will be exercised. Either men and women will follow God's mandate for dominion or they will exercise dominion for themselves, according to their standards. True and lasting dominion results from acknowledging the authority of Jesus Christ and obeying His commandments (Matthew 28:18-20). The arena of dominion is the earth and all its environs (Genesis 1:26-28; Matthew 28:18-20 and 6:10). It includes destruction of "fortresses," all "speculations," and "every lofty thing raised up against the knowledge of God" (2 Corinthians 10:4, 5). Why does Paul seem so militant? He realizes that unless Christians actively oppose ideas which energize contrary movements, hostile principles will dominate the world and impede Christian dominion. There is an offensive strategy as well. Every thought is to be brought captive to the obedience of Christ (v. 5). We are no longer to think and act like unbelievers. Rather, Christians are to formulate their ideas according to the standards of Jesus Christ and implement them wherever His lordship extends, remembering that His lordship is universal.

Second, man's bent toward rebellion often makes him a destroyer of God's good creation. When men and women fail to follow God's laws regarding the care of the earth, abuse soon follows. For example, one of the reasons the Israelites were taken into captivity for seventy years was their failure to allow the land to rest every seven years (Leviticus 25:4). In their absence, the land would have its rest (2 Chronicles 36:21; Jeremiah 50:34).

George Washington Carver *devoutly believed that a personal relationship with the Creator of all things was the only foundation for the abundant life.*

In the 19th century farmers in the southern United States suffered a similar fate by planting cotton year after year. In time, the nitrogen in the soil, necessary for cotton production, was depleted. By abusing the land, the South was held in "captivity" to land that would no longer produce one of their most valued crops. Moreover, as a basically one-crop economy, they were at the mercy of their more economically diverse manufacturing neighbors. Only after practicing crop rotation (which was a way of allowing the soil to "rest") and soil conservation on a large scale could the South once again enjoy a booming agricultural economy.

Care for the earth does not mean to venerate or worship the earth as pantheistic religionists would have us do. Care for the earth means to act as God's stewards. Having dominion over the earth does not in itself lead to abuse. "Our polluted regions of the earth are rebelling against man's rebellious, lawless rulership, not against rulership as such" (Gary North, *The Dominion Covenant: Genesis*, p. 33). Sin leads to abuse and "sin is lawlessness" (1 John 3:4). If companies were held responsible for chemical spills and were made to pay restitution, then such "crimes" would indeed be scarce (cf. Exodus 22:6). The "ecological crisis" that we experience today is "really only one aspect of the pervasive moral and cultural crisis of our time, and the cause of this crisis is pride. For too long we have believed that no bounds need be placed on human ambition and desire, but now it has been discovered that even scientific technology, the instrument of modern man's intended self-deification, must bow to the finitude of reality" (R. V. Young, Jr., "Christianity and Ecology," *National Review* [Dec. 20, 1974]).

4. The original Great Commission, the Dominion Covenant of Genesis 1:26-28, did not include evangelism. The command to subdue the earth was given before the fall, and thus there was no need for a command to evangelize. Since the fall, however, the preaching of the gospel is necessary and mandatory. Fallen men and women need new hearts regenerated by the power of God's Spirit before dominion can take place in the name of Jesus Christ. The Christian's *first* task, therefore, is to bring the word of God, the gospel of Jesus Christ, to men and women who are in need of personal dominion, subduing the desires of a rebellious heart and will. Societal dominion cannot take place by those who will not first see their need of personal responsibility before God. Pat Robertson, in his book *The Secret*

67

Kingdom, shows the proper relationship between personal dominion and societal dominion: "When man, through Jesus, reasserts God's dominion over himself, then he is capable of reasserting his God-given dominion over everything else. That is the way everything on earth will be freed from the cycle of despair, cruelty, bondage, and death" (p. 203). Only then will we understand that our task is a stewardship, working under the sovereign decree of our Creator.

Jesus' command to His Church was to preach the gospel (regeneration) and make disciples of all the nations (training for dominion), bringing the world under the sway of His law-word (tool of dominion): "It was the sovereign Christ who sovereignly charged His church with the Great Commission, 'All authority hath been given unto me in heaven and on earth. Go ye therefore, and make disciples of all the nations, baptizing them into the name of the Father, and of the Son, and of the Holy Spirit: teaching them to observe all things whatsoever I commanded you: and lo, I am with you always, even unto the end of the world' (Matt. 28:18-20 ASV)" (R.B. Kuiper, *God-Centered Evangelism*, p. 62).

The Christian's first task is to bring the word of God, the gospel of Jesus Christ, to men and women who are in need of personal dominion, subduing the desires of a rebellious heart toward God. Societal dominion cannot take place by those who will not first exercise personal dominion under God.

Evangelism should never be limited to conversion, however. Regeneration certainly must be the first step, but by limiting evangelism to conversion the newly redeemed sinner often receives the impression that he has been saved for his own sake rather than for the Lord's sake. This is certainly not the case: "Evangelism presents the total claims of the triune God upon man and his whole life and world. Man is not saved merely to enjoy heaven but to serve the Lord with all his heart, mind, and being (Matt. 22:35-40), and his neighbor as himself. This means seeking *first* the Kingdom of God and His righteousness. Our salvation thus has a purpose beyond ourselves: it is the Kingdom of God and our service to Him. It is a restoration to our dominion calling (Gen. 1:26-28; 9:1-7; Ps. 8:6; Joshua 1:1-9; Matthew 28:18-20). It begins with regeneration, it continues with sanctification and dominion" (R.J. Rushdoony, "Evangelism and Dominion," *The Journal of Christian Reconstruction*, Symposium on Evangelism, ed. Gary North, Vol. VIII, No. 2 [Winter, 1981], p. 15).

5. The dominion task can only be accomplished through *many* Christians, the body of Christ, operating under the *one* head, Jesus Christ. Because man is not God, he is not able to exercise comprehensive cultural dominion as a single individual. Neither can man *institutionally* exercise comprehensive dominion (Genesis 11). A successful plan for dominion must include a proper balance between central direction and local involvement. Like the Trinity, who is one God yet three Persons, Christian organizations must be both one and many, centrally directed yet locally administered. Without a "head," there can be no rational, integrated program (Ephesians 1:22; Colossians 2:19). Without the "members" and their various gifts and talents there can be no successful implementation of the program (1 Corinthians 12; Ephesians 4:11-16).

The family is the first created structural organization that integrates the one and many concept. There is one head, the husband, with many members. When the children are grown and married, another head emerges with additional members: "It is important to understand that the division of labor within the family was designed to extend men's dominion over nature. The family unit was to be broken with each generation, even before the Fall of man. Speaking of marriage, Adam said: 'Therefore shall a man leave his father and his mother, and shall cleave unto his wife: and they shall be one flesh' (Gen. 2:24). The harmony of the family before the Fall was never to be intended to keep sons and daughters in the same immediate household. They were to leave, to bring the whole earth under dominion . . . Isaac did not live with Abraham; Jacob did not live with Isaac" (Gary North, *The Dominion Covenant: Genesis*, p. 99n).

The division of labor principle applies to the church, business establishments, political movements, voluntary service organizations, the judicial system, and every other aspect of society. No one organization can accomplish the task. The division of labor principle must be adopted and implemented at all levels of society. For example, there is one church, the body of Christ, but many local churches throughout the world. In each of these local churches there are many members. Among the many members there are a variety of gifts that should be used for "the building up of the body of Christ" (Ephesians 4:12). By dividing responsibilities among the various churches and their many members the dominion task does not seem so awesome.

The division of labor principle is despised by those who want to see a monolithic state rule all things and thus curtail the God-ordained method of dominion, i.e., many Christians exercising their many gifts through many institutions. Families, independent schools, churches, and voluntary organizations are a threat to a state that sees itself as "God Marching on Earth." Individualism is called into question because it is seen as contrary to the ideals of the state. Laws that give the state power to confiscate the lawful transfer of wealth to family members through inheritance are implemented in order to diffuse the power of families. Private schools are permitted to exist as long as they meet state minimum standards. Churches can receive a tax "exemption" from the state if they meet the criteria of what constitutes a church, also defined by the state. The list could go on.

The early church was able to grow and have influence because it was decentralized. When the Christians were persecuted in Jerusalem, they moved on to Judea and Samaria (Acts 8:1-6). Even Rome, the center of apostate political power, was populated with Christians. Spain was next in Paul's missionary plans (Romans 15:28). The decentralized church was the growing and elusive church. No political power on earth could curtail its efforts. Christians, because ultimately they serve God, take their religion with them wherever they go. Families no longer look to the state for care. Education is seen as a parental responsibility. Statist education is opposed.

Alternative educational establishments are constructed. Care for the needy is seen as a Christian responsibility and not the obligation or right of the state. There was little need for "fair" business laws because Christian employers treated their employees with dignity, as individuals created in the image of God. These early Christians were persecuted for their "individualistic" beliefs, but with the Roman Empire crumbling around them, in time, Christians found themselves in positions of power and authority.

6. The book of Acts depicts the beginning of the opposition. Peter and John were imprisoned because they jeopardized the prevailing religious ideology (Acts 4:1-23). Stephen was executed by men from the Synagogue, led by a Pharisee named Saul (6:8-8:3). Israel had suffered a similar fate centuries before: "For both prophet and priest are polluted; even in My house I have found their wickedness" (Jeremiah 23:11). Even from within the church opposition arose that threatened the cause of Christ and the advancement of His kingdom: "It suffered from political rivalries that sometimes motivated religious zeal (Phil. 1:15), was plagued by false teachers (2 Pet. 2:1-3) and perverse and destructive leaders (Acts 20:29f., Jude 4), preached a false gospel (Gal. 1:6-9), practiced divisiveness (3 John 9, 10), and harbored servants of Satan disguised as servants of Christ (2 Cor. 11:3-15)" (Herbert Schlossberg, *Idols for Destruction*, p. 234).

One of the greatest obstacles to dominion in the name of Christ is the church's identification with the ways of the world. Thus it becomes difficult to differentiate between the Kingdom of God and the kingdoms of this world. Just as Israel was told to separate itself from pagan practices of the surrounding cultures, the early church was to separate itself from the beliefs and practices of a society energized by Greek and Roman thought: "And do not be conformed to this world, but be transformed by the renewing of your mind, that you may prove what the will of God is, that which is good and acceptable and perfect" (Romans 12:2; cf. 1 Peter 1:14). The task of dominion is curtailed when the church seeks to be "relevant" by adopting the standards of the world and preaching them as the "gospel."

Such "preaching" creates a breeding ground for "doctrines of demons" (1 Timothy 4:1). The battle, however, is not between two equal forces. The defeat of evil powers came as the result of divine satisfaction of justice. The death of Jesus was not primarily to defeat Satan and his forces; rather, it was to

71

The book of Acts depicts the beginning of the opposition to both personal and societal dominion. Peter and John were imprisoned because their message jeopardized the prevailing religious ideology (Acts 4:1-28). Stephen was executed by men from the Synogogue for the proclamation of the gospel (above). As time went on, the early church was accused of upsetting the world and *saying that there is another king, Jesus* (Acts 17:7, 8).

fulfill all righteousness. When Jesus cried out, "It is finished!" (John 19:30), He declared every aspect of divine justice satisfied. The wrath of God had been diverted from the unrighteous sinner to the righteous Savior: "He [Jesus] was pierced through for our transgressions, He was crushed for our iniquities; the chastening for our well-being fell upon Him, and by His scourging we are healed" (Isaiah 53:5; cf. 2 Corinthians 5:21). Satan has nothing to do with the people of God because he can no longer bring a charge against God's elect (Romans 8:33-39); this is why Satan must flee when resisted (James 4:7). Good always triumphs over evil because God controls both: "And we know that God causes all things to work together for good to those who love God, to those who are called according to His purpose" (Romans 8:28). If Satan is ruling in a particular area of our society (e.g., civil government), it is only because men have allowed him to rule (cf. Judges 9:14, 15). The Bible's injunction is clear: "Do not give the devil an opportunity" (Ephesians 4:27).

Christians must understand that dominion means more than simply being ready to act when confronted by the devil. Satan wants us to believe it is the Christian's duty to fight him, to engage in a defensive war, to spend all our energy opposing his actions. While we must have our defenses up (otherwise there would not be much use in putting on armor), it is more important to restore our world according to God's commandments and thus put the enemy on the defensive (Matthew 16:18). No one ever won a war by remaining on the defensive. Christians must effect change in their society by *implementing* the word of God. For example, being against abortion is biblical, but ignoring those who want to abort their babies is not. Government give-a-way programs are wrong, but ignoring those who are truly in need is worse. Opposing state-controlled teaching in public schools is necessary, but failing to establish parent-funded Christian schools allows the state to control our children. Christians can best oppose the enemy by *creating* a godly social order.

7. Absolute governmental sovereignty manifests itself in two ways. *First,* by refusing to acknowledge God as the only true sovereign, the people desire the kingship of another and thus "vote" themselves a protector. Instead of acknowledging that the rise of foreign aggressors is the result of ethical rebellion and the answer is repentance (2 Chronicles 7:14), the people seek a *political* solution. The nation Israel transferred absolute sovereignty from God

73

to an earthly *dependent* and *subordinate* sovereign king and suffered the consequences: "And he [king Saul] will take the best of your fields and your vineyards, and your olive groves and give them to his servants" (1 Samuel 8:14).

Second, as the period of oppression increases, the governing powers take property by force, claiming a *divine* right. Since "the earth is the LORD'S" (Psalm 24:1) and whatsoever is under the whole heaven is God's (cf. Job 41:11), and since the earthly rulers represent God on earth, kings often assume that they have a *divine right* to act as gods. The claim of absolute sovereignty by Jezebel over Naboth's vineyard is the classic case of the usurpation of God's sovereign claim over property. Ahab and Jezebel claimed a divine right. Ahab coveted Naboth's vineyard and offered him a "better vineyard" (1 Kings 21:2, 6). Naboth refused the king's offer as he had every right to do because he saw his land as an inheritance that he desired to keep in his family: "The LORD forbid me that I should give you the inheritance of my fathers" (v. 3). For Naboth, possession of the land meant a stake in the future. He was dominion-minded. Giving up his land to despotic rulers meant giving up the future and present liberty.

Jezebel, the wife of Ahab, would not take no for an answer. She chided her husband: "Do you now reign over Israel? Arise, eat bread, and let your heart be joyful; I will give you the vineyard of Naboth the Jezreelite" (v. 7). Jezebel denied God's sovereign claim to the earth and His *delegated* sovereignty (stewardship) to His faithful people. Jezebel claimed what only belonged to God: "*I* will give you [Ahab] the vineyard." A plot was manufactured to confiscate Naboth's land. Eventually he was murdered because he would not cooperate (vv. 8-16). The just end of these tyrants is established through the mouth of the prophet Elijah: "Thus says the LORD, 'Have you murdered, and also taken possession?' . . . Thus says the LORD, 'In the place where the dogs licked up the blood of Naboth the dogs shall lick up your blood, even yours' " (1 Kings 21:19; cf. 1 Kings 22:38).

When the people lose their land, they lose the future, and dominion is curtailed. This is why the Bible is land-oriented, both in the Old and New Testaments. Forty years of dominion were lost because Israel could not occupy the land (Numbers 14:33, 34). Seventy years were spent under the dominion of Babylon because of Israel's repeated sins (Jeremiah 25:1-26; 29:10; Daniel 9:1, 2). Israel's land was occupied by Rome for generations. But the Bible promises that those who are "humble will inherit the land, and will delight themselves in abundant prosperity" (Psalm 37:11; cf. Matthew 5:5). A nation that continues to reject God as the sovereign over all things faces eviction from the land, and dominion will be postponed.

If Christians are to take dominion, their educational institutions must be built upon the Rock, Jesus Christ. The purpose of Harvard College was plainly stated by its leaders: *Let every student be plainly instructed, and earnestly pressed to consider well, the main end of his life and studies is, to know God and Jesus Christ which is eternal life (John 17:3) and therefore lay Christ in the bottom, as the only foundation of all sound knowledge and learning.*

And Jesus entered the temple and cast out all those who were buying and selling in the temple, and overturned the tables of the moneychangers and the seats of those who were selling doves. And He said to them, "It is written, 'MY HOUSE SHALL BE CALLED A HOUSE OF PRAYER'; but you have made it a robber's den" (Matthew 21:12, 13).

Lesson 4

Sovereignty
and
Ownership

God's sovereignty includes ownership of all His creation. Melchizedek, in blessing Abram, said, "Blessed be Abram of God Most High, *Possessor of heaven and earth* (Genesis 14:19; cf. v. 22). The Bible continues the relationship between sovereignty and ownership by declaring to Israel that all the earth is His (Exodus 19:5). God demands obedience from His people because they live in the midst of His creation. They are responsible as *stewards* of God's order. They cannot claim independent sovereignty or independent ownership. The Psalmist records God's words: "Hear, O My people, and I will speak; O Israel, I will testify against you; I am your God . . . For every beast of the forest is Mine, the cattle on a thousand hills . . . For the world is Mine, and all it contains" (Psalm 50:7, 10-12). The New Testament continues the relationship between sovereignty and ownership: "For the earth is the Lord's, and all it contains" (1 Corinthians 10:26). No aspect of the created order lies outside God's claim of absolute ownership.

Because God is absolutely sovereign, no earthly institution can claim independent and absolute ownership of property. Only God can claim such a right. Man's claim to absolute sovereignty is foolish in light of the fact that "God is the Creator, and therefore the Proprietor, Owner, and Lord of all things; apart from him there is neither existence nor ownership; he alone has absolute authority; his will is decisive everywhere and always. Again and again Scripture makes mention of God's sovereign will" (Herman Bavinck, *The Doctrine of God*, p. 223). This does not mean, however, that individuals, families, and corporations cannot own property. Rather, it means that the ownership of property is regarded as a stewardship to be governed by the word of God. The accumulation of property through theft (Exodus 20:15), confiscation of property by governmental decree (1 Kings 21), and the willful destruction of property by the envious (Genesis 26:12-17) are lawless acts, destructive to an orderly society. The possession of property is a way for the godly to fulfill their dominion assignment under God. God gives His creatures possession of the earth to extend the boundaries of the kingdom as they fulfill their calling in obedience to His word; therefore, the confiscation of property is an attack upon the kingdom and its advance.

Since the family is the primary institution whereby the Dominion Covenant is to be extended, laws were given to protect the property of families. The Jubilee laws of Leviticus 25 insured a family that it would always have land so that dominion could be exercised. Property could not be taxed. Even the father could not dispossess his family from the land because of carelessness, poor stewardship, or debt. Fathers were instructed to lay up an inheritance for their children so that the work of dominion under God could continue.

When a man is secure in the possession of his property, he has an area of liberty and dominion which is beyond the reach of other men. If no man and no state can reach in to tax and confiscate his property, man can enjoy true liberty and great security, whether he be prosperous or poor. Every attack on private property is, therefore, an attack on man's liberty. Man's freedom and security in the possession of his property is not only basic to man's independence, but it is also basic to his power. A man has power if he can act independently of other men and the state, if he can make his stand in the confidence of liberty. Every attack on private property therefore is also an attack on the powers of free men as well as their liberty (R. J. Rushdoony, *Law and Liberty*, p. 65).

Is it any wonder, therefore, that Karl Marx in his *Communist Manifesto* declared the right to hold individual private property was a crime against the state? His first "commandment" called for the "abolition of property in land and application of all rents of land to public purposes." His third "commandment" abolished "all right of inheritance." Both of these edicts sought to overrule the biblical order where laws against theft operate and inheritance laws are the norm. Marx understood that "property is power." The Bible secures private property for *many* individuals and *many* families. Communism consolidates power under the umbrella of the *one* state. From this position of consolidated power the state controls the individual, the family, church, school, and every other institution God ordained for the proper ordering of society. The state therefore becomes both sovereign and owner, displacing God as the absolute sovereign and owner over all creation. The direction of the people comes from the state's central planning committee. This committee determines what is "best" for the people.

God is the Creator, and therefore the Proprietor, Owner, and Lord of all things; apart from him there is neither existence nor ownership; he alone has absolute authority; his will is decisive everywhere and always. Again and again Scripture makes mention of God's sovereign will.

–Herman Bavinck

Those who wish to deny private property, and thus, the biblical mandate of stewardship, fail to recognize God's order for society. A person's property is tied to the past and has meaning for the future because it is seen in the context of the family as God's means of insuring future dominion. This is why Naboth was unwilling to sell his vineyard: "The LORD forbid that I should give you [Ahab] the inheritance of my fathers" (1 Kings 21:3). Property must be seen in the context of a man and his family's calling under God. The commandments "You shall not steal" and "You shall not covet" (Exodus 20:15, 17) are meaningless unless there are prior owners responsible to God as faithful stewards of *His* property.

Since the creature's relationship is one of steward under His heavenly Master, we can expect God to require an accounting of property He places in our possession. A steward manages the household and resources of his owner. The parable of the unfaithful steward shows how serious God is about the resources He places in our care. He expects a return on His investment. The

Christian is told to "do business" until Jesus returns: "A certain nobleman went to a distant country to receive a kingdom for himself, and then return. And he called ten of his slaves, and gave them ten minas, and said to them, 'Do business with this until I come back' " (Luke 19:12, 13). The slave who refused to develop and extend the stewardship that was given to him lost even the original possession: "Take the mina away from [the poor steward], and give it to the one who has the ten minas" (v. 24). When the bystanders protested, Jesus silenced them with these words: "I tell you, that to everyone who has shall more be given, but from the one who does not have, even what he does have shall be taken away" (v. 26).

Those who fail to recognize their ownership as a stewardship seldom understand that without the hand of God they would have nothing. Even the ability to use the property God gives us comes from Him. It is God who gives gifts to men (Ephesians 4:8) and supplies resources for productivity:

It is God who gives rain upon the earth, and sends water upon the fields. He makes His sun to rise upon the evil and the good, and sends rain on the just and the unjust. He clothes the grass of the field, causing the grass to grow for cattle and herb for the service of man. He feeds the birds of heaven. Not a sparrow falls to the ground without His knowledge and will. He gives us our daily bread . . . He crowns the year with goodness and the paths drop fatness. He even gives that which is abused and used in the service of another god. He gave grain and new wine and the oil and multiplied silver and gold which they used for Baal. He makes the wind His messengers and flames of fire His ministers. The whole earth is filled with His glory. So that the pious contemplation of His working brings forth the exclamation of adoration, "O Lord, how manifold are thy works! in wisdom hast thou made them all: the earth is full of thy riches" (Job 5:10; Matt. 5:45; Ps. 104:4; 104:24; 65:11; Hos. 2:8) (John Murray, *The Sovereignty of God*, p. 9f.).

The unrighteous steward claims to be the absolute sovereign. He claims absolute ownership because he fails to recognize that all good things come from God's gracious hand. God will have His day of accounting where He will determine the faithfulness of our stewardship under Him (Matthew 25:21). The unrighteous steward considers himself the source and distributor of wealth. He is accountable to no one for how he uses "his" property.

Questions For Discussion

1. Over what does our Sovereign God claim ownership? What right does God have in claiming ownership?

a. Genesis 1:1; 14:19, 22; Leviticus 25:23; Psalm 24:1; 50:10; 89:11

_____
_____
_____
_____
_____
_____

b. Colossians 1:16; Job 1 and 2; 1 Kings 22:19-23

_____
_____
_____
_____
_____

c. Genesis 2:16, 17; Deuteronomy 4:20

_____
_____
_____
_____
_____

d. Jeremiah 25:1-12; Romans 13:1; Colossians 1:16

_____
_____
_____
_____
_____
_____

2. How does God manifest His absolute and unlimited sovereign ownership of all aspects of creation? (Exodus 5:1, 2; Ezekiel 46:18; cf. Matthew 21:43; 23:37-24:3; 26:24; John 18:33-37)

_____

_____

_____

_____

_____

_____

_____

_____

3. In what way is man's ownership a _stewardship_? How is this stewardship to manifest itself in the ownership of property? (Genesis 1:26-28; 2:15; Matthew 21:33-46; Luke 19:11-27)

_____

_____

_____

_____

_____

_____

_____

4. How did Adam and Eve's denial of God's ownership of all creation affect the property of their posterity who continue to be stewards of God's creation? (Genesis 4:1-8, 23, 24; 6:1, 2; 14:10, 12; 26:12-15)

_____

_____

_____

_____

_____

_____

_____

_____

5. What instructions regarding ownership has God given to compensate people and institutions from theft? (Exodus 22:1-9; Deuteronomy 19:14; 27:9; Luke 19:1-10; Ephesians 4:28)

_____

_____

_____

_____

_____

6. How may one legitimately acquire property?

a. Genesis 41:57; 42:2-10; Jeremiah 32:6-15; Proverbs 31:16; 1 Timothy 5:18; Deuteronomy 25:4; 1 Corinthians 9:9-11

_____

_____

_____

_____

_____

b. Proverbs 19:14; 2 Corinthians 12:14

_____

_____

_____

_____

_____

7. Can people claim "common" ownership in the name of "social justice"? Do poor people have the _right_ to the property of the wealthy? (Exodus 20:15; Acts 4:32-5:6)

_____

_____

_____

_____

_____

_____

8. What did Jesus teach concerning property? (Matthew 4:21; 20:1-16; Mark 1:19, 20; 19:16-26; Mark 10:17-31; Luke 6:19-31; 12:16-34; 18:18-30)

_____

_____

_____

_____

_____

_____

_____

_____

_____

Summary

"The Bible infers that man has a right to own property. We recall that Abraham entered the land of Canaan as a stranger. In the Old Testament we read that he purchased a piece of property in the land upon which there was the cave of Machpelah (Genesis 23). He was free to choose this property, to buy it, and to use it for whatever legitimate purpose he desired.

"The land was later divided among the twelve tribes of Israel, and the individuals of those tribes had the right to own private property and to leave it to their descendants (Joshua 13-17).

"Naboth, who owned a piece of land on which was a fine vineyard, had inherited this land from his ancestors. King Ahab wanted it. Naboth did not want to sell it. Stirred by his evil wife, Jezebel, Ahab took the land and had Naboth and his family executed. This was theft plus murder; and for these crimes, the judgment of God fell upon Ahab and his wife (I Kings 21:1-16).

"The New Testament ratifies the teaching of the Old Testament on this subject. The parables of Jesus have economic implications. The talents were distributed unequally among the servants. Each man was given according to his ability (Matthew 25:15). It was the right of each one to keep that property and to use it as he chose. In the parable of the pounds the men were afforded equal opportunity, but each one improved upon his opportunity differently — it was his right to do so" (John R. Richardson, _Christian Economics_, p. 97).

Naboth, who owned a piece of land on which was a fine vineyard, had inherited this land from his ancestors. King Ahab wanted it. Stirred by his evil wife, Jezebel, Ahab took the land and had Naboth and his family executed. This was theft plus murder; and for these crimes, the judgment of God fell upon Ahab and his wife [above] (I Kings 21:1-16).

Answers to Questions for Discussion

1. a. (Genesis 1:1; 14:19, 22; Leviticus 25:23; Psalm 24:1; 50:10; 89:11): God claims ownership over all creation because He created all things: "The earth is the LORD'S, and all it contains, the world, and those who dwell in it" (Psalm 24:1; cf. Genesis 1:1; 14:19, 22). God claims ownership over all the earth and its resources: "For every beast of the forest is Mine, the cattle on a thousand hills" (Psalm 50:10).

b. (Colossians 1:16; Job 1, 2; 1 Kings 22:19-23): God also owns that which is invisible: "For by Him all things were created, both in the heavens and on earth, visible and invisible, whether thrones or dominions or rulers or authorities — all things have been created by Him and for Him" (Colossians 1:16). Even Satan, God's enemy, acknowledges God's ownership over him. Satan is a member of God's court and his followers do God's bidding (cf. Job 1 and 2 and 1 Kings 22:19-23).

c. (Genesis 2:16, 17; Deuteronomy 4:20; 1 Corinthians 6:20; 7:23; Acts 20:28; 1 Peter 1:18f.): God's ownership includes man, the crown of creation. God has the right to dictate the terms of His ownership because He is the Creator: "And the LORD God commanded the man, saying, 'From any tree of the garden you may eat freely; but from the tree of the knowledge of good and evil you shall not eat, for in the day that you eat from it you shall surely die' " (Genesis 2:16, 17). The nation Israel was God's special "possession" (Deuteronomy 4:20). The Christian is owned in a special way because he or she has been "bought with a price" (1 Corinthians 6:20; cf. 7:23; Acts 20:28; 1 Peter 1:18f.; 2 Peter 2:1; Revelation 5:9).

d. (Jeremiah 25:1-12; Romans 13:1; Colossians 1:16): God owns the political powers of the nations, and they do His bidding. God chose Nebuchadnezzar as His servant to punish His people for seventy years (Jeremiah 25:1-12). All earthly authority comes from God: "Let every person be in subjection to the governing authorities. *For there is no authority except from God, and those which exist are established by God*" (Romans 13:1; cf. Colossians 1:16).

Moreover, God's position as the sovereign owner affects the way the created order is governed: "And He [Jesus] is the radiance of His glory and the exact representation of His nature, and upholds all things by the word of His power" (Hebrews 1:3). God's word is our starting point for consideration as to how creation should function and whose laws should rule. The evolutionary theory of origins places ownership of the created order, what evolutionists call "Nature," in the hands of man. Man, therefore, is left to formulate his own laws and standards of conduct. The upholding of all things is now accomplished by the word of man rather than the word of Jesus Christ. Unlike the evolutionary system of thought, biblical Christianity affirms that "Jesus Christ is the same yesterday and today, yes and forever" (Hebrews 13:8), and we can expect His laws for the government of the created order to remain the same (Matthew 5:17-29; cf. Malachi 3:6). The Christian, knowing God's unchanging character, knows God will providentially sustain, direct, and rule all things according to His good pleasure, according to the council of His will (cf. Ephesians 1:11).

Karl Marx abhorred the right of *private property*. He considered it a crime against the State. He called for the *abolition of property in land and application of all rents of land to public purposes.* He also wanted to abolish *all right of inheritance.*

2. Only God can claim *absolute* ownership of the created order. And only God can delegate a *limited* sovereignty to whomever He wishes. Moreover, only God can remove the limited sovereignty He gives to His servants. Sovereignty had been removed from Nebuchadnezzar's hand because he claimed it originated from himself: "King Nebuchadnezzar, to you it is declared: sovereignty has been removed from you" (Daniel 4:31). God's absolute sovereignty gave Him the right to bring judgment upon Egypt because "the earth is the LORD'S" and Pharaoh refused to acknowledge God as the true Sovereign (Exodus 9:29). Jesus claimed the same divine right of ownership in a variety of ways: "The cleansing of the Temple by Jesus [John 2:13-22; Matthew 21:12-17], both at the beginning and at the end of His ministry, was an assertion of His eminent domain [sovereign right of ownership] over the church. His condemnation of Jerusalem (Matt. 24:1ff.), His declaration that the Kingdom of God was taken from Israel and given to another (Matt. 21:43), His assertion of divine Kingship before the Sanhedrin (Matt. 26:64), and His declaration of His Kingship before Pilate (John 18:33-37), were all assertions of eminent domain over the state, whether Judea or Rome" (R.J. Rushdoony, *Politics of Guilt and Pity*, p. 327).

The cleansing of the temple by Jesus, both at the beginning (John 2:13-22) and at the end of His ministry (Matthew 21:12-17) was an assertion of His eminent domain, His sovereign right of ownership, over the church.

3. God delegated the responsibility for the care of the earth to Adam and Eve, the representative family of mankind: "Then God said, 'Let Us make man in Our image, according to Our likeness; and let them rule over the fish of the sea and over the birds of the sky and over the cattle and over all the earth, and over every creeping thing that creeps on the earth' " (Genesis 1:26-28). God reminds us that ours is a delegated and limited ownership. What we have comes from God's gracious hand; therefore, to act independent of God's absolute ownership will bring God's wrath upon us (Genesis 2:15-17; 3:1-24). Acting independently means to act contrary to God's commandments.

Man's authority to subdue and rule is a delegated responsibility. Man was created to exercise dominion *under* God. God has not relinquished His sovereignty to man. The parable of the landowner who put his servants in charge while he went on a journey indicates what God requires of His servants and the payment He will demand if faithful stewardship is neglected. The landowner's servants proved to be thieves and murderers because they denied the sovereign rights of their owner (Matthew 21:33ff.). The faithful steward treats God's creation with respect, causing it to grow and bring forth fruit, with the knowledge of the Creator's prior ownership.

God expects His people's stewardship to prove productive. The good steward will "do business" until the owner returns (Luke 19:13). The good servants occupy — produce a profit — for their Lord, utilizing their talents to the maximum in terms of His law-word. The wicked servant produces no profit because he does not use his talent to produce the largest increase he can. Consequently, the good servants are rewarded when the Master returns, while the wicked servant is not. Those philosophical and religious movements that look upon profit-making as ungodly neglect the point of this parable. Part of being a good steward is to be productive through exercising one's God-given gifts in cultivating the created order for God's glory. Those who refuse to increase the usefulness of their talents will have them taken away (19:20-27). The Christian should be reminded that profits are not necessarily tangible assets (see Matthew 6:19-21).

God's laws must be the standard for our delegated stewardship under God. The creature must not rule in terms of his own laws (cf. Genesis 3:4, 5). God has not left His creatures to carry out the task of stewardship without an authoritative law-word. This means we must not view profit-making as an end

Profits should be invested to advance God's kingdom through care for the poor, Christian education, orphanages, adoption agencies, medical centers, hospitals, universities, *apprenticeship programs*, care for the elderly, and every other kingdom enterprise.

in itself. Profits should be invested to advance God's kingdom through care for the poor, Christian education, orphanages, adoption agencies, medical centers, hospitals, universities, apprenticeship programs, care for the elderly, and every other kingdom enterprise. Only God's word can set a standard for determining how we should exercise our stewardship.

Recreational activities are part of kingdom life. We should not feel guilty when we enjoy God's good gifts. The first question of the Westminster Shorter Catechism (1648) begins with this question: "What is man's chief end?" Answer: "Man's chief end is to glorify God, and *to enjoy him forever* (Ps. lxxiii. 25, 26, 27, 28)." Enjoyment includes more than thoughts about God and heaven. For example, David sang (Psalm 7:1) and played musical instruments (1 Samuel 16:23; Psalm 33:1-3; 57:9). Play is a normal part of child development: "And the streets of the city will be filled with boys and girls playing in its streets" (Zechariah 8:5; cf. Luke 7:32). Jesus celebrated the marriage of a family friend and also added to the festivities by performing his first public miracle (John 2:1-11). Since all things are from God (Romans 11:36), we should not denounce pursuits that we enjoy. As in all things "abstain from every form of evil" (1 Thessalonians 5:22) remembering that "things" are not evil in and of themselves (cf. Colossians 2:20-23).

All individuals, families, businesses, and governments are obligated to follow God's laws of stewardship. No individual, family, or government is permitted to claim another's stewardship as his own. "The earth is indeed the Lord's, as is all dominion, but God has chosen to give dominion over the earth to man, subject to His law-word, and property is a central aspect of that dominion . . . The ownership of property does not leave this world when it is denied to man; it is simply transferred to the state...God grants *dominion* to man under His law, but He does not grant His *sovereignty*. God alone is absolute Lord and Sovereign. To deny God's sovereignty is to transfer sovereignty from God to man, or to man's state" (R.J. Rushdoony, *Institutes of Biblical Law*, p. 451).

MANUFACTURER OF SQUARES, CHISELS, SAWS, AXES, HATCHETS, AUGERS, BITTS &c. &c.
Importer and general Dealer in Foreign and Domestic Hardware.

4. Adam and Eve's initial sin, the denial of God's absolute property rights, led sinful men to deny the right of delegated ownership (stewardship) to others. If sinful men and women steal what rightfully belongs to God, what will prohibit them from stealing what belongs to other men and women who seek to be faithful stewards of God's absolute property? Before we can answer this question adequately, we must define the term *property*.

First, property is both material and non-material. It includes not only physical things an individual, family, partnership, or business acquires, but also non-physical faculties that are God-given or are gained by experience and concentrated learning. These may include intelligence, wisdom, knowledge, spiritual gifts, formulated ideas, and religious opinions. "By the term *property* or *private property* we mean the individual's ownership and effective control over his self — his mind, his body, his labor-power and the physical wealth he has produced or accumulated through the expenditure of his own mental and physical efforts. Where man does not have effective discretionary control over his person and his own physical wealth, the *raison d'etre* [reason or justification for being] of economic science disappears" (Tom Rose, *Economics: Principles and Policy from a Christian Perspective*, p. 92). Those who think only of physical properties external to man, hold to a very narrow view of property.

Ideas are property when those ideas are constructed in such a way that a commodity results. Books, music, and magazine articles are copyrighted. The creative ideas that are put to paper in a unique way become the property of the originator of the idea. In order to use the copyrighted material permission must be secured and a fee paid to the copyright holder.

Inventors have to go through a long and involved process to protect their innovative ideas, and it is often difficult for the courts to determine who came up with the idea first, especially when patents are submitted for similar inventions. Thomas Alva Edison engaged in various forms of invention for more than 50 years. His inventions include an electric vote recorder (his first patented invention), the incandescent lamp ("light bulb"), a "speaking machine" (phonograph), the "kinetoscope camera" (motion picture camera), and more than 1,000 additional patented inventions. In each case, Edison had to prove the invention was his own and that there were no previous patents given for a similar device. The use of a copyrighted article without the author's permission is theft.

Thomas Alva Edison engaged in various forms of invention for more than 50 years. His inventions included an electric vote recorder, the incandescent lamp, the phonograph (above), the "kinetoscope camera," and more than 1,000 additional patented inventions. In each case, Edison had to prove the invention was his own and that there were no previous patents given for a similar device.

Alexander Graham Bell had a number of patent fights. Elisha Gray, while working with telegraphic relays, experimented with the transmission of tones (vibrations) through wires. Gray also experimented with the concept of a "telephone" about the same time Bell was preparing his work for the patent office. Alexander Graham Bell received Patent Number 174,465 for what we now call a Telephone and was initially the sole owner of the patent. Elisha Gray claimed as his invention "the art of transmitting vocal sounds or conversations telegraphically, through electric-circuit" (Robert V. Bruce, *Alexander Graham Bell and the Conquest of Solitude*, p. 169). While Gray attempted to patent an *idea*, Bell patented a working model of his idea.

Second, a person's life constitutes property. The effect of the fall on the lives of individuals was dramatic: "And it came about when they [Cain and Abel] were in the field, that Cain rose up against Abel his brother and killed him" (Genesis 4:8; cf. 4:23, 24). The death penalty was instituted very early in biblical history: "Whoever sheds man's blood, by man his blood shall be shed, for in the image of God He made man" (Genesis 9:6; cf. Exodus 21:14).

Third, material possessions constitute property. The commandment tells us that we are not to steal (Exodus 20:15). This commandment assumes the privilege and right of ownership by individuals, families, business establishments, corporations, partnerships, and churches. Stiff penalties are meted out to dissuade a potential thief, or, in the case of a theft, have the thief make restitution to compensate the victim (Exodus 22:1-15).

Fourth, kidnapping (manstealing), a crime against a person, is an evil that is punished severely: "And he who kidnaps a man, whether he sells him or he is found in his possession, shall surely be put to death" (Exodus 21:16).

Fifth, the Bible even sets forth prohibitions so civil governments cannot claim a "divine right" to confiscate property. Small but powerful city-states (civil governments ruled by despotic kings) arose and sought to confiscate the lives and property of other less powerful city-states: "They *took* all the goods of Sodom and Gomorrah and all their food supply, and departed. And they also took Lot, Abram's nephew, and his possessions and departed . . ." (Genesis 14:11, 12; cf. 1 Kings 21).

5. The Bible protects private property by prohibiting theft and establishing a system of restitution to compensate the offended party and punish the thief. "You shall not steal" (Exodus 20:15), implies private property is a reality. One cannot steal something unless there is a prior owner. The eighth commandment does not specify what constitutes theft, however. There are other laws, case laws, that specify what constitutes theft and how restitution should be carried out when a thief is found guilty. For example, the Bible instructs us that we are not to move the boundary marker of our neighbor's land (Deuteronomy 19:14; cf. 27:17). All property rights are to be respected (cf. Exodus 22:1-9).

Possessions of an individual or family also were protected by case laws prohibiting theft and requiring restitution to be paid to the victim: "If a man steals an ox or a sheep, and slaughters it or sells it, he shall pay five oxen for the ox and four sheep for the sheep" (Exodus 22:1). In most cases only double restitution was to be paid (cf. Exodus 22:4). Multiple restitution teaches that theft is not profitable. Breeding capabilities of livestock required multiple restitution if the animal was sold or slaughtered. To steal animals capable of breeding meant stealing not only present but future goods.

The New Testament continues the concept of protecting property by sanctioning the laws of restitution for those engaged in theft. Zaccheus, an unscrupulous tax-gather (a thief), made restitution by returning "four times as much" as he had secured by fraud (Luke 19:8). The Apostle Paul instructs the thief to stop stealing and make restitution by giving to those in need (Ephesians 4:28). This assumes that restitution cannot be made to the victim.

6. Property can lawfully be acquired in two ways:

a. *Property can be purchased* (Genesis 41:57; 42:2-10; Jeremiah 32: 6-15; Proverbs 31:16; 1 Timothy 5:18; Deuteronomy 25:4; 1 Corinthians 9:9-11): Abraham purchased a burial place for his deceased wife with "four hundred shekels of silver" (Genesis 23:16). When there was a famine in the land all the people "came to Egypt to buy grain from Joseph" (Genesis 41:57). The Prophet Jeremiah purchased land from his uncle, paying "seventeen shekels of silver" (Jeremiah 32:9). The godly woman works and earns enough capital to purchase land: "She considers a field and buys it; from her earnings she plants a vineyard" (Proverbs 31:16).

The Bible teaches us to pay a hired man for the job he was contracted to perform. Even animals must not be neglected: "For the Scripture says, 'You shall not muzzle the ox while he is threshing,' and 'The laborer is worthy of his wages' " (1 Timothy 5:18; cf. Deuteronomy 25:4; 1 Corinthians 9:9-11). The Bible emphatically instructs employers not to withhold wages from a hired man: "You shall not oppress your neighbor, nor rob him. The wages of a hired man are not to remain with you all night until morning" (Leviticus 19:13). An individual can purchase property by trading his earnings for other types of property: land to produce his crops, work implements to make his work easier and more efficient, a home, furniture, education to increase his skills in an ever-increasing competitive market, etc.

b. *Property can be inherited* (Proverbs 19:14; 2 Corinthians 12:14): Property often is acquired through gifts and inheritance. Such property must belong to a legitimate property owner before transfer, however. No third party can transfer property unless the third party is lawfully designated to do so. A will falls into this category. A third party, the executor, is hired by the owner of an estate to insure that his wishes will be carefully carried out after his death. God is the greatest example of one who bestows gifts according to His good pleasure. He gives life, property, food, shelter, salvation, and all good things. "The inheritance of believers is a total one: The Kingdom of God (Matt. 25:34; 1 Cor. 6:9, 10; 15:50; Gal. 5:21; Eph. 5:5; James 2:5). They inherit the earth (Ps. 37:29; Matt. 5:5). They are heirs of salvation (Heb. 1:14), or a blessing (1 Peter 3:9), of glory (Rom. 8:17, 18), and of incorruption (1 Cor. 15:50)" (R. J. Rushdoony, *Law and Society*, p. 181).

The Christian is to imitate God as he is able. Inheritance is a type of gift. The one receiving an inheritance has not earned it through labor. Rather, an inheritance is a legitimate transfer of wealth from one family member, usually the father, to other family members, the wife and children: "House and wealth are an inheritance from fathers. . ." (Proverbs 19:14). The Bible insists that gains through dishonesty have no place in the Christian's life (Ephesians 4:28; cf. Proverbs 1:1; 2:6, or Hosea 2:7; Micah 6:10, 11).

Inheritance is a type of gift. The one receiving an inheritance has not earned it through his own labor. An inheritance is a legitimate transfer of wealth from one family member, usually the father, to other family members.

7. The Bible makes no provision for *involuntary* common ownership. The only exception to this might be when children are "involuntarily" born into an already structured system of ownership. The child is then "forced" to comply with an already existing law-structure established by the head of the family. Modern-day proponents of common or state ownership (e.g., Communism, Socialism, and so-called "Christian" Socialism) advocate an "involuntary" common ownership in the name of social justice where the state confiscates the wealth of one group of citizens and redistributes the "excess" wealth to another group of citizens making everyone "equal." True social justice is obedience to God's laws. God's word prohibits the expropriation of people's property through envy, covetousness, and redistributive theft by the governing powers for whatever reasons, no matter how noble the intention.

Property may, however, be given away by property holders *voluntarily* (Acts 4:32-35). For example, in order to meet the *temporary* needs of the early church, Christian land owners in Jerusalem *voluntarily* sold some of their land holdings. "On the day of Pentecost, when Jews from around the Roman Empire had gathered in Jerusalem, Peter preached a sermon which immediately added 3,000 new believers to the church (Acts 2:41). Shortly thereafter, 5000 more were converted (4:4). *Because of the urgent necessity of receiving instruction in the faith, most, if not all of these new converts stayed in Jerusalem* (2:41, 42). They had brought enough with them for their stay during the feasts, but they had not planned on staying in Jerusalem indefinitely. Nevertheless, there they were, and the early church was faced with an immediate economic crisis of gigantic proportions. God commands aid to needy brethren, and the Jerusalem Christians stepped in to supply for the needs. Many of the needy were apparently from Israel, but many also were 'Hellenized' Jews from other nations (2:9-11; 6:1). It was a special situation, and required special measures to deal with it. So believers in Jerusalem who owned property liquidated it as the need arose, using the proceeds for charity" (David Chilton, *Productive Christians in an Age of Guilt-Manipulators*, p. 181f.)

Moreover, the early church had been warned by Jesus that Roman armies would destroy the city of Jerusalem within their generation (cf. Matthew 24:15-18, 34; Mark 13; Luke 21:20-24). It would be pointless to hold parcels of land soon to be confiscated by hostile forces. The sale of property, therefore, probably included additional land holdings some of the Jerusalem Christians could part with to meet the *temporary needs* of the brethren. Their action was

97

a *voluntary* act, not for the benefit of all, but to benefit new converts in need. The distribution was handled on the local level by the *Church* leadership and not by a governmental agency. Those in need and those in leadership positions did not demand the property to be sold to resolve the crisis situation. A further study of the New Testament shows the tithe and *voluntary* giving as the prescribed way of helping the needy, not confiscation.

8. Jesus never condemned private ownership of property. James and John were owners of their own fishing business, along with their father Zebedee (Matthew 4:21). Jesus did not disapprove of their work, nor did He criticize them because they owned boats and fishing equipment and hired workers (Mark 1:19, 20). Apparently, the business remained theirs throughout the time they were with Jesus because they returned to their livelihood after the death and resurrection of Jesus (John 21:1-11). Jesus was frequently a guest in the homes of people who owned property. While He healed many people, upheld the law, and dealt with a variety of sins, He did not denounce their ownership of property (Matthew 8:6, 14; 9:23, 28; 10:12-14; 26:6-13; Mark 2:15-17; Luke 10:38-42; 19:1-10; etc.).

At times, however, Jesus dealt with the *abuses* of property and taught that riches can blind an individual from seeing the real kingdom and the way to enter. Of course, because something can be abused does not make it an evil thing. Power, knowledge, and even spiritual gifts are often abused (cf. 1 Corinthians 12-14). Should we attempt to abolish all power, knowledge, and spiritual gifts because certain people abuse them? Certainly not. The Bible instructs us to correct our abuses of God's good gifts. There are a number of accounts of Jesus dealing with the abuses of property. The Rich Young Ruler's problem was not his wealth; rather, it was the state of his heart. His great wealth was a hindrance to entering God's kingdom (Matthew 19:16-22). Compare the response of the Rich Young Ruler with the response of Zaccheus (Luke 19:1-10). For some people power may be the obstacle that blinds them (see Daniel 4).

The parables of the Laborers in the Vineyard (Matthew 20:1-16) and the Rich Fool (Luke 12:16-34) and the story of the Rich Man and Lazarus (Luke 16:19-31) all deal with how money can possess a man and distort God's blessings. The problem, however, is not with the money but with the sinner who attempts to use his God-given property his own way.

If ownership of property is not a reality then the selling of goods cannot take place. Goods can be confiscated but not sold. The commandments *You shall not steal* and *You shall not covet* make no sense if one cannot claim his property as his own.

And Melchizedek king of Salem brought out bread and wine; now he was a priest of God Most High. And he blessed him and said, "Blessed be Abram of God Most High, Possessor of heaven and earth; and blessed be God Most High, Who has delivered your enemies into your hand." And he gave him a tenth of all (Genesis 14:18-20).

Lesson 5

Financing the Work of God's Kingdom

One of God's most neglected commandments is the requirement to tithe. Our failure to tithe leaves the church of Jesus Christ without a financial base to carry on God's kingdom work. Where God's people started schools, colleges, voluntary self-help agencies, orphanages, and hospitals, the state has assumed the responsibility: tax-supported education (from pre-school to university level), federal departments of Health and Welfare and state-run orphanages and hospitals. These state-run agencies reflect the state's religious ideals. In its attempt to be religiously "neutral" (an impossibility), the state denies the Christian faith and embraces a political faith financed through its own substitute for the tithe, the tax.

There is no way to battle humanism's destructive effects unless Christians develop and financially support institutions to train future generations of Christians in the "whole purpose of God" (Acts 20:27). The Psalmist declares that fathers are not to conceal the commandments of God from their children: "They should teach them to their children; that the generation to come might know, even the children yet to be born, that they may arise and tell them to their children . . ." (Psalm 78:5, 6). This can only come through financing the future. This means investing in the kingdom of God to counteract effects of anti-Christian policies that seek to make the state the all-encompassing provider. In order to finance its ever-growing state programs, taxes are levied against the people. As we lose control of the use of our money through a coercive tax, power and authority are lost as well. With a larger tax bite, the state controls more and more areas of society that biblically belong to individuals, families, churches, and voluntary organizations which should be supported by the tithe and free will offerings.

101

If every true Christian tithed today, we could build vast numbers of new and truly Christian churches, Christian schools, and colleges, and we could counteract socialism by Christian reconstruction, by creating Christian institutions and a growing area of Christian independence. Consider the resources for Christian reconstruction if [for example] only 25 families tithed faithfully! Socialism grows as Christian independence declines. As long as people are slaves within, they will demand slavery in their social order. The alternative to a godly society, as God made clear to Samuel, is one in which men, having forsaken God, make man their lord. And, when their decision finally comes home to them, and they cry out to God, God refuses at that late date to hear them (I Samuel 8:18) (Edward A. Powell and Rousas John Rushdoony, *Tithing and Dominion*, p. 4).

Many gifts are . . . given sorrowfully, where the giver is induced to give by a regard to public opinion, or by stress of conscience. This reluctance spoils the gift. It loses all its fragrance when the incense of a free and joyful spirit is wanting.

–Charles Hodge

In reality there is no way to avoid paying the tithe. Either we will pay it to God with a willing heart or to the state through coercion. "Many gifts are . . . given sorrowfully, where the giver is induced to give by a regard to public opinion, or by stress of conscience. This reluctance spoils the gift. It loses all its fragrance when the incense of a free and joyful spirit is wanting" (Charles Hodge, *A Commentary on 1 and 2 Corinthians*, p. 595). Israel did not learn this lesson, even after God told them what it would mean to choose the state as the agency of salvation. The king they wanted would act like all the other nations. The sign that he was playing God would be the tax he would demand from the people: "He will take a tenth of your seed and of your vineyards . . . . He will take a tenth of your flocks, and you yourselves will become his servants" (1 Samuel 8:15, 17). There is no escaping the tithe. By refusing to pay the tithe to God, an individual proclaims that God has no claim on him. Of course, it means that the man-centered state has now claimed him. Wherever our tithe is paid, there is our God.

The heavy tax burden that most citizens must bear relates directly to the failure of most Christians to pay the tithe, and their reluctance to assume responsibility for supporting programs that seem outside the context of spiritual activity. As the people of God gave up their God-ordained responsibilities in the area of education, disaster relief, financial counseling, charity loans, legal aid, and care for the poor, the state assumed them. As responsibilities for these agencies were assumed by the state, there was less need for the tithe. But the funding of these programs was still necessary. In order to fund these agencies and other statist programs, the graduated income tax was instituted. The tax bite has steadily increased year by year.

The tithe also diversifies power and authority. Because of man's sinfulness he is often prone to abuse the power that is given to him. When millions of Americans pay their taxes each year, the tax monies go to one huge bureaucratic agency (Internal Revenue Service) that makes the assets available to Congress and non-elected officials in federal agencies. If those in power deny the Constitution they are sworn to uphold, the tax-payer loses control over the use of his money. The tithe, however, is not paid to a single agency. Rather, it is paid by *many* Christians, who belong to *many* local churches, in *many* different locales, to *many* worthy agencies that support the work of *many* kingdom activities. No one sphere of society can control a nation if the ability to fund a variety of programs is diversified. This is one of the principles that serves to restrict unbridled and corrupt power. If an organization is not using the tithe biblically, then the tither can remove his support and seek another worthy work. The tax-payer has no such freedom.

While the tithe is certainly beneficial to society in general and the church in particular, there is, however, a more significant element attached to the tithe. God tells us that failure to pay the tithe is tantamount to theft: "Will a man rob God? Yet you have robbed Me! But you say, 'How have we robbed Thee?' In tithes and contributions" (Malachi 3:8). Certainly God does not need our money. Even so, He demands that we acknowledge His lordship over our life and livelihood by returning a tenth of our increase to Him. Failure to pay the tithe will mean calling the curse of God down on the entire nation: "You are cursed with a curse, for you are robbing Me, the whole nation of you" (v. 9). There are some real economic disadvantages attached in failing to pay the tithe. Crop failures and general agricultural problems often result from this one act of disobedience. God will remove the curse only when the tithe is paid: " 'Then I will rebuke the devourer for you, so that it may not destroy the fruits of the ground; nor will your vine in the field cast its grapes,' says the LORD of hosts" (v. 11).

The tithe, therefore, reminds us that we do not own ourselves or the creation upon which we make our living. When we pay the tithe we are acknowledging our sole dependence upon God for life and all things (Acts 17:24, 25). Sinful men and women are prone to rely upon their self-sufficiency, believing that they do not need God. This is a fatal mistake. God warns us never to come to the place where we say, "My power and the strength of my hand made me this wealth" (Deuteronomy 8:17). The tithe keeps our minds focused on God as the One who supplies us with *every* good and perfect gift (James 1:17).

God expects His people to be stewards of His creation. The good steward will *do business* until the owner returns (Luke 19:13). Good servants occupy — produce a profit — for their Lord, utilizing their talents to the maximum in terms of God's law-word.

Questions For Discussion

1. What is the tithe's origin and significance? (Genesis 14:17-24 [Hebrews 7:1-4]; Leviticus 27:30-33)

_____

_____

_____

_____

_____

_____

_____

_____

2. What is the purpose of the tithe? (Deuteronomy 26:1-11; Matthew 28:18-20; Deuteronomy 14:28, 29)

_____

_____

_____

_____

_____

_____

_____

3. Why is the local nature of the tithe so important in caring for those in need? (Deuteronomy 14:28, 29; Acts 6:1-6; 2 Thessalonians 3:10)

_____

_____

_____

_____

_____

_____

_____

4. How does the tithe restore authority and power to the church? (Acts 2:43-47; 4:32-35; 6:1-6)

_____

_____

_____

_____

_____

5. Are the people of God obligated to pay the tithe today? (Malachi 3:8-12; Matthew 22:21; 23:23; Deuteronomy 15:10; 16:17 and 2 Corinthians 8:12; 9:6-8, 15)

_____

_____

_____

_____

_____

6. What happens to a nation if God's people fail to honor Him through payment of the tithe? (Deuteronomy 28:1, 2, 12, 13, 15, 43, 44; 1 Samuel 8; Malachi 3:7-12)

_____

_____

_____

_____

_____

7. Who has authority to enforce the tithe? Explain. (Proverbs 3:9, 10; Malachi 3:8-10)

_____

_____

_____

_____

Summary

"Tithing is the solution no one talks about. Solution to what? Answer: many more problems indeed than we have thought. If every professing Christian would tithe, every congregation would be free of financial worries and could begin truly to be 'the salt of the earth' (Matt. 5:13). If every Christian would tithe the church would begin to make an impact on the world that could change it. The church instead is paralyzed. Tithing Christians could make a big difference.

"But because most Christians do not tithe, the church remains in a generally discouraged state. It struggles to pay its own bills: electricity, water, heat, pastor's salary. Perhaps the church will do something about redecorating its premises or improving the manse if there is any extra. In the meantime money that might go to missions has to be kept at home: a handful of the faithful carry on most Christian work with precious little money" (R. T. Kendall, *Tithing: A Call to Serious, Biblical Giving*, p. 13f.)

Honor the LORD from your wealth, and from the first of all your produce; so your barns will be filled with plenty, and your vats will overflow with new wine (Proverbs 3:9, 10).

107

Answers to Questions for Discussion

1. The tithe is first mentioned in Genesis 14:18-20. Abraham, the father of the faithful, paid tithes (10%) to Melchizedek, and all the true sons of Abraham (cf. Romans 4, Hebrews 7) are obligated to pay the tithe to the greater Melchizedek, Jesus Christ. The tithe apparently was an established practice originating in the revelation given to Adam. Certain aspects of the tithe could have been practiced by Cain and Abel (Genesis 4:4), similar to the obligation to offer a sacrifice consisting in the shedding of blood given Noah prior to the Mosaic legislation (Genesis 8:20, 21). Jacob also spoke of the tithe: "And this stone, which I have set up as a pillar, will be God's house [Bethel]; and of all that Thou dost give me I will surely give a tenth to Thee" (Genesis 28:22).

Mosaic legislation regarding the tithe deals with the fruit of one's labor, the admission that all things are from God: "Thus all the tithe of the land, of the seed of the land or of the fruit of the tree, is the LORD'S; it is holy to the LORD" (Leviticus 27:30). Since the economy of Israel was basically agricultural, the tithe is spoken of in agricultural terms. The application is clear, however; the "fruit" of one's labor must be tithed to the Lord as a declaration of the Christian's submission to God's ownership and the acknowledgment of sonship: "God's requirement of the tithe is simply a declaration that He is Lord and King over His covenant people. To deny the tithe is to deny God's covenant and to deny that God is Lord and King. It is simply another way of saying, 'We have no King but Caesar' (John 19:15), a cry not only of the chief priests who crucified our Lord, but of the antinomians [anti-law people] who crucify Him afresh today. The tithe is a royal tax: it is God's claim on us as Lord and King" (Edward A. Powell and Rousas John Rushdoony, *Tithing and Dominion*, p. 16f.).

2. The purpose of the tithe is four-fold. *First*, the tithe is a reminder that God owns us; that God is our Father, King, and Redeemer. The first-fruits, therefore, belong to God (Deuteronomy 26:1-11). Failure to pay the tithe is a denial of the lordship of Jesus Christ over every area of our life. Moreover, for the state to tax citizens more than God taxes His children is to say that the state has a prior and greater claim over us.

Truly I say to you, this poor widow put in more than all the contributors to the treasury; for they all put in out of their surplus, but she, out of her poverty, put in all she owned, all she had to live on" (Mark 12:42-44).

Second, the tithe reminds us that God is the source of all we have: "Beware lest you forget the LORD your God by not keeping His commandments and His ordinances and His statutes which I am commanding you today; lest, when you have eaten and are satisfied, and have built good houses and lived in them, and when your herds and your flocks multiply, and your silver and gold multiply, and all that you have multiplies, then your heart becomes proud,

109

and you forget the LORD your God who brought you out of the land of Egypt, out of the house of slavery . . . In the wilderness He fed you manna which your fathers did not know, that he might humble you and that He might test you, to do good for you in the end. Otherwise, you may say in your heart, 'My power and the strength of my hand made me this wealth.' But you shall remember the LORD your God, for it is He who is giving you power to make wealth, that He may confirm His covenant which He swore to your fathers, as it is this day" (Deuteronomy 8:11-18).

Third, the tithe is the means for financing the work of God's kingdom. God has commanded His people to go into all the world and "make disciples of all the nations. . . teaching them to observe all that [Jesus] commanded" us (Matthew 28:18, 20). *"Our goal should be the reconstruction of Western culture, and this takes money.* It takes donated money. It takes schools, hospitals, churches, the arts, and all sorts of charity-supported activities. If our main political and economic problem today is the huge, impersonal, ever-expanding bureaucratic State, then *we must be prepared to take over many of the State's activities.* Either we pay for these activities and programs with money voluntarily donated to organizations that must give an account of their actions, or else we pay for them with higher taxes, and nobody is willing to take responsibility for anything. The discipline of the tithe is related to the discipline of saving. The sooner we and our children learn such discipline, the sooner we will see our hope filled" (Gary North, *Government by Emergency*, p. 243f.) ;

Fourth, the tithe is to be used in caring for those who are in *immediate* need because of certain economic set-backs. The tithe was not established to fund the creation of a welfare state, however. The tithe is not a remedy for poverty. Provision is made in Scripture for caring for the long-term poor through the biblical poor laws (see Lessons 9 and 10).

3. For the most part, the tithe was used to handle local concerns. Each town was a distribution center for the tithe to care for those who had no means of support: aliens, the fatherless, and widows (Deuteronomy 14:29).

The focus of Christian social concern was not to be some unnamed and distant "humanity" in the abstract, but individuals whom we see daily. The tithers knew those who needed help, with all their faults and shortcomings. Thus, the tithe was also (at least primarily) directed to *help* the poor by those who knew the circumstances and needs of prospective recipients (not to make everyone socially or economically equal!). Are the recipients worthy of aid (those who *cannot* work), or are they unworthy (those who are able-bodied but *will not* work, 2 Thessalonians 3:10)? Such a screening process could only be carried out on a local level by local officials.

When needs arise that cannot be met on the local level, the more prosperous brethren are to aid their less fortunate brothers and sisters in Christ. Disasters of many types usually precipitate such action: "Now at this time some prophets came down from Jerusalem to Antioch. And one of them named Agabus stood up and began to indicate by the Spirit that there would be a great famine all over the world. And this took place in the reign of Claudius. And in the proportion that any of the disciples had means, each of them determined to send a contribution for the relief of the brethren living in Judea. And this they did, sending it in charge of Barnabas and Saul to the elders" (Acts 11:27-30).

The Salvation Army, a voluntary aid society, supplied coal to needy families during the cold winter months.

The church's first responsibility is to help those closest to home. Thus, the tithe was to be administered in a way that would produce maximum efficiency in distribution with no large, self-interested bureaucracy built into the system like our present-day governmental agencies. True compassion and love for people is doing good to them in a personal way whenever possible. False humanitarianism promises love that is done at a distance in an impersonal way. This false humanitarianism has created a system of wealth redistribution that steals from several classes of citizens to create another class of citizens that becomes dependent upon constant bureaucratic handouts. The Bible places the responsibility to care for the poor in the hands of God's people at the *local* level where the potential for an uncontrolled bureaucracy can be alleviated.

4. If the people of God fail to tithe, they then transfer the obligation for social financing to another agency, usually the state because it has the power to enforce the tax. If the tithe is operating effectively, the state's power, authority, and influence will diminish considerably. If vast amounts of capital are in the hands of God's people through funds derived from the tithe, then the funding of a number of institutions, schools, and social agencies will propagate the ideals of the kingdom of God and not the kingdom of man. These institutions will be financed: either the people of God will do it through the tithe, or the state will do it through its power to tax.

The early church learned this lesson well. When needs arose within the local community, the people of God were ready with resources to meet the needs. Those with extra land holdings sold some of their property so new converts would have food and shelter for their prolonged stay in Jerusalem (Acts 2:45). There was no appeal to the state for financial assistance. Control remained in the hands of the people of God so that "there was not a needy person among them" (4:34). As other matters surfaced, the leaders of the church settled problems quickly. When there was a dispute between the Hellenistic (Greek) Jews and the native Jews about the daily serving of food and the way Greek widows were being overlooked, the problem was solved within the confines of the local believing body. The Hellenistic Jews were to care for their own (6:1-6). It is interesting to note that those chosen to care for the Greek widows were Greeks. Control remained with the people of God on the *local* level.

5. The New Testament assumes the validity of the tithe. When Jesus denounced the practices of the Pharisees and scribes, it was not because they failed to tithe. Rather, He criticized their failure to keep the weightier matters of the law: "Woe to you, scribes and Pharisees, hypocrites! For you tithe mint and dill and cummin, and have neglected the weightier provisions of the law: justice and mercy and faithfulness; but these are things you should have done *without neglecting the others*" (Matthew 23:23). Jesus assumes the validity of the tithe along with justice, mercy, and faithfulness. Jesus corrected the scribes and Pharisees because they were only concerned with externals of the law.

On an earlier occasion Jesus was confronted by the Pharisees and Herodians about the validity of paying taxes to Caesar. Jesus' answer was to the point: "Render to Caesar the things that are Caesar's; and to God the things that are God's" (Matthew 22:21). The question was about money and one's *obligation* to pay money in the form of taxes (vv. 17-19). One cannot *voluntarily* give what is *due* someone, whether it is to the state or to God. Caesar is *due* money in the form of taxes and God is *due* money in the form of tithes. The Apostle Paul, dealing with the validity of the governing powers, reinforces the non-voluntary nature of paying taxes: "Render to all what is due them: tax to whom tax is due; custom to whom custom; fear to whom fear; honor to whom honor" (Romans 13:7).

Some believe, however, that after the resurrection of Jesus things changed regarding the obligatory nature of the tithe. Many Christians believe the obligatory nature of giving has been exchanged with voluntary giving. They use the Apostle Paul's remarks in 2 Corinthians 8 and 9 to support this thesis. Does Paul negate the tithe or does he encourage the Corinthian church to give *gifts* above the tithe to help the saints in Jerusalem (an emergency situation)? In his previous letter to the Corinthians, Paul instructed the church to put aside some money for the needs of the saints in Jerusalem (1 Corinthians 16:1ff.). Paul, in his second letter to the Corinthians, is applying the concept of the "weightier matters of the law." While the tithe is obligatory as Jesus made clear, justice, mercy, and faithfulness are also required. Moreover, the Corinthian church had made arrangements to have a gift ready: "So I thought it necessary to urge the brethren that they would go on ahead to you and arrange beforehand *your previously promised bountiful gift*, that the same might be ready as a bountiful gift, and not affected by covetousness" (2 Corinthians 9:5).

To assume that Paul replaces the tithe with voluntary giving is unfounded. Paul's entire discussion reflects the Old Testament concept of giving to those in need: "You shall generously give to him, and your heart shall not be grieved when you give to him, because for this thing the LORD your God will bless you in all your work and in all your undertakings" (Deuteronomy 15:10). Paul's ideas are not "New" Testament laws as opposed to "Old" Testament laws. Rather, he encourages the Corinthian believers to follow what already has been written.

Render to Caesar the things that are Caesar's; and to God the things that are God's (Matthew 22:21).

This objection needs further comment: "A common objection to tithing is that the New Testament supposedly sets a new and *voluntary* standard, whereby men give as they are able. The supposed authority for this is II Corinthians 8:12, and 9:7. But the statement in its original form is in Deuteronomy 16:17: 'Every man shall give as he is able, according to the blessing of the Lord thy God which He hath given unto thee.' The law does not negate tithing: it has reference to the due proportion of our prosperity as something which is due the Lord who gives it. Tithes *and* gifts are basic to both Testaments" (R.J. Rushdoony, *Law and Society,* p. 700).

If the Christian wishes to claim voluntary giving *better* than mandatory giving (the tithe), it follows that voluntary giving should result in greater giving. Moreover, while the tithe continues, greater gifts should also continue because of God's greater gift to us: "Thanks be to God for His indescribable gift!" (2 Corinthians 9:15). The writer to the Hebrews says we have a "better covenant" with greater blessings; therefore, our giving should reflect how God has prospered us, not how guilty some might make us feel for not following *their* laws of giving.

Finally, the Christian must understand how the biblical view of "voluntary" giving differs from some modern views. Some understand voluntarism as an *option,* while the Bible sees it as an *obligation,* but *from the heart.* The modern view teaches a Christian should not give if he does not *feel* like giving, because he would be hypocritical. The Bible commands us to love whether or not we feel like it, love being defined as keeping God's commandments (Romans 13:8-10; James 2). Obviously our hearts should express love, as should our actions, but love remains mandatory whether or not our feelings match our actions. Should the Christian not *feel* like tithing, this does not remove his obligation to tithe; it simply means he must repent of his covetousness and ask God to make him a "cheerful giver" (2 Corinthians 9:7).

6. A nation that fails to honor God through payment of the tithe will incur the curse of God: "Now it shall be, if you will diligently obey the LORD your God, being careful to do all His commandments [including the tithe] which I command you today, the LORD your God will set you high above all the nations of the earth. . . . But it shall come about, if you will not obey the LORD your God, to observe to do all His commandments and His statutes with which I charge you today [including the tithe], that all these curses shall come upon you and overtake you" (Deuteronomy 28:1, 15). God considers failure to pay the tithe as robbery (Malachi 3:8-12).

The entire nation is affected by failing to pay the tithe: "You are cursed with a curse, for you are robbing Me, *the whole nation* of you" (Malachi 3:9). This curse has reference to the curses delineated in Deuteronomy 28. Many of these curses are economic and can be attributed in failing to pay the tithe: "The alien who is among you shall rise above you higher and higher, but you shall go down lower and lower. He shall lend to you, but you shall not lend to him; he shall be the head, and you shall be the tail" (vv. 43, 44). When a nation pays the tithe God's "good storehouse" will be opened (v. 12).

God will exact His "tax" (tithe), when the people fail to give as they have been commanded, by bringing in oppressors like king Saul (1 Samuel 8) and Caesar (Matthew 22:15-22). Only when a nation restores the tithe will the governments of tyranny cease to exist. Because God believes in restitution, He will exact His due payment. If it is theft to rob another man of his property, how much more is it theft to rob God of what rightfully belongs to Him?

7. There are some laws in the Bible that prohibit certain actions, yet require no civil penalties for non-compliance. For example, the ox is not to be muzzled when he treads out the corn, but there is no civil penalty if this is not done (Deuteronomy 25:4; cf. 1 Corinthians 9:9; 1 Timothy 5:18). Apparently, the state has no authority to enforce such a law. In the long run, however, the farmer will pay for his disobedience because his ox probably will suffer the effects of neglect or will not produce in the same way as a competitor's ox. The reason for this is not always obvious: "Scripture is silent in regard to which human agency has the power to force payment of God's Levitical or Social taxes. It is silent in this regard, because Scripture does not acknowledge that *any* human agency has such power. The Word of God does not give *any* human agency the power to *force* compliance to God's laws of taxation, because whoever claims such power is virtually claiming to be as God on earth. Whoever can use the sword to force payment of God's taxes [tithes] will, by necessity, define what is good and evil for society. And that is equivalent to claiming to be as God" (Edward A. Powell and Rousas J. Rushdoony, *Tithing and Dominion*, p. 135).

Moreover, the agency that has the power to enforce compliance also has power to determine who receives the benefits. For example, if the tithe is used for education and the state has power to enforce compliance and also determine who receives the money, the state could support any institution it wished. What if the state rejects God's truths and funds atheistic institutions? The tither would be powerless to channel his money to the cause of truth. Even if the church were given power to enforce the tithe, a particular church or denomination could reject the truth, take the tithe, and fund schools, seminaries, and social causes opposed to the truth of Scripture, all in the name of the tithe.

This does not mean, however, that the tithe is not enforced. God is the enforcing agent when His tithe is not paid. God blesses those who obey and curses those who do not. The blessings and curses are in economic terms: "Honor the LORD from your wealth, and from the first of all your produce; so that your barns will be filled with plenty, and your vats will overflow with new wine" (Proverbs 3:9, 10).

A nation that fails to honor God through payment of the tithe will incur the curse of God: *You are cursed with a curse, for you are robbing Me, the whole nation of you* (Malachi 3:9).

Constitutionally it is clear the Federal government's authority is limited in nearly every respect. Taxes only should be collected for those stated functions. *MILLIONS FOR DEFENCE. NOT A CENT FOR TRIBUTE.*

Lesson 6

Financing the Responsibilities of the State

The Bible establishes the right of governmental authorities to exist: "Let every person be in subjection to the governing authorities. For there is no authority except from God, and those which exist are established by God" (Romans 13:1). Our forefathers understood that governmental power ultimately was established by God, and they structured our nation accordingly. They also understood that giving unlimited power to any man-made institution, even an institution established by God, results in tyranny.

At the time the United States Constitution was drafted, an almost universal belief held that governmental authority found its legitimacy in the Creator. Benjamin Franklin's address to George Washington and the Constitutional Convention of 1787 made it clear that no nation can claim its authority to rule, independently of the God who rules the universe:

I have lived, sir, a long time, and the longer I live the more convincing proofs I see of this truth, that God governs in the affairs of men. And if a sparrow cannot fall to the ground without His notice, is it probable that an empire can rise without His aid? We have been assured, sir, in the sacred writings, that 'except the Lord build the house, they labor in vain that build it.' I firmly believe this and I also believe that, without His concurring aid, we shall succeed in this political building no better than the builders of Babel; we shall be divided by our little, partial, local interests, our projects will be confounded and we ourselves shall become a reproach and a byword down to future ages. And, what is worse, mankind may hereafter, from this unfortunate instance, despair of establishing government by human wisdom and leave it to chance, war and conquest . . .

119

(Benjamin Franklin, "Motion for Prayers in the Convention," *The Works of Benjamin Franklin*, Federal edition, Vol. II. ed. John Bigelow, pp. 377-378).

Prayer alone did not create a national government designed to limit the potential unrestrained power of the state. Prayers must be acted upon (cf. Joshua 7:6-15). To appeal to God for wisdom means that God must also be consulted for the standard wherein wisdom is found. Because man is a sinful creature, his potential for evil must be curtailed, especially when great power is involved. A careful division of powers had to be instituted at the federal level of our civil government. By limiting the function of civil government to specifics, powers of taxation would be limited.

The written Constitution "checks" the powers of the federal government by carefully delineating and specifying the powers of each branch. If the Constitution does not grant the federal government power to perform a particular activity, the government cannot legally perform it: "The powers not delegated to the United States by the Constitution, nor prohibited by it to the States, are reserved to the States respectively, or to the people" (Amendment X of the Bill of Rights). This becomes an extremely important point when any discussion of taxation arises. The federal government's authority to tax is only as great as its stated function. If the Constitution does not specify a particular function for the federal government to perform then the United States Congress has no Constitutional right to collect taxes from citizens for the proposed unconstitutional activity.

Obviously, all levels of civil government — federal, state, city, county — need money to operate. Every Christian should be willing to pay the governmental authorities the taxes "due them" (Romans 13:7). The question remains: What is due them? Constitutionally it is clear the federal government's functions are *limited* in nearly every respect. There is no provision for the federal government to redistribute wealth from one group of people to another in order to satisfy the Marxist-Leninist objective "from each according to his ability; to each according to his need" (See Karl Marx, *The Communist Manifesto*, pp. 54-55). Our Constitutional fathers incorporated no such leveling device:

Those who devised the Constitution of the United States followed the precedent, and benefited from the experience, of their English heritage by reposing in the Congress the power of levying taxes, and specifically conferred upon the House of Representatives (the body which represents the people directly) the sole authority to originate revenue bills. So that the instrumentality of taxation could not be converted into a device of special Privilege or be used as a leveling device or as a weapon of class-warfare in the hands of an irresponsible majority, the Congress was prohibited levying any direct tax on the citizens of the states unless in proportion to the census or enumeration. Thus the taxes which Congress was authorized to levy were per capita only [see United States Constitution, Article I, Section 8] (Thomas O. McWhorter, *Res Publica*, p. 89).

The power to tax involves the power to destroy; [and] the power to destroy may defeat and render useless the power to create; there is a plain repugnance in conferring on one government a power to control the constitutional measures of another . . .
— John Marshall

The tax-limiting effects of Article I, Section 8 of the Constitution seemingly were nullified with passage of the Sixteenth Amendment in 1913. This Amendment effectively gave the federal government unlimited taxing power. Moreover, by redefining "general Welfare" to mean wealth redistribution, "[i]n time, the structure of the federal tax on personal incomes became steeply graduated exactly as advocated by Karl Marx as a prime means of making 'despotic inroads on the rights of property' " (Thomas O. McWhorter, *Res Publica*, p. 89).

The Bible, for the most part, is silent on the positive aspects of taxation. The reason for this is easy to understand — taxation in the hands of fallen creatures often is used as a device to establish a messianic political order where the state is the god of its citizens. In the famous Supreme Court case, *M'Culloch v. Maryland* (1819), Supreme Court Chief Justice John Marshall wrote these famous words: "The power to tax is the power to destroy; that the

121

power to destroy may defeat and render useless the power to create; that there is a plain repugnance in conferring on one government a power to control the constitutional measures of another . . ."

The modern state ignores Justice Marshall's words and "finds the masses harassed and helpless, like sheep without a shepherd, needing a savior" (Herbert Schlossberg, *Idols for Destruction*, p. 185). The collection of tax monies to help the wayward sheep is seen as an act of grace. In its attempt to save it enslaves. Those whose wealth is confiscated are *coerced* into turning over more and more of their "unnecessary" wealth to the state while those who receive the "excess" wealth of the rich become *dependent* on the graciousness of the state to supply their needs. It was President Lyndon B. Johnson who articulated this unbiblical and unconstitutional view of the purpose of taxation: "We are going to try to take all the money that *we* think is unnecessarily being spent and take it from the 'haves' and give it to the 'have nots' that need it so much" (White House speech, January 15, 1964. See *Congressional Record*, Vol. 110, No. 22, Feb. 6, 1964, p. 2227, for official text).

Who determines what is "unnecessarily being spent"? Will it be an unrestrained federal government with no biblical or constitutional guidelines? The state has failed to heed the Bible's warning: "Except the Lord build the house, they labor in vain that build it" (Psalm 127:1). The state cannot save no matter how much it taxes the citizens in order to fulfill its statist dream of heaven on earth. "In the United States, federal tax policy illustrates the government's unconscious rush to be the god of its citizens. When a provision in the tax law permits the taxpayer to keep a portion of his money, the Internal Revenue Service calls this a 'tax expenditure,' or an 'implicit government grant.' This is not tax money that the state has collected and expended but money it has allowed the citizen to keep by not taking it. In other words, any words, any money the citizen is permitted to keep is regarded as if the state had graciously given it to him. Everything we have is from the state, to which we owe gratitude. In fact, we are the property of the state, which therefore has the right to the fruit of our labor" (Herbert Schlossberg, *Idols for Destruction*, p. 187). The state must be returned to its delegated and limited function under God, to punish the evil doer and praise the good and not act like the Roman Caesar Domitian who demanded that the people address him as *dominus et deus*, "my lord and God."

God warned the people in Samuel's day that their rejection of Him as their true King would mean the confiscation of their property by an oppressive state: "And [the king] will take the best of your fields and your vineyards and your olive groves, and give them to his servants. And he will take a tenth of your seed and of your vineyards, and give to his officers and to his servants . . . He will take a tenth of your flocks, and you yourselves will become his servants" (1 Samuel 8:14-17). The day is long past when we can say that the Federal Government of the United States has taken a tenth of what we own. The percentage is much greater. What will the judgment be?

We have been assured . . . in the sacred writings, that "except the Lord build the house, they labor in vain that build it" (Benjamin Franklin).

Questions For Discussion

1. Are certain forms of taxation by civil governments biblical? For what purposes can legitimate taxes be collected and used? Explain. Familiarity with Article I, Section 8 of the United States Constitution will help in answering these questions. (Matthew 22:15-22; Romans 13:1-8)

_____

_____

_____

_____

_____

_____

_____

2. What circumstances bring about excessive tyranny and oppression through taxation? (1 Samuel 8; 1 Kings 12; 2 Kings 15:17-20; Ezra 4:12, 13, 18-22)

_____

_____

_____

_____

_____

_____

3. How does excessive taxation by the state affect other governing institutions (e.g., the family) and society as a whole? (1 Samuel 8)

_____

_____

_____

_____

_____

_____

4. What was the political situation in Israel's history that led to this question: "Tell us [Jesus], what do you think? Is it lawful to give a poll-tax to Caesar, or not?" (Genesis 47:13-19; Judges 3:15-23 [especially vv. 15 and 17]; 1 Samuel 8:10-18; 2 Kings 23:31-35; Matthew 22:1

_____

_____

_____

_____

_____

_____

_____

_____

_____

5. Why doesn't the Bible establish regulations for governmental agencies to institute a property tax? (Deuteronomy 10:14; Psalm 50:10-12)

_____

_____

_____

_____

_____

_____

_____

6. Are any property (land) taxes legitimate? Explain. (2 Kings 23:31-33)

_____

_____

_____

_____

_____

_____

_____

_____

7. Should churches be tax-exempt? Explain. (Ezra 7:24; Ephesians 5:23).

_____

_____

_____

_____

_____

_____

_____

_____

_____

_____

_____

_____

Summary

"One of the problems in trying to comprehend federal spending is that the units involved — billions of dollars — are so large as to be almost meaningless to many citizens. To visualize what a billion dollars means, imagine that some organization had been spending a thousand dollars a day _every day since the birth of Christ_. They would not yet have spent a billion dollars. In the year 2000 they would still be more than 250 million dollars short of one billion dollars. Government agencies of course spend not one but many billions of dollars annually. HEW alone spends about 82 billion dollars annually. To get a figure comparable to what the entire federal government spends annually, change the one thousand dollars per day to _half a million dollars per day_, every day since the birth of Christ. At the end of two thousand years the grand total would amount to less than three quarters of what the federal government spent in 1978 alone" (Thomas Sowell, _Knowledge and Decisions_, p. 306).

Answers to Questions for Discussion

1. The proper function of civil government first must be understood before we can study legitimate taxation by the state. For example, if the federal government of the United States is given free rein to formulate any program it wishes, because the proper function of civil government never is defined, citizens can be compelled to pay taxes to fund any governmental program Congress might propose. When the extent of taxing authority never is defined, the coercive power of the state can enforce non-compliance of failure to pay taxes through fines, confiscation of property, and/or imprisonment.

A legitimate governmental function is the maintenance of a police force.

How is it possible to limit the taxing power of federal, state, county, and city governments? Once an elected representative assumes his ministerial governmental position, what guides his decision-making in the area of taxation? Does he depend on his constituents' wishes, his own desires, testimony of economic experts, or a written set of laws that establish limits for governmental taxing powers? History is a good teacher in answering these questions. The Constitution of 1787 set forth the taxing powers of the federal government in relation to its function. Taxes only could be collected for governmental functions as they were actually listed in the Constitution. If the Constitution did not specify a particular function, the federal government (Congress) had no power to collect taxes for it. The created national government was governed by the Constitution.

On the federal level taxes were essentially "Duties, Imposts and Excises" whose purpose was "to pay the Debts and provide for the common Defense and general Welfare of the United States" (Article I, Section 8). What constituted "general welfare" was set forth in the following section of the Constitution. A careful reader will note that "general welfare" did not mean aid to *some* individuals or states at the expense of some or all the states as James Madison was quick to point out: "But what color can the objection have [that the phrase 'general welfare' is not specified by particulars], when a specification of the objects alluded to by these general terms immediately follows and is not even separated by a longer pause than a semicolon? . . . Nothing is more natural nor common than first to use a general phrase, and then to explain and qualify it by a recital of particulars . . ." (*The Federalist Papers*, No. 41). The modern concept of general welfare is most often defined in terms of wealth redistribution where some members of society ("the rich") are taxed heavily in order to benefit the "welfare" of others ("the poor"). General welfare, according to the Constitution, means welfare that benefits *everybody*. This can be clearly seen in providing "for the common Defense." Taxes collected to defend the nation benefit everybody *generally*.

A study of some decisions of the legislative and executive branches of the federal government in the area of "general Welfare" will support the thesis that taxes could not be used to aid states or individuals: "President Monroe vetoed a bill for the improvement of Cumberland Road because he did not believe the work came within this clause. President Jackson for the like reason, vetoed every bill for public improvements that was not clearly for

National welfare, as distinguished from local or State advantage . . . River and harbor bills were vetoed by Presidents Tyler, Polk, Pierce, Grant, Arthur, and Cleveland. A bill appropriating $19,000,000 was passed over President Arthur's veto in 1882, and a bill which President Cleveland vetoed in 1896, appropriating $80,000,000 was repassed by Congress. The Presidents regarded the appropriations as largely for local rather than National purposes, and therefore, as President Arthur put it, 'beyond the powers given by the Constitution to Congress and the President.' Declaring that when the citizens of one state found that money of all the people was being appropriated for local improvements in another State they naturally 'seek to indemnify themselves . . . by securing appropriations for similar improvements', he concluded: 'Thus as the bill becomes more objectionable, it secures more support.' President Cleveland deplored 'the unhappy decadence among our people of genuine love and affection for our Government as the embodiment of the highest and best aspirations of humanity, and not as the giver of gifts' " (Thomas James Norton, *The Constitution of the United States: Its Sources and Its Applications*, pp. 45-46).

President Chester Alan Arthur (1881-1885) declared that when the citizens of one State found that money of all the people was being appropriated for local improvements in another State they naturally *seek to indemnify themselves . . . by securing appropriations for similar improvements.*

129

What then is the legitimate function of civil government? Romans 13:1-8 tells us that civil government is to be a minister of justice: "It is a minister of God, an avenger who brings wrath upon the one who practices evil" (v. 4). Civil government has been established by God to protect the good and punish the evil doer (vv. 3 and 4). "Keeping the peace" would be a good way of summing up its function. As it has already been pointed out, Article I, Section 8 of the Constitution describes how the National government is given power to keep the peace. With fifty relatively independent states bound by their own individual constitutions, governing bodies, tax structures, and business establishments, theoretically, it becomes necessary for a single governing body to keep war from breaking out between the states over state-related issues.

A ministry of justice requires the establishment of a judicial system to hear cases of those accused of crimes (Leviticus 19:15; Deuteronomy 16:19, 20), development of a restitution system for those convicted of crimes (Exodus 22:1-17), and a well-ordered militia to protect citizens from domestic and foreign enemies (Numbers 26:2, 3; Deuteronomy 20). Moreover, judges and courts must be maintained, as well as local police powers. Taxes are needed to make law enforcement a reality. This means a system of enforcing laws regarding restitution must be financed to ensure that restitution is paid and records kept on incorrigible criminals (repeat offenders). Most of these functions could and should be carried out on a local level, reserved for the states. Taxation could provide the needed revenue to maintain such services. Fines could be levied against convicted criminals to pay court costs. The tax burden would be placed on the offenders rather than the law abiding citizen.

The maintenance of standards of weights and measurements could also come under the jurisdiction of civil authorities. Consumers would be assured that a gallon on the west coast was the same as a gallon on the east coast. The Bible commands the maintenance of just weights and measures: "You shall have just balances, just weights, a just ephah, and a just hin: I am the LORD your God, who brought you out from the land of Egypt" (Leviticus 19:36). While civil governments have the authority to enforce just weights and measures, they do not have the authority to determine what manufacturers can charge for a commodity.

The statement of Jesus, addressing the Pharisees and Herodians, to pay what is *due* Caesar is legitimate if "what is due" is stressed (Matthew 22:21; cf

Romans 13:7). Moreover, every nation's "Caesar" is different. (It must be remembered that Israel was a subject nation under Roman rule. All Israeli laws were subject to Roman laws. We must be careful, therefore, in drawing exact parallels between our present constitutional government and Israel's subjugation under the Romans. Rome executed Jesus even with Pilate's claim that he found no fault with Him.) In the United States the Constitution is our "Caesar." We are bound to pay what it stipulates is our due. But neither citizens nor civil representatives must assume that Jesus gave rulers a blank check in the area of taxation. Paul informs citizens they are to pay taxes *due* the civil authorities (Romans 13:7). Notice that Paul does not say "what they want." The state must limit taxing authority to those areas specified by God's word. For the most part, our original Federal Constitution has been faithful to the biblical mandate of limited taxation for a specified limited function.

If a fire breaks out and spreads to thorn bushes, so that stacked grain or the field itself is consumed, he who started the fire shall surely make restitution (Exodus 22:6).

131

Christians must begin to elect representatives who will abide by the Constitution, not only in word but in deed. All candidates running for public office should be required to take a comprehensive test on the Constitution with the results of the test published so all can see that they really know and understand the Constitution they will swear to uphold. All schools should offer courses on our Constitution's history, purpose, and application today. Citizens should understand the Constitution so they can vote intelligently on issues which confront them daily. Responsibility must return to the people while we still have some of our freedoms intact.

2. Tyranny and oppression begin when a nation fails to recognize its true King, the Lord God, Possessor of heaven and earth (1 Samuel 8:7). When people reject their heavenly King, they place their hopes in an earthly ruler whom they expect to satisfy their wants. This can be done only as he promises and delivers unlimited prosperity. In attempting to accomplish this impossible enterprise, taxes are levied to pay for prosperity programs the people know must cost money. (They never quite seem to believe that the programs cost *them* money.) Israel did not come under oppression with blinders on: "This will be the procedure of the king who will reign over you: he will take your sons and place them for himself in his chariots and among his horsemen and they will run before his chariots . . . And he will take the best of your fields and your vineyards and your olive groves, and give them to his servants. And he will take a tenth of your seed and of your vineyards . . ." (1 Samuel 8:11-15). When Samuel finished telling the elders of the people how oppressive the king would be, this was their response: "Nevertheless, the people refused to listen to the voice of Samuel, and they said, 'No, but there shall be a King over us . . .' " (v. 19).

As the blessings of God began to diminish because of the rejection of their true King (see Judges 2:11-23; 17:6), the people cried out to the state to save them from the tyranny brought on them by their constant rebellion against God (Judges 8:22, 23; 1 Samuel 8 and 1 Kings 12). Political oppression results from a nation's rejection of God as its King (see Psalm 2). The world's governments continue to follow in Israel's footsteps. As a nation rejects God as its true King, the curses of God begin to have their effect. A strong ruling power is seen as the solution to its problems. The people are told that more tax revenue must be raised to save the nation. This is really an attempt to overrule God's judgments (see Deuteronomy 28:15ff.). The people see the solution to their national ills as political rather than ethical, so they elect a new regime that promises them security. In order to pay for the promises, taxes are raised, industry is nationalized, and freedoms are curtailed. The newly installed governing authority becomes more powerful and despotic and the people suffer under the load of heavy taxation and oppression. Discontent resurfaces, the old regime is voted out (or thrown out), and a new political solution is installed. The cycle is repeated until the stability of the country is threatened by outside forces, also the result of God's judgment.

In order to postpone inevitable judgment by foreign nations, an attempt is made to "purchase" peace: "Pul, king of Assyria, came against the land, and [king] Menahem gave Pul a thousand talents of silver so that his hand might be with him to strengthen the kingdom under his rule. Then Menahem exacted the money from Israel, even from all the mighty men of wealth, from each man fifty shekels of silver to pay the king of Assyria. So the king of Assyria returned and did not remain there in the land" (2 Kings 15:19, 20). The recurring theme of tyranny is the king's demand for a tax (cf. Ezra 4:13, 20).

God calls all nations to repentance. All the rulers of the earth must rule under God, obeying His commandments for the proper ordering of society. The people must turn to Jesus Christ as Savior and Lord, and turn away from the state as their savior. There is no other solution: "And there is salvation in no one else; for there is no other name under heaven that has been given among men, by which we must be saved" (Acts 4:12).

3. When a nation turns to the state for salvation, we can assume this does not happen overnight. There has been a general and gradual breakdown in society which finally leads a people to such desperate action. The historical circumstances of 1 Samuel 8 must be seen in the light of the period of the Judges where "every man did what was right in his own eyes" (Judges 17:6). The desire for a king such as all other nations had was evidence that the people had officially severed their allegiance with Jehovah: "And the LORD said to Samuel, 'Listen to the voice of the people in regard to all that they say to you, for they have not rejected you, but they have rejected Me from being king over them'" (1 Samuel 8:7). The people believed that the source of their nation's decline was in external circumstances.

Like Adam and Eve, the people of Israel were blame-shifting (cf. Genesis 3:9-13). Instead of repenting of their personal and corporate sins, they saw their nation's problems as institutional. By changing the structure of government, they believed their nation would be saved. If only we adopt what other nations have, we will be secure! By increasing the power of the state, the people believed they could be assured of protection from their foreign enemies. Of course, as it turned out, Israel was constantly at war with her Philistine neighbors. The people of Israel failed to realize that oppression from internal and external powers is the result of God's judgment upon the sins of His people.

Where God once commanded service from His people, the state now commands service which results in slavery. The family, the basic institution of a society is stripped of its influence. Children are raised to continue the power of the state:

> This will be the procedure of the king who will reign over you: he will take your sons and place them for himself in his chariots and among his horsemen and they will run before his chariots. And he will appoint for himself commanders of thousands and of fifties, and some to do his plowing and to reap his harvest and to make his weapons of war and equipment for his chariots. He will also take your daughters for perfumers and cooks and bakers (1 Samuel 8:11-13).

A non-elected ruling class emerges to live off the people's productivity. Resources needed for godly dominion are consumed by the state and its many agencies. Societal reform is curtailed because the agencies of reform — the family, church, and voluntary associations — are prohibited from acting, or their resources are depleted through taxation and bureaucratic restrictions. Reform now comes solely from the state, in the name of the state, and for the state:

> And he will take the best of your fields and your vineyards and your olive groves, and *give them to his servants*. And he will take a tenth of your seed and of your vineyards, and *give to his officers and to his servants* (vv. 14, 15).

Their hope for security rested in a limited and temporal power. They wanted someone to fight their battles, the very thing God had done for them since the time of the Exodus: "Moses said to the people, 'Do not fear! Stand by and see the salvation of the LORD which He will accomplish for you today; for the Egyptians whom you have seen today, you will never see them again forever. The LORD will fight for you while you keep silent' " (Exodus 14:13, 14; cf. 15:3; Deuteronomy 1:30; 3:22). The nation wanted salvation through the agency of man and his weaponry.

The coin brought to Jesus, similar to this one, had the following inscription: TI[berius] CAESAR DIVI AUG[usti] F[ilius] AUGUSTUS, or, in translation, *Tiberius Caesar Augustus, son of the deified Augustus.*

4. Israel had been subjected to oppressive taxation throughout her long history. During the reign of the Pharaohs, Israel experienced tyrannical civil government. By the famine's end, the people were reduced to slavery: "Why should we die before your eyes, both we and our land? Buy us and our land for food, and we and our land will be slaves to Pharaoh. So give us seed, that we may live and not die, and that the land may not be desolate" (Genesis 47:19). Israel was not immediately affected by Egyptian oppression until the sons of Israel were seen as a threat: "Now a new king arose over Egypt, who did not know Joseph. And he said to his people, 'Behold, the people of the sons of Israel are more and mightier than we. Come, let us deal wisely with them, lest they multiply and in the event of war, they also join themselves to those who hate us, and fight against us, and depart from the land.' So they appointed taskmasters over them to afflict them with hard labor" (Exodus 1:8-11).

God's mighty hand freed Israel by destroying Pharaoh and his army. Israel's later rebellion against God brought judgment, however. One aspect of this judgment was having to pay "tribute" to a foreign ruler: "But when the sons of Israel cried to the LORD, the LORD raised up a deliverer for them, Ehud the son of Gera, the Benjamite, a left-handed man. And the sons of Israel sent tribute by him to Eglon the king of Moab" (Judges 3:15). Israel's continued rebellion brought a tax burden for which they "voted." Even when Israel was warned about the oppressive nature of their chosen king, the Israelites still wanted him — they failed to listen to the warnings of Samuel (1 Samuel 8:19-22). During the reign of Jehoiakim the land was taxed in order "to give it to Pharaoh Neco" (2 Kings 23:35).

When the tax question was put to Jesus, the Pharisees failed to take into account Israel's long history of rebellion against God. Time and time again they had rejected God as their true King. Present Roman occupation of the land depicted the condition of Israel's true worship. They chose for themselves their own system of salvation and law. They even rejected their long-awaited Savior. The coin brought to Jesus had the following inscription: " 'TI[berius] CAESAR DIVI AUG[usti] F[ilius] AUGUSTUS,' or, in translation, 'Tiberius Caesar Augustus, son of the deified Augustus' " (Merrill C. Tenney, *New Testament Times*, p. 152). This offended the Jews because the attributes of deity were being attributed to a mere man. The Jews believed that by paying the tax they would be acknowledging the divinity of Caesar. It was only a matter of time before their true allegiance would be known: "We have no king but Caesar" (John 19:15).

The Pharisees were not interested in why Israel suffered at the hands of Rome. They desired to remove Rome's external oppression without acknowledging their sin and their need for a Savior of the whole man. Jesus stated that taxes were paid by subject nations (Matthew 17:25, 26). Israel was a subject nation and they must pay the tax. Caesar was their god: "If the Jews rendered the poll tax to Caesar, they were admitting that he was their rightful ruler — admission which they made articulate when they cried out in Pilate's court, 'We have no king but Caesar' (John 19:15)" (Merrill C. Tenney, *New Testament Times*, p. 153). Oppressive taxation for Israel, therefore, was the result of rejecting Jesus Christ as the true King and forsaking His commandments as the only law system for individuals, families, churches, business establishments, and civil governments (Mark 7:1-13).

5. No governmental agency is given biblical directives to tax the land because the state possesses no land to tax. "The earth is the *LORD'S*" (Psalm 24:1). Not even God taxes the land. He does, however, tax the *fruit* or *increase* of the land. When the state has the power to tax the land, it also has the power to dispossess families of their land. According to biblical law, a family could not lose its land. "It was impossible to dispossess men of their inheritance under the law of the Lord as no taxes were levied against land. Regardless of a man's personal commitments he could not disinherit his family by being dispossessed of his land forever" (Howard H. Rand, *Digest of Divine Law*, p. 111).

If a government agency is given the power to tax land, a land owner eventually could be dispossessed of his land through a gradually increased property tax. Failure to pay the tax would result in confiscation of his or her land. For example, a retired couple may be living debt-free on their land with very little income, but must continue to pay property tax. In time their income could be consumed by the property tax, with little left for living expenses. Conceivably, a retired couple could lose their land for failure to pay the taxes. Moreover, they would hesitate to make improvements because of the added value to the property and the resultant increase in property taxes. The incentive to make property improvements is lost through the tax.

No governmental agency is given biblical directives to tax the land because the state possesses no land to tax: *The earth is the LORD'S* (Psalm 24:1).

While the land laws regarding the Jubilee are no longer applicable, there is an underlying principle that those possessing the land possessed the future. If an all-powerful civil government had power to tax the land there would be no way of securing the future for the next generation of godly families. The taxation of property often leads to state ownership of the land, an attempt by the state to own the future. State ownership robs an individual and his family of their ability to produce freely, to live out their calling under God.

6. A tax on property (land) is a sign of oppression and tyranny. Pharaoh Neco, in order to show the people of Jerusalem that their king and nation were in his control, "imposed on the land a fine of one hundred talents of silver and a talent of gold" (2 Kings 23:33). After imprisoning Jehoahaz, Pharaoh Neco made Eliakim (Jehoiakim), the son of Josiah, king (v. 34). Jehoiakim continued to pay tribute in the form of a land tax: "So Jehoiakim gave the silver and gold to Pharaoh, but he taxed the land in order to give the money at the command of Pharaoh. He exacted the silver and gold from the people of the land, each according to his valuation, to give it to Pharaoh Neco" (v. 35). Israel knew nothing of a land tax until they rejected God as their King and had a tyrannical foreign government in the position of power and authority. While the people still had possession of the land, the decision-making power remained with Pharaoh Neco.

Our modern conception of the property tax falls in the area of a *privilege* or *use* tax. A property owner is given the *privilege* of the *use* of the property through the graciousness of the state *as long as the tax is paid.* In this capacity, the state assumes the status of owner. The occupant of the land, in a technical sense, rents the land from the state. According to the Bible, only God can grant use of land because only He owns the land. The state can make no such claim.

Police and fire protection could be financed through a service fee, similar to insurance premiums. Police offer protection against vandals and thieves. Fire protection is directly related to property and its value. Those who have much property to be protected should pay a higher fee. The occupant of the property is paying for a service in order to *protect* himself, his family, and his possessions, including his land. Failure to pay the fee would mean the termination of protection, similar to lapsing premiums for automobile or health insurance. Of course, failure to pay the fee would make a property owner liable for damage done to a neighbor's property because of fire. There is an Old Testament case law that places responsibility on the property owner where fire originated to make restitution for any damages: "If a fire breaks out and spreads to thorn bushes, so that stacked grain or the standing grain or field itself is consumed, he who started the fire shall surely make restitution" (Exodus 22:6). A fund could be established by neighborhood charity agencies and church groups to help those unable to pay the fee.

Property taxes for education purposes have no biblical warrant and are inequitable. For example, the parents of two children who own property valued at $100,000 will pay more in property taxes than parents of four children who own a $50,000 piece of property. The children receive the same education, but the family with 2 children pays much more in taxes. A more equitable solution would be to abolish the property tax for educational purposes and have each family pay for the education of its children. This would allow families to "shop around" for the best education at the best price. Those with no children would not be burdened with a tax used to provide another family's education. Moreover, when the children no longer attend school, the parents could begin to save so an inheritance is left to the next generation. This savings could also help pay the tuition of grandchildren, nieces and nephews, and those with limited financial means.

Since it is the obligation of parents to educate their children (Deuteronomy 6:4ff.), of families to care for their own members (1 Timothy 5:8), and of private citizens, through churches or locally established charities, to care for the welfare of others (Acts 4:34, 35; 6:1-7), a property tax to finance these functions is unwarranted. Placing responsibility for these services in the hands of the state effectually removes power and authority from family, church, and local voluntary agencies and consolidates it within one monolithic governmental agency.

7. Churches should remain tax-exempt because of the nature and function of the church, not because the church is a non-profit institution. The state does not hold jurisdiction over the internal matters of churches, their laws, government, and doctrine. Jesus Christ is head of the church; therefore, the church's domain is outside the state's jurisdiction and taxing authority. In many instances, the modern state believes it has the authority to *grant* tax-exempt status to the churches; therefore, churches must meet certain "public

policy" requirements before they can be legally designated a church. "If the church pays taxes to the state, it means that the church then exists in the state and by grace of the state, and is a subject or citizen of the state. This the true church can never recognize nor permit. Emperor worship does not become respectable and holy by its transfer from Rome to the United States" (R.J. Rushdoony, *The Nature of the American System*, p. 56f.).

Even the pagan king Artaxerxes understood the relationship between taxation and control. He commanded that the ecclesiastical function of Israel was to be exempt from taxation: "We also inform you that it is not allowed to impose tax, tribute or toll on any of the priests, Levites, singers, doorkeepers, Nethinim, or servants of this house of God" (Ezra 7:24).

An analysis of how churches are persecuted behind the Iron Curtain is telling. Underground evangelist Jan Pit lists the restrictions placed on religious activities:

1. The churches and their members must be registered. This becomes a means for the state to control church functions and to have access to the membership rolls.

2. Christians are permitted to worship and to talk about the Lord only inside the registered church building. Public evangelism is prohibited in most Communistic countries.

3. Christians are forbidden to teach religion to children; therefore Sunday schools and youth gatherings are not allowed. Even within the home, Christian training is not to take place.

4. Christians are given the less desirable menial jobs; their children are not allowed a university education. They are, in effect, second class citizens (*Persecution: It Will Never Happen Here*, pp. 42-43).

The frightening thing about Jan Pit's analysis is that many of these same restrictions are present in our country. For example, in order for a church to "obtain exemption from taxation" a form of registration must be filed. (Churches are not *exempt* from taxes but *immune* and therefore do not need to be declared exempt by the state.) Churches are required to possess federal tax numbers. More and more states are imposing restrictions on Christian schools maintaining that they must be licensed and regulated by the state. Zoning laws are used to restrict many neighborhood Bible studies and house churches. Churches are now being taxed through new Social Security laws. The list could go on.

The church of Jesus Christ is a sovereign agency. No agency of civil government should possess the destructive power of taxation over God's church. Sovereignty is the issue. The authority (power) to tax is the symbol. Property owned by the Federal government is immune from taxation as well. Supreme Court Chief Justice John Marshall wrote, "The power to tax is the power to destroy." He maintained that the sovereignty of the Federal government makes it immune from taxation by any other civil government. The church of Jesus Christ can be thought of in no less terms.

Jesus Christ is head of the church; therefore, the church's domain is outside the state's jurisdiction and taxing authority.

Money is a *commodity*, a real thing which people value. It is the *most marketable commodity*. In the Bible, money is always gold and silver.

Lesson 7

Biblical Economics

Can economics be studied from a Christian perspective? Is there a distinctly *Biblical* Economics, or is the biblical approach to economic issues only one approach among many? Some might maintain that economics is a "neutral" enterprise where religion in general and Christianity in particular are irrelevant. This, however, is not the Christian view. Economics deals with relationships, the exchange of goods, just weights and measures, just business dealings, contracts, investments, future planning, and charity. How is the individual, family, church, business establishment or civil government able to determine how each will govern its financial affairs? There must be a *standard*. Will that standard be according to man and his word, or according to God and His word? There is no third way. To say, therefore, that economic matters should be evaluated from a neutral premise is to say that God is not concerned about the economic ordering of society.

While the humanist has reservations about Christian involvement in economics, too often even Christians have reservations about Christians bringing the Bible to bear on economic issues. Of course, their reasons are quite different. The humanist does not want to be confronted with absolutes. His economic system is designed to serve himself. An example of a humanistic economic decision to serve the purposes of man is the abolition of the gold standard. Man, through the agency of the state, can now create money at will to fund any governmental program proposed by the state. This humanistic economic policy has been disastrous for our country, with inflation and worthless money as the result.

For the Christian, the subject of economics often is looked upon as solely "secular" or "material" and, therefore, outside the realm of spiritual, and thus, biblical considerations. A dichotomy between spiritual (religious) and material (secular) aspects of reality results, as if the Bible does not speak to both. Such thinking effectually cuts Christians off from important earthly endeavors. The Bible, however, makes no such distinction. Material things are not evil in themselves. When God finished His creative work, He looked upon what He had made and evaluated it: "And God saw all that He had made, and behold, it was very good" (Genesis 1:31). Gary North, commenting on the goodness of the created order, writes:

> The first chapter of Genesis repeats this phrase, "and God saw that it was good," five times (vv. 10, 12, 18, 21, 25), in addition to the final summation in verse 31. God's creative acts were evaluated by God and found to be good. They reflected His own goodness and the absolute correspondence among His plan, His standards of judgment, His fiat word, and the results of His word, the creation. The creation was good precisely because it was solely the product of God's sovereign word. God therefore imputed positive value to His creation, for He created it perfect (*The Dominion Covenant: Genesis*, p. 37).

The Apostle Paul reiterates God's evaluation of the created order with the following value judgment: "For everything created by God is good, and nothing is to be rejected, if it is received with gratitude; for it is sanctified by means of the word of God and prayer" (1 Timothy 4:4, 5). To declare that matter (the make-up of physical things) is somehow evil, is to call God's creation less than good. God and His creation are dishonored by those who say Christians should not concern themselves with such material (secular) questions as economics.

There were those in the church at Colossae who were persuaded that by avoiding material things they would avoid sin. Paul's words bring the subject into proper perspective: "If you have died with Christ to the elementary principles of the world, why, as if you were living in the world, do you submit yourself to decrees, such as, 'Do not handle, do not taste, do not touch!' (which all refer to things destined to perish with the using) — in accordance with the commandments and teachings of men? These are matters which have, to be sure, the appearance of wisdom in self-made religion and self-abasement and severe treatment of the body, but are of no value against fleshly indulgence" (Colossians 2:20-23). Material things are not evil. Rather, sinful man's *use* of what is created *can* be sinful. For example, money is not evil, but the *love* of money is (1 Timothy 6:10). Therefore, to take a vow of poverty will in no way eradicate the love for material possessions because sin is not in the *things* of this world but in the attitudes man holds toward them and their usage (cf. Mark 7:15, 20-23).

Gold and silver, containing great value in a small compass, and being therefore of easy conveyance, and being also durable and little liable to diminution by use, are the most convenient metals for coin or money, which is the representative of commodities of all kinds of lands, and of every thing that is capable of being transferred in commerce.

–Noah Webster

The Christian is called to a dominion task, bringing every area of life in submission to Jesus Christ and His commandments (cf. Genesis 1:26-28; Matthew 28:18-20; 2 Corinthians 10:5, 6). This dominion task cannot be accomplished without involvement in our world, including its economic affairs. How can goods be exchanged when there is no concept of value?: "Of how much more value then is a man than a sheep!" (Matthew 12:12). How can an individual claim ownership and stewardship for his assets without laws to protect property?: "You shall not steal" (Exodus 20:15). How can civil governments be prevented from inflating the money supply without laws to protect against debasement of currency?: "You shall have just balances, just weights, a just ephah, and a just hin" (Leviticus 19:36). How can lawful trade take place if there are no laws to protect the poor, the consumer, and the businessman if, at will, "the bushel [can be made] smaller and the shekel bigger" (Amos 8:5)? How can present-day civil governments, in the name of "social justice," be prohibited from stealing from the rich in order to supply the needs of the poor?: "You shall not do injustice in judgment; you shall not be partial to the poor nor defer to the great, but you are to judge your neighbor fairly" (Leviticus 19:15).

145

How can citizens be assured that their currency is backed up by a commodity (gold or silver) and not a promise (paper money)? Our nation's money system had gold and silver as the standard of value. It was written into our Constitution. Paper "money" only "represented" owner-held gold or silver. Noah Webster, in his *American Dictionary of the English Language* (1828), gives us some of the practical reasons: "Gold and silver, containing great value in a small compass, and being therefore of easy conveyance, and being also durable and little liable to diminution by use, are the most convenient metals for coin or money, which is the representative of commodities of all kinds of lands, and of every thing that is capable of being transferred in commerce." The Bible informs us that "gold. . .is good" (Genesis 2:12a).

An economic system of some kind will prevail in a society. Economic dominion will be instituted and followed according to some standard. When an economic system is formulated, based on certain religious presuppositions, the next step is implementation of that system. If the system is rooted in the unchanging law of God, the process of implementation must also be biblically based. Conformity to the biblical system comes from within, based upon the regeneration of the heart (self-government under God). Conformity to a humanistic economic system comes from without, usually in terms of violent revolution and eventual governmental tyranny.

Men have always had to choose between two methods of social change: regeneration and revolution. The Christian first seeks to discipline *himself* to God's standard. He then publishes the gospel and attempts to peacefully implement the laws of God into the life of his culture, trusting in the Spirit of God for the success of his efforts. He knows that there is not, and never will be, a perfect society in this life. He knows that the Kingdom of God spreads like leaven in bread — not by massive, disruptive explosions, but by gradual permeation. He knows that justice, righteousness and peace result from the outpouring of the Spirit in the hearts of men (Isaiah 33:15-18); a nation's legal structure, is therefore, an indicator, not a cause, of national character. Law does not save (David Chilton, *Productive Christians in an Age of Guilt-Manipulators*, p. 100).

Economic principles derive their authority from religious principles. Socialistic economic systems see the state as messianic, and therefore, given authority to disrupt any "unequal" social order by whatever means deemed necessary. This usually occurs through state ownership of the means of production. When this process is viewed as too slow, violent revolution usually follows. Contrary to Socialism, a biblical economic system puts the power of economic decision making in the hands of individuals who transact millions of economic decisions every day. The exchange of goods happens freely. If a man wishes to purchase an automobile, he may do so. The automobile dealer freely exchanges his product for the consumer's money. Each believes he got the better deal. There is no coercion to buy or sell. Economic power remains with the many. If the consumer does not like the deal, he can take his business elsewhere. A free economy allows for competition between automobile manufacturers. In a socialistic system there is little if any competition.

Christians, however, must be aware of those who want to create a "free" market without the unchanging economic laws of God that really govern our freedom. Any economic system that omits God, not only as a factor in production and economic prosperity, but also as the *key* to economics and economic prosperity, is a false system no matter how anti-statist it may be. The espousal of freedom carries with it certain responsibilities. For example, our Constitution guarantees freedom of speech, but it does not guarantee freedom to bear false witness or to yell "Fire!" in a crowded movie theater. There is no such thing as unrestricted, autonomous freedom, every man doing what is right in his own eyes, as long as an action does not hurt others (cf. Judges 17:6). While the Christian should be opposed to all forms of Socialism and Marxism because of their collectivistic policies (making the state sovereign), the Christian also should steer clear of unbridled freedom where individual relativism reigns (making the individual sovereign). The Bible is the Christian's standard, not the independent voice of the individual or the collective voice of the majority.

Questions For Discussion

1. What is wealth and who supplies it? (Genesis 13:2, 6, 7; Deuteronomy 8:18a; 1 Kings 3:1-15 [especially verses 6-9]; Job 28:12-28; 42; Psalm 50:10-12; 112:1-3; Proverbs 2 and 3; Matthew 6:19-21, 33; Matthew 16:26; 1 Peter 1:7; Psalm 19:9, 10).

_____

_____

_____

_____

_____

_____

_____

_____

2. How is wealth preserved? (Deuteronomy 8 [especially vv. 11-20]; Psalm 49; 112:1-3; Proverbs 11:28; 13:11, 22; 15:16; 18:11; Matthew 6:24)

_____

_____

_____

_____

_____

_____

3. What is the purpose of wealth? (Matthew 25:14-30; Luke 12:35-48 [especially v. 48]).

_____

_____

_____

_____

_____

4. What dangers are attached to the accumulation of wealth? Is the accumulation of wealth always a sign of God's blessings? (Deuteronomy 8; Psalm 52 [especially v. 7]; Proverbs 11:4; Luke 12:16-21; 16:19-31; Revelation 3:14-22)

_____

_____

_____

_____

_____

_____

_____

_____

5. How does the curse, man's nature, and the scarcity of resources affect economics? (Genesis 3:17-19; Isaiah 56:9-12; Luke 12:13-21).

_____

_____

_____

_____

_____

_____

_____

_____

6. What is money? Why are gold and silver looked upon as money? (Genesis 2:12; 24:22; 1 Kings 15:18-22; 20:3; 2 Kings 5:5; 12 [especially v. 13])

_____

_____

_____

_____

_____

_____

_____

7. When are gold, silver and precious stones not money? (Genesis 47:13-19)

_____

_____

_____

_____

_____

_____

Summary

"[R]eligion (so-called) has much to do with creating the atmosphere and delineating the boundaries within which positive science is applied and objective truth is perceived.

"The most popular 'religion' of our day is humanism (as contrasted with Christianity, which Christians regard not as 'religion,' but as Biblical revelation direct from the Creator). The humanist regards man as the apex of an evolutionary process that has taken place through eons of time (a religious supposition itself!). Therefore, he may scoff at any attempt to view the science of economics through a Christian's eyes as 'unscientific.' The Christian, on the other hand, can only ask: What did the apostle Paul mean when he, speaking of Christ, said, 'In whom are hid all the treasures of wisdom and knowledge'? Does this not include *all* knowledge, the world of science as well as everything else?

"[A]ll the hidden treasures of wisdom and knowledge, even those of the sciences, can be sought most successfully and profitably *only* if the seeker constantly keeps his eyes focused on the Person of Jesus Christ. If all that we regard as knowledge is not continually tested against the Immovable Benchmark, Jesus Christ, our Savior and Lord, the seeker of truth may very likely come up with only a pseudo-science which leads him away from reality instead of toward it" (Tom Rose, *Economics: Principles and Policy From a Christian Perspective*, p. 15).

Answers to Questions for Discussion

1. Wealth is an accumulation of what God values. What an individual considers wealth (valuable) may not in fact be wealth. For example, the ungodly may value certain immoral acts, but the day of judgment will certainly prove them of no value. In fact, they will prove to be liabilities. The Christian may value some of his works which are in reality worthless: "Now if any man builds upon the foundation [that Jesus Christ laid] with gold, silver, precious stones, wood, hay, straw, each man's work will become evident; for the day will show it because it is to be revealed with fire; and the fire itself will test the quality of each man's work. If any man's work which he has built upon it remains, he shall receive a reward. If any man's work is burned up, he shall suffer loss; but he himself shall be saved, yet so as through fire" (1 Corinthians 3:12-15).

Wealth, therefore, must be evaluated in terms of God's word. Wealth is described in a number of ways. *First*, the Bible tells us that there is *spiritual* wealth that will follow the Christian beyond the grave if he forsakes his sin and unconditionally surrenders himself to the lordship of Jesus Christ. We are to lay up for ourselves "treasures in heaven, where neither moth nor rust destroys, and where thieves do not break in or steal; for where your treasure is, there will your heart be also" (Matthew 6:20, 21). This certainly does not mean to abandon earthly things. Rather, our *use* of God's good and perfect gifts, both spiritual and material, will serve as indicators of our faithful stewardship. The Apostle Paul informs the rich not to depend upon their material wealth as a way of gaining acceptance before God: "Instruct those who are rich in this present world not to be conceited or to fix their hope on the uncertainty of riches, but on God, who richly supplies us with all things to enjoy. Instruct them to do good, to be rich in good works, to be generous and ready to share, storing up for themselves the treasure of a good foundation for the future, so that they may take hold of that which is life indeed" (1 Timothy 6:17-19).

Second, king Solomon considered "an understanding heart [wisdom] to judge" the people as accumulation of great wealth that would serve him and the nation well (1 Kings 3:9). God honored Solomon's request for wisdom and added to it "both riches and honor" (v. 13). Job compares the finding of wisdom more significant than pure gold, silver, pearls, and crystal: "Pure gold cannot be given in exchange for it, nor can silver be weighed as its price. It cannot be valued in the gold of Ophir, in precious onyx, or sapphire" (Job 28:15, 16). The pursuit of wisdom is considered a precious commodity: "Make your ear attentive to wisdom, incline your heart to understanding" because "she is more precious than jewels; and nothing you desire compares with her" (Proverbs 2:2 and 3:15).

King Solomon considered *an understanding heart to judge* the people as an accumulation of great wealth that would serve him and the nation well (1 Kings 3:39). God honored Solomon's request for wisdom (above) and added to it *both riches and honor* (v. 13).

The Book of Proverbs makes it clear that, although there are advantages accruing from material wealth, there is something of far greater *intrinsic* value — righteousness and wisdom: "Riches do not profit in the day of wrath, but righteousness delivers from death" and "How much better it is to get wisdom than gold! And to get understanding is to be chosen above silver" (Proverbs 11:4 and 16:16).

At this point a word of caution is in order. The Christian does not have to deny material wealth in order to obtain wisdom and righteousness. Scripture *compares* wisdom and righteousness with gold, silver, and jewels. The Bible nowhere states that you cannot have one (riches) without the other (wisdom). The truly wise man will understand how to accumulate wealth, make it available to those in need, support worthwhile business and charitable organizations, and avoid the allurement of riches.

Third, material wealth also comes from the hand of God. Material wealth is not evil in itself, however: "For everything created by God is good, and nothing is to be rejected, if it is received with gratitude; for it is sanctified by means of the word of God and prayer" (1 Timothy 4:4, 5). Material wealth is put to good purpose when "sanctified by means of the word of God and prayer," i.e., set apart with the word of God as a standard for properly using God's good gifts. The Bible does not denigrate the rich; rather, it rebukes those who abuse and distort God's good gift of wealth. Abram was a rich man and received no condemnation for it: "Now Abram was very rich in livestock, in silver and in gold" (Genesis 13:2). Job also was directly prospered by God: "And the LORD restored the fortunes of Job when he prayed for his friends, and the LORD increased all that Job had twofold. . . And the LORD blessed the latter days of Job more than his beginning, and he had 14,000 sheep, and 6,000 camels, and 1,000 yoke of oxen, and 1,000 female donkeys" (Job 42:10, 12).

In the New Testament we find wealthy individuals of whom Jesus approved (Matthew 27:57; Luke 19:1-10), and others of whom Jesus disapproved (Matthew 19:16-26; Luke 16:19-31). In each case, it is how these men used their wealth that Jesus considered, not that they were wealthy.

God is the source of all wealth: "But you shall remember the LORD your God, for it is He who is giving you power to make wealth. . ." (Deuteronomy 8:18a). He has supplied all there is through His creative and redemptive acts (Genesis 1; Matthew 6:33; 1 Corinthians 1:5; Ephesians 2:7). Psalm 112:1-3 declares: "Praise the Lord! How blessed is the man who fears the LORD, who greatly delights in His commandments. His descendents will be mighty on the earth; the generation of the upright will be blessed. Wealth and riches are in his house, and his righteousness endures forever."

Fourth, there are a number of items few would think to value. Jesus compares the world with the value of a man's soul: "For what will a man be profited, if he gains the whole world, and forfeits his soul? Or what will a man give in exchange for his soul?" (Matthew 16:26; cf. Mark 8:36, 37). A good name is compared to silver and gold: "A good name is to be more desired than great riches, favor is better than silver and gold" (Proverbs 22:1; cf. 2 Corinthians 8:18). The good name follows those who fear God rather than men (Exodus 18:21). The trials that God sends our way refine us so that our faith is strengthened: "In this you greatly rejoice, even though now for a little while, if necessary, you have been distressed by various trials, that the proof of your faith, being more precious than gold which is perishable, even though tested by fire, may be found to result in praise and glory and honor at the revelation of Jesus Christ" (1 Peter 1:6, 7). Finally, "the judgments of the LORD are true, they are righteous altogether. They are more desirable than gold, yes, than much fine gold" (Psalm 19:9b, 10).

The Bible does not denigrate the rich; rather, it rebukes those who abuse and distort God's good gift of wealth. Abram was a rich man and received no condemnation for it: *Now Abram was very rich in livestock, in silver and in gold* (Genesis 13:2).

154

2. Wealth is preserved in at least four ways: *First*, wealth is preserved by acknowledging that God gives man power to make wealth. When an individual, family, church, business, or civil government forgets who is the Source and Preserver of wealth, that individual, family, church, business, or civil government will be judged: "And it shall come about if you ever forget the LORD your God, and go after other gods and serve them and worship them, I testify against you today that you shall surely perish" (Deuteronomy 8:19). Once God has prospered a people, too often He is forgotten as the source of their wealth; therefore, God reminds the forgetfulness of man through judgment: "Otherwise, you may say in your heart, 'My power and the strength of my hand made me this wealth' " (v. 17).

Second, to preserve one's wealth means to reject it as an object of trust: "He who trusts in his riches will fall. . ." (Proverbs 11:28a). The unrighteous rich man sees his wealth as his security: "A rich man's wealth is his strong city, and like a high wall in his own imagination" (Proverbs 18:11). If the ungodly continue to trust in riches as a way of salvation, they will eventually lose their wealth to the righteous: "The wealth of the sinner is stored up for the righteous" (Proverbs 13:22b). An individual, if he is to be truly wealthy, must place his trust in Jesus Christ.

Third, "Wealth is preserved and expanded by means of character and lawful stewardship (Abraham, Jacob, Joseph), and it is lost by those with poor character and no respect for God's law (Lot, Laban, Esau)" (Gary North, *The Dominion Covenant: Genesis*, p. 241). This means following God's economic laws of hard work (Proverbs 13:11), honest personal and business dealings (Ephesians 4:28); sound (biblical) economic principles (Exodus 22:25-27; Romans 13:8a), charity (Leviticus 25:35-38), and the tithe (Malachi 3:8-10). "Wealth obtained by fraud dwindles, but the one who gathers by labor increases it" (Proverbs 13:11).

Fourth, wealth can be preserved by passing one's inheritance to godly generations: "A good man leaves an inheritance to his children's children" (Proverbs 13:22a; cf. Ezra 9:12). This principle insures that the ongoing work of the kingdom will be continued by those who have been taught kingdom principles. The next generation of Christians will not have to start from scratch to fund the work of the Great Commission (Matthew 28:18-20). A tax on a family's inheritance is a tax on the work of the kingdom. This means parents must be examples of good stewardship for their children. Moreover, children who do not exhibit righteous living while their parents are alive should be cut off from an inheritance. For example, Reuben, Jacob's first-born lost the privileges of the first-born. This meant he did not receive a double portion of his father's inheritance (Genesis 35:22): "Reuben, you are my first-born; my might and the beginning of my strength, preeminent in dignity and preeminent in power. Uncontrolled as water, you shall not have preeminence, because you went up to your father's bed; then you defiled it — he went up to my couch" (Genesis 49:3, 4). Reuben was a man of ungoverned passions. He should not be trusted with great wealth.

3. Wealth is simply a tool for expanding productivity so the work of God's kingdom can flourish. This means that riches not put to use (invested) are not really wealth. The farmer who does not use his land to produce crops is not wealthy. The master craftsman whose tools lie idle is sinning before God because he is squandering the potential for wealth that could be used in the extension of the kingdom: "For to everyone who has shall more be given, and he shall have an abundance; but from the one who does not have, even what he does have shall be taken away," and "from everyone who has been given much shall much be required; and to whom they entrusted much, of him they will ask all the more" (Matthew 25:29 and Luke 12:48). Pat Robertson, in his book *The Secret Kingdom*, speaks about the responsibility that goes with wealth, no matter its form: "Using a parable on watchfulness and preparation, He [Jesus] made clear that rejection of this law leads to suffering. Those who are given understanding, ability, goods, money, authority, or fame have a responsibility that the less favored do not bear; failure to fulfill it produces fearful punishment"(p. 144).

God has given His people wealth of every kind to fund the activities of the kingdom of God in all its operations: caring for the poor, helping the widow and orphan, investing in godly business enterprises, funding evangelistic outreach, building such Christian institutions as colleges and universities, and every other aspect of kingdom work. Because Christians have neglected God's command to use their wealth wisely, the work of the kingdom has been financially starved. Christianity has a long history of philanthropic work that led to the building of such Christian educational institutions as Harvard, Yale, and Princeton. The history of present-day Christianity tells another story. "Where are the Christian orphanages? I am not referring to Christian orphanages operated by Christians in Korea or some other foreign land. Where are the orphanages run by Christians in their own nations? Where are the Christian homes for the retarded? Where are the Christian schools for the deaf and blind? There are almost none. Why not? Because there is no tithing. Because there is no vision of a Christian social order. Because there is a futile faith in neutrality, so that Christians assume that the State has the right [and obligation] to educate the deaf and blind — that education is essentially technical, and that so long as a competent instructor is located and financed by taxes, the handicapped children will receive all the education they need, irrespective of the theology held by the technically proficient instructor" (Gary North, "Comprehensive Redemption: A Theology for Social Action," in *The Journal of Christian Reconstruction*, Symposium on Social Action, ed. Gary North, Vol. VIII, No. 1 (Summer, 1981), p. 33).

The farmer who does not use his land to produce crops is not wealthy. The master craftsman whose tools lie idle is sinning against God because he is squandering the potential for wealth that can be used in the extension of God's kingdom.

4. Man's sinfulness often perverts God's good gifts. Wealth in its many forms is no exception. It has been noted that wealth is a gift from God; therefore, wealth is good. Too often, however, wealth is seen as the way to self-sufficiency, no longer needing God (Deuteronomy 8:11-18). The rich are prone to reject God as their refuge: "Behold, the man who would not make God his refuge, but trusted in the abundance of his riches" (Psalm 52:7). On the day of judgment a man's material possessions will not be the standard of righteousness: "Riches do not profit in the day of wrath, but righteousness delivers from death" (Proverbs 11:4). The *use* of possessions, however, will be taken into account by God (cf. Luke 12:16-21).

Even the people of God can become self-sufficient in their wealth, living their lives without regard for God and His word. God calls the church in Laodicea back to Himself by urging them to repent of their fleeting earthly sufficiency: "I advise you to buy from Me gold refined by fire, that you may become rich, and white garments, that you may clothe yourself, and that the shame of your nakedness may not be revealed. . ." (Revelation 3:18).

An economic paradox is found in Deuteronomy 8. While blessings are from the hand of God as the result of a society's obedience to God's commandments, there is a time when the blessings can also mean that a society is nearer to judgment: "The paradox is this: blessings, while inescapable for a godly society, are a great temptation. Blessings are a sign of God's favor, yet [in time] — the society's response to the temptation of autonomy — blessings can result in comprehensive, external, social judgment. Thus, there is no way to conclude simply from the existence of great external wealth and success of all kinds — the successes listed in Deuteronomy 28:1-14 — that a society is facing the prospect of continuing positive feedback or imminent negative feedback, namely destruction. *Visible success is a paradox: it can testify to two radically different ethical conditions*" (Gary North, an unpublished paper, p. 6). Material wealth, therefore, can be a sign that God is prospering His people because of obedience, or that His people have rejected Him, believing God to be irrelevant in the accumulation of wealth. Only the word of God can be the standard or gauge by which a nation can evaluate its present position before God. Economic prosperity may still be evident but the nation may be close to lawlessness and judgment. External blessings are therefore no sure indicator that God still favors an individual or nation (cf. Deuteronomy 8:17, 18; Jeremiah 9:23, 24).

5. *First,* "God has cursed the earth (Gen. 3:17-19). This is the starting point for all economic analysis. The earth no longer gives up her fruits automatically. Man must sweat to eat. Furthermore, among the able-bodied, Paul wrote, 'if any would not work, neither should he eat' (II Thess. 3:10)" (Gary North, *An Introduction to Christian Economics,* p. ix). Even prior to the fall man had to work, but his labor was entirely pleasant: "Man was simply fulfilling his purpose and exercising his God-given talents. 'To labor is human,' but in the garden, it was without a curse. God added vast new costs to labor, reducing efficiency, while simultaneously reducing the psychological pleasure and incentive attached to labor. Man would now be *compelled* to labor by his *environment*; no longer would his mere humanity be relied on by God in order to encourage man to fulfill the terms of the covenant of dominion" (Gary North, *The Dominion Covenant: Genesis,* p. 112f.).

Second, because man is a finite being he is not able to secure all he might want. He is therefore limited in what he can produce and save. "The idea of scarcity in the study of economics means that man does not have unlimited means of choice at his disposal; that is, that he must choose at any one instant in time between two or more alternatives. In eternity, where time is endless, we can assume that the time constraint will be gone. Therefore, in eternity the fact of scarcity which we face in this world will vanish" (Tom Rose, *Economics: Principles and Policy From a Christian Perspective,* p. 53). This is both a curse and a blessing. It is a curse to the godly because the task of humanistic dominion is made more difficult and time consuming. It is a blessing to the godly because the ungodly are unable totally to dominate a culture economically and thus frustrate the dominion mandate given to Christians. The ungodly assume time is on their side: " 'Come,' they say, 'let us get wine, and let us drink heavily of strong drink; and tomorrow will be like today, only more so' " (Isaiah 56:12; cf. Psalm 10:6; Luke 12:13-21). The godly are to overcome the curse of the ground through the faithful proclamation of the gospel, hard work, and faithful adherence to God's commandments.

Third, scarcity of resources forces men and women to "economize" and cooperate. Planning for the future must be part of every individual's perspective. It is not possible to consume all of one's assets in the present and be assured that there will be future assets. Moreover, because no individual can gather all the needed resources for life, economic cooperation is a necessity. The farmer must cooperate with the truck driver, the truck driver must cooperate with the trucking company, the trucking company must cooperate with the truck manufacturers, truck manufacturers must cooperate with part suppliers, and consumers must be satisfied with the product being sold at market.

6. "Money is a *commodity*, a real thing which people value. It is the most *marketable commodity*. In the Bible, money is always gold and silver. Money makes exchange easier, because people can trade their goods for money and use the money to buy other things they want" (David Chilton, *Productive Christians in an Age of Guilt-Manipulators*, p. 270). Cattle, grain, people (slaves), salt, sugar, and other scarce commodities have served as money throughout history. Obviously, these types of monies can prove to be difficult to transport, especially over long distances. This is one of the reasons why gold and silver are used as media of exchange. It is easier to carry coinage than to haul a ton of grain. This allows the consumer to exchange his gold or silver for needed commodities without having to find individuals who need the only commodity he has to sell. For example, if a farmer has grain to sell and he wants to buy cattle, but the cattleman does not need grain, the grain farmer will have to negotiate a second deal with someone who wants grain plus a commodity the cattleman may want. This can become very involved and time consuming. But if there is an agreed upon scarce commodity that cannot be easily counterfeited, then it can act as the medium of exchange for all other commodities and services.

In Eden, gold has a special position established by God: "And the gold of that land is good. . ." (Genesis 2:12a). "God provided high quality gold for Adam, and Adam and his heirs were (and are) expected to recognize God's generosity in this regard. The gift of gold was a fine one indeed. It still is" (Gary North, *The Dominion Covenant: Genesis*, p. 80). Gold and silver have certain qualities which allow them to function as money: durability, divisibility, transportability, recognizability, and scarcity. Whatever the culture, gold and silver are recognized as money: "Then Asa [king of Judah] took all the silver and the gold which were left in the treasuries of the house of the LORD and the treasuries of the king's house, and delivered them into the hand of his servants. And King Asa sent them to Ben-hadad the son of Tabrimmon the son of Hezion, king of Syria, who lived in Damascus" (1 Kings 15:18; cf. Genesis 24:22). A kingdom outside of Judah recognized and accepted gold and silver as a standard of value. Moreover, since these metals are easily divisible, they can be weighed in order to test their "value": "And I [Jeremiah] signed and sealed the deed, and called in witnessss, and weighed out the silver on the scales" (Jeremiah 32:10).

7. When another essential commodity (e.g., food) is more scarce than gold, then gold and silver cease to be money for a time. For example, a famine may overtake a people and all the gold in the world will not satisfy a nation's hunger (cf. Genesis 41:56). During Joseph's rulership in Egypt, a famine came upon the world (Genesis 47:13). While gold was looked upon as money in the past, other commodities proved to be more valuable as circumstances changed: livestock, land, and people. But grain remained the most sought after commodity: "Buy us and our land for food, and we and our land will be slaves to Pharaoh. So give us seed, that we may live and not die, and that the land may not be desolate" (v. 19). At this point in time there was a complete breakdown in Egypt's economy. The people were not concerned about the future value of gold. Since the population was doing everything possible to stay alive, the people had no desire to possess gold and silver or any commodity other than food. Gold and silver are valued because people believe these metals will be valued in the future. In the case of famine, however, the future is discounted to practically zero; therefore, a desire to own gold declines considerably.

There are modern-day examples of food being the most desired commodity. During Germany's hyper-inflation period (1922-23), food became the most valued commodity for those who did not have it. The farmers received the "valuables" of the city dwellers because inflation destroyed the purchasing power of the German mark. Value was now defined in terms of what an individual needed to survive but did not have. This is why "[t]here was a steady stream of pianos, furniture, family heirlooms, gold watches, jewelry, and gold coins *toward the farms*, and a stream of food flowing the other way. We are talking about the disintegration of money and the markets that money had made possible. *It was food, not gold, that was king.* What does the term 'valuables' mean? Gold, silver, jewelry, precious stones? Why do we call them 'precious'? In short, what are 'valuables'? It depends upon *external circumstances* and the *evaluations* of buyers and sellers concerning these circumstances" (Gary North, *Successful Investing in an Age of Envy*, p. 169).

Historical chart of the paper money of the United States from the earliest settlement of the country to the commencement of the Revolutionary War.

Lesson 8

The Enemies
of Biblical
Economics

Failure to follow God's economic laws results in disaster for individuals, families, corporations, and nations. This is easily understood by those who make daily economic decisions. If a family fails to pay its bills, or writes bad checks to postpone bill collection, it suffers the consequences of having bill collectors call. What is true of the individual is also true of the nation. The effects of poor money management are not readily seen on the national level, however. While a "reminder" notice may be sent in thirty days to a family because of an overdue account, it may take decades before a national government gets its overdue notice in the form of inflation and/or depression.

If families or nations fail to honor the word of God as the standard for economics, they must evaluate their economic decisions on the basis of practical results. Economic policy becomes pragmatic: Let's try it to see if it works. The problem with developing economic theory based on pragmatism is that the consequences are often known too late. The gamble can be very costly. For example, the great German inflation (1914-23) was very effective in the short run. The inflation policies of the Weimar Republic benefited a large number of German farmers who were able to pay off their debts with the lower valued marks. The industrialists who borrowed to expand or replace their plant equipment paid off their debts with ease. The German government was an enormous debtor that virtually wiped out its entire public debt with its new inflation policies. The long-term effects were disastrous. Near the end of the inflationary period, from July to December, 1923

[p]rices spiraled upward into "the wild blue yonder" as small change

bank notes of 100,000 marks (25 cents) in July were succeeded by 1,000,000 mark notes in August (likewise 25 cents) to be followed in time by 1,000,000,000 mark notes in late September and finally 1,000,000,000,000 (one trillion) mark notes in early November. It was taking the efforts of 30 paper mills and 200 printing presses working continuously to produce the money fast enough (Donald L. Kemmerer, "Reflections on the Great German Inflation," *Journal of Christian Reconstruction*, Symposium on Inflation, ed. Gary North, Vol. VII, No. 1 [Summer, 1980], p. 46).

Pragmatism can never match the absolute mandates of Scripture; therefore, entire nations can be crippled when biblical economic laws are ignored. History offers ample proof that "God is not mocked; for whatever a man sows, this he will also reap" (Galatians 6:7). The German inflation of 1914-23 was the worst inflationary period the modern world has seen. It was the attempt of rebellious man, through the agency of the state, to create something out of nothing — a power only God possesses (cf. Genesis 1:1; Hebrews 11:3). When finite man attempts to play God, we can expect less than perfect results.

Our nation is not immune. The United States suffered a runaway inflationary period considered the world's worst until surpassed by Germany. Several of the early colonies in the late 1600s issued paper money to pay debts incurred by the individual states. In time, the paper would be redeemed for a "hard" currency. As long as the colonists believed the paper would be bought back or redeemed, it was accepted. If doubts arose, the paper "notes" were rejected. The results were obvious to all who understood basic biblical economic principles:

The "invention" of paper money in the colony of Massachusetts in 1690 — the government issued promissory notes acceptable for taxes and thus for virtually any transaction — made it easier for governments to borrow and hence increase the money supply at a more rapid pace than before. In some of the American colonies in the eighteenth century, the price level rose twenty- or even thirtyfold. The worst inflation of that era was that of the paper dollars issued by the Continental Congress to help finance the American Revolution. By 1781 it took 1000 "continentals" to buy what one had bought six years before, a situation that led to the expression, "not worth a continental" (Donald L. Kemmerer, "Reflections on the Great German Inflation," in *The Journal of Christian Reconstruction*, Symposium on Inflation, ed., Gary North, Vol. VII, No. 1 [Summer, 1980], p. 40f.)

Inflation manifests covetousness and greed. Man wants something for nothing, or for as little as he can get away with. He desires wealth for himself without following the commandments of God. John Calvin, in his commentary on Matthew 6:19-21, writes of the dangerous effects of covetousness: "This deadly plague reigns everywhere throughout the world. Men are grown mad with an insatiable desire of gain. Christ charges them with folly, in collecting wealth with great care, and then giving up their happiness to *moths* and to *rust*, or exposing it as a prey to thieves" (*Commentary on a Harmony of the Evangelists*, 1:332). The insatiable desire for wealth can be destructive to an individual, especially those who hold unlimited political power. He can be so intent on securing for himself the "treasures" he deems most important that the real treasures of life pass him by. The covetous man believes that having enough of what the world values will solve his problems, no matter what they might cost him. If political power is desired, then votes can be "bought" by promising voters that certain programs will be instituted that can only be fulfilled through a disregard of biblical law and constitutional principles and the levying of higher taxes and the hidden tax of inflation.

This deadly plague [of covetousness] reigns everywhere throughout the world. Men are grown mad with an insatiable desire of gain. Christ charges them with folly, in collecting wealth with great care, and then giving up their happiness to moths *and to* rust, *or exposing it as a prey to thieves.*
–John Calvin

The people have insatiable desires. Only a steady stream of promises backed up by fiat currency will fulfill those desires. If there is not enough money to meet man's desires, civil governments create it. If gold and silver are too difficult to dig out of the ground, then paper money officially declared by the state to be "legal tender" will do just as well. Civil governments cannot be trusted to maintain a sound monetary policy without restraints. History shows us that the gold standard was the stabilizing force behind a sound monetary policy.

Covetousness that leads to currency debasement (inflation) is just one of the enemies of biblical economics. The freedom to make a profit and the right to own property are also under attack. An attack on these two essential aspects of economics will destroy the foundation of a truly free society. There are many who see private ownership and the ability to make a profit as somehow contrary to biblical principles. The Bible does not condemn men and women for being wealthy or owning property: Abraham struck a deal to purchase property so he would have a burial place for his family (Genesis 23); the Eighth and Tenth commandments prohibit theft and the desire to have what belongs to someone else (Exodus 20:15, 17); *privately* owned fields were opened up to the poor only *after* the harvest was completed (Ruth 2); property rights were even acknowledged by kings (1 Kings 21); the debasement or the "watering down" of commodities is a reason for judgment (Isaiah 1:21, 22); businessmen as well as those dealing with the insurance of currency values (civil governments) must not have "differing weights and differing measures" (Proverbs 20:10); and God expects His stewards to return a profit for Him (Matthew 25:14-30). In each of these examples, ownership of property is the norm.

The free exchange of goods by property owners and the risk-taking of entrepreneurs in a free society brings about tremendous growth in capital and goods whereby all can benefit. When the freedom of the market is destroyed due to governmental policies like "windfall profits" taxes, inflation, price controls, tariffs, unnecessary regulations, and other freedom-inhibitors, a nation can be expected to decline in its productivity. The harder an individual works, the less he realizes profits for reinvestment and hiring of additional personnel. Why be productive if the profits are subject to excessive taxation? The incentive to make a profit is part of God's plan for His people:

The universal spark of economic progress comes from man's hope of
adding to his wealth through economic production. God made man
in such a way that he responds favorably to the hope for profit, so we
must recognize that man's universal drive to accumulate wealth is a
wholesome motivating force. And in a free market where competition reigns, the producers of goods and services will strive to accumu-

late wealth by serving consumer needs (Tom Rose and Robert Metcalf, *The Coming Victory*, p. 108f.)

Either many individuals making many individual and independent decisions will decide economic matters or a single controlling agency will do it. There is no possible way that profit-making will be eliminated. The individual will have freedom to exercise his talents under God for God's glory, or the state will confiscate the "excesses" of production to further the ideals of the state. The *many* individuals will profit, or profits will be absorbed by the *one* state.

When gold and silver function as money, paper can only *represent* owner-held gold and silver. These early examples of paper certificates promise to pay the *Bearer* the designated amount in gold or silver.

Questions For Discussion

1. What is inflation? How does the condition of the heart manifest itself in a debased (inflated) currency? (Isaiah 1:22; Jeremiah 9:7; Ezekiel 22:13-31; Proverbs 25:4, 5).

_____

_____

_____

_____

_____

_____

_____

2. How does a commodity like gold restrain civil governments from inflating the currency of a nation?

_____

_____

_____

_____

_____

_____

3. How does the Constitution of the United States prohibit the debasement of our nation's currency and therefore the evils of inflation? (see Article 3, section 8 and Article 1, section 10)

_____

_____

_____

_____

_____

_____

4. What authority should civil governments have in the area of monetary control? (Leviticus 19:35-37; Deuteronomy 25:13-15; Proverbs 11:1; 20:10, 23; Amos 8:5, 6; Micah 6:10-12)

_____

_____

_____

_____

_____

_____

_____

_____

5. Who is usually affected by inflation before other groups of people? (Isaiah 1:21-26; Amos 8:4-6)

_____

_____

_____

_____

_____

_____

_____

6. Why should the Christian avoid debt? (Exodus 22:25-27; Deuteronomy 28:43, 44, [cf. vv. 12, 13]; Proverbs 22:7; Romans 13:8; 1 Corinthians 7:23)

_____

_____

_____

_____

_____

_____

_____

169

7. Should Christians plan and save for the future, or is the state responsible for our future needs? (Proverbs 13:22; 21:20; 27:23-27; Luke 14:28-30; 1 Timothy 5:8)

_____

_____

_____

_____

_____

_____

_____

_____

_____

_____

8. Why do the ungodly often prosper? (Deuteronomy 6:10, 11; 8; Psalm 69:22; Proverbs 13:22; Ecclesiastes 2:26)

_____

_____

_____

_____

_____

_____

_____

_____

9. How is covetousness an enemy to biblical economics? (Luke 12:13-21)

_____

_____

_____

_____

_____

_____

_____

_____

Summary

"During this century, several breakdowns have occurred in the political-economic realm. One of the greatest of these failures was in the government-sponsored departure from sound money — that is, of money redeemable in gold.

"Ideally, money should be 100% gold or some other valuable commodity which has been raised to monetary status by the value that men freely place upon these commodities. Correctly defined, money is not what government rulers define as legal tender, but rather, money is anything that the people freely and generally accept in payment for goods and services. Over eons of time, gold and silver have become the most generally acceptable commodities used by man for money, but some other scarce and valuable commodities might, at least in theory, be used. The key factor is that whatever commodity is used for money should be raised to the role of money by the free value imputations of the people rather than by government fiat" (Tom Rose and Robert Metcalf, *The Coming Victory*, p. 115).

Paper money was issued by the Continental Congress to help finance the American Revolution. By 1781 it took 1,000 "continentals" to buy what one had bought six years before, a situation that led to the expression, "not worth a continental."

Answers to Questions for Discussion

1. Inflation is an increase in the money supply and/or of the supply of credit (including personal debt). Higher prices, therefore, are the *result* of inflation (an increase in the money supply); they are not inflation itself. When the money supply increases (*usually by government action*), the purchasing power of money held by consumers falls in value because it is cheapened by an over-supply of paper dollars or debased coins in circulation. Therefore, whoever controls the money supply is responsible for inflation. Historically, civil governments have inflated currencies through a variety of means: adding cheap metals (tin) to expensive metals (silver), printing paper money not redeemable in hard currency (gold or silver), adding non-existent money supply figures to financial records, increasing the national debt, etc. The purpose is to increase the money supply to fund certain governmental programs (e.g., wars, welfare programs, public work projects, statist education, etc.) without having to raise taxes. Moreover, in order to stay in public office many politicians promise government programs which only can be financed with more money. Since gold and silver cannot be created, and since only so much tax revenue can be raised before taxpayers rebel, civil governments "create" money by printing it.

Monetary inflation is a manifestation of self-inflation. The condition of man's heart is shown by the actions of his hands and ideas of his mind: "Take away the dross from the silver, and there comes out a vessel for the smith; take away the wicked from before the king, and his throne will be established in righteousness" (Proverbs 25:4, 5). God's evaluation of Judah's deeds was expressed in terms of a refiner's fire and the assayers test of metallic purity: "Behold, I will refine them and assay them" (Jeremiah 9:7). God easily tests the condition of the heart, using His commandments as an assayer uses a touchstone to determine the purity of gold. Inflated currency can be traced back to an inflated heart, a heart that is impure, mixed with the dross of covetousness and greed. In Ezekiel 22:13-31 "Jerusalem is described as being smitten for making dishonest gain (v. 13). The house of Israel had become dross; fit only to be melted in the fire of God's wrath (vv. 18, 21). The prophets, priests, and princes are each singled out by God (vv. 25-28). Finally, so are the people: 'The people of the land have used oppression, and exercised robbery, and have vexed the poor and needy: yea, they have oppressed the stranger wrongfully. And I sought for a man among them, that should make up the hedge, and stand in the gap before me for the land, that I should not destroy it: but I found none" (Ezek. 22:29-30) (Steven Alan Samson, "The Character of Inflation," in *Biblical Economics Today*, [Feb./March 1983], Vol. VI., No. 2).

The Bible's critique of inflation is as valid for our day as for Isaiah's. People then debased their commodities, thus cheating their customers, by adding water to wine and base metals to gold and silver and labeling the commodity "pure": "Your silver has become dross, your drink diluted with water" (Isaiah 1:22). For example, if water is added to wine at the rate of 10% per bottle, the seller automatically reaps a 10% profit without an increase in production. The silver merchants added a less valuable commodity to their silver (tin) and called the entire ingot "silver." "It is when men as citizens or government officials tamper with the gold and silver content of the currency that disaster results. When men's hearts are dross, they risk the production of dross currency and dross consumer goods (Isa. 1:22)" (Gary North, *The Dominion Covenant: Genesis*, p. 81). Debasement of currency (inflation) is nothing more than tampering with the weights and measures God has established as a standard for honest trade: "A just balance and scales belong to the LORD; all the weights of the bag are His concern" (Proverbs 16:11).

2. By taking a nation off the gold standard and using a paper "money" standard, governments can accomplish political goals, but with disastrous results. All a government must do to fund its programs is print more "money." Since the paper standard cannot be regulated (because the gold standard has been eliminated), governments can print all the "money" they need. Over a period of time, however, the purchasing power of the dollar *decreases* because there is an abnormal *increase* in the money supply without an equal increase in goods. The increase in the money supply puts more dollars in the buyer's hands, but the increased paper substitutes are chasing the same number of market goods. Greater demand causes prices to rise.

When gold and silver act as money, and paper only *represents* owner-held gold and silver, the only legitimate way to inflate the monetary supply is to add more gold to the market. Since gold and silver are rare (scarce) commodities, inflation at worst is very gradual. An increase in the gold supply can be compensated by a corresponding increase in goods. Since unbacked paper can be printed at will, the temptation to inflate is great. A return to the gold standard would do much to help alleviate present inflationary policies.

Very few leaders will take the political risks needed to stop the printing presses that fund unbiblical and unconstitutional political programs. Since inflation seems very gradual, those who vote for inflationary programs are usually not concerned with inflation's long-term effects. The results of inflation, therefore, must be passed on to future generations of political leaders and citizens. As the programs of inflation continue, it becomes harder and harder to stop the inflationary cycle, especially as citizens learn to expect the government programs from which they supposedly benefit.

3. The Constitution gives no governmental branch or independent organization (Federal Reserve System) authority to tamper with weights and measures. The Federal government has authority "to coin money, regulate the value thereof, and of foreign coin, and fix the standard of weights and measures" (Article 3, section 8). Article 1, section 10 makes it clear that to coin money means "gold and silver Coin," commodities that cannot easily be inflated: "No State shall enter into any Treaty, Alliance, or Confederation; grant Letters of Marque and Reprisal; coin Money; emit Bills of Credit; make any Thing but gold and silver Coin a Tender in Payment of Debts . . ." This section of the United States Constitution is ignored by our national and state governments. Debts no longer are paid with gold or silver. Paper Federal Reserve Notes are now "legal tender," a clear violation of the Constitution, and more importantly, of biblical law.

Today's "silver" coins are made from an alloy of 75 percent copper and 25 percent nickel, bonded to a core of pure copper. They are completely debased. There is no silver content. There was a time in our nation's history (not long ago) when goods were purchased with gold and silver coins, or paper dollars that could be redeemed in gold and silver (gold and silver certificates *representing* owner- or bank-held gold and silver). Gold coinage ceased in 1934 by governmental decree. The mints produced the last silver dollars in 1935; silver quarters, half-dollars, and dimes were discontinued for general circulation in 1965. If God's indictment of Israel was for a significant but not total debasement, how will He judge us for a completely debased currency?

Roger Sherman, during the debate on Article I Section 10 of the Constitution, moved to insert after the words *coin money* the words *nor emit bills of credit, nor make any thing but gold and silver coin a tender of payment of debts.*

175

While governments certainly are guilty of creating an illusion of prosperity by inflating the money supply, many citizens are equally guilty of accruing tremendous debt through deficit (credit) spending. When consumers establish a sense of prosperity through credit purchases, they in effect are increasing the money supply (inflation) and thus driving up prices (the result of inflation). Too often voters seem indifferent to governmental spending and creation of debt because it is no different from their own daily spending habits. Before we can expect our Federal government to reduce deficit spending, our spending habits must be trimmed as well. "Owe nothing to anyone except to love one another. . ." (Romans 13:8).

4. The authority that the Bible puts in the hands of civil governments is the ministry of justice (Romans 13:3-5). Justice in economic matters means to ensure "just weights and measures": "You shall do no wrong in judgment, in measure of weight, or capacity. You shall have just balances, just weights, a just ephah [volume] and a just hin [volume]: I am the LORD your God . . ." (Leviticus 19:35-37). Ezekiel declares that a false weight is despoiling the people, and contrary to the law: "Thus says the Lord GOD, 'Enough, you princes of Israel; put away violence and destruction, and practice justice and righteousness. Stop your expropriations from My people,' declares the Lord GOD. 'You shall have just balances, a just ephah [volume], and a just bath [volume]' " (Ezekiel 45:9, 10).

God considers tampering with weights and measures similar to "violence and destruction." Princes, representatives of civil governments, are to assure the people that their money is "hard" currency, gold and silver. Men are not permitted even to *own* false weights and measures: "You shall not have in your bag differing weights, a large and a small. You shall not have in your house differing measures, a large and a small" (Deuteronomy 25:13, 14). There is a promise attached to keeping a true system of weights and measures: "You shall have a full and just weight; you shall have a full and just measure, that your days may be prolonged in the land which the LORD your God gives you" (v. 15). The same promise is given to those who honor their parents (Exodus 20:12). Moreover, civil authorities have a duty to punish those who break economic laws such as counterfeiting, theft, broken contracts, false advertising, etc. If these sins continue, the future of the nation is jeopardized and greater governmental control arises.

5. The poor usually are affected by inflation before any other group of people because they receive the ability to purchase goods when the effects of inflation already have ravaged the economy. The poor may be unemployed or hold low paying jobs with little or no increases in salary. If inflation increases 10-15% per year and wages only 2-5%, a reduction in purchasing power results. Of course, those not able to work, dependent on charity, experience an even more grievous condition. The Bible maintains that inflation has its greatest effects on widows and orphans: "Your silver has become dross, your drink diluted with water. Your rulers are rebels, and companions of thieves; every one loves a bribe, and chases after rewards. They do not defend the orphan, nor does the widow's plea come before them" (Isaiah 1:22, 23). Inflation rewards the corrupt and tramples the poor. A nation increases the number of poor with its policy of inflation. Ironically, the very policies instituted in our country to help the poor created the massive debt that now has turned on the poor and made them even more dependent upon government assistance. To deliver the promised programs of prosperity, the United States federal government took our nation off the gold standard and inflated the dollar with more and more paper "currency," since the gold standard prohibited our political leaders from tampering with the money supply.

When the official protector of weights and measures, the civil magistrate, disregards commandments regarding sound money, what stops the general populace from gouging the poor as well? The merchants of Amos' day were cheating their poorest customers by making the bushel smaller when selling grain, adding base metals to the shekel, and tampering with the scales for trade: "Hear this, you who trample the needy, to do away with the humble of the land . . . so as to buy the helpless for money and the needy for a pair of sandals, and that we may sell the refuse of the wheat" (Amos 8:4-6).

Here is an area where civil government has legitimate authority to ensure that what is advertised as a certain volume is true (e.g. a gallon is truly a gallon). Civil governments, however, have no authority to regulate the monetary supply, or replace true money, gold and silver, with such easily inflated "legal tender" as paper and debased coinage that destroy the poor. Governmental programs intended to help the poor harm them because they cause inflation and decreased purchasing power for those holding the inflated dollars. By the time the poor can save enough money to purchase goods, the price has been affected by inflation.

Since the civil magistrate is a minister of justice he also should punish those who defraud consumers through theft and misrepresentation. In Israel the poor were sold "the refuse of the wheat" for the real, advertised commodity (Amos 8:6). Because the poor had no means of defense, unscrupulous businessmen continued to oppress them. Civil authorities should force such fraudulent businessmen to make restitution to cheated consumers by following the laws of restitution as outlined in Exodus 22:1-15.

You shall do no wrong in judgment, in measure of weight, or capacity. You shall have just balances, just weights, a just ephah and a just hin: I am the LORD your God . . . (Leviticus 19:35-37).

6. The Christian is to avoid debt. The reason for the prohibition is clearly stated: "The rich rules over the poor, and the borrower becomes the lender's slave" (Proverbs 22:7). A nation of borrowers is a sign of God's curse: "The alien who is among you shall rise above you higher and higher, but you shall go down lower and lower. He shall lend to you, but you shall not lend to him; he shall be the head, and you shall be the tail" (Deuteronomy 28:43, 44). The Christian is instructed to "owe nothing to anyone except to love one another . . ." (Romans 13:8). Debt is restricted to six years and multiple indebtedness is prohibited (Deuteronomy 15:1-6 and Exodus 22:26, 27). "The believer cannot mortgage his future. His life belongs to God, and he cannot sell out his tomorrows to men, nor bind his family's or country's future. This means that long-term personal loans, deficit financing, and national debts involve paganism" (R. J. Rushdoony, *Politics of Guilt and Pity*, p. 249). The Christian who avoids debt refuses to be a slave (cf. Exodus 21:1-6).

If the Christian family stays constantly in debt, family members cannot involve themselves in kingdom work. Time and energy are expended keeping creditors from the door. The interest exacted by creditors prohibits fathers and mothers from saving, and thus insuring an inheritance for their children. Moreover, if untimely death occurs the debt will be passed to the wife, who may not be in the job market and thus she may be unable to handle the debt load. The wife probably will have to work outside the home, placing her children in the care of others for education and discipline. The long-term effects of debt are many. God's gracious commandment, therefore, is to avoid debt!

7. By planning for the future and caring for one's family members, need for governmental programs should disappear. The state is not responsible to care for the elderly, the infirm, the crippled, and the destitute. These are individual, family, and church concerns: "But if anyone does not provide for his own, and especially for those of his household, he has denied the faith, and is worse than an unbeliever" (1 Timothy 5:8; cf. Romans 12:13). Christians should provide for future generations through inheritance: "A good man leaves an inheritance to his children's children" (Proverbs 13:22a). The godly man works and saves with his grandchildren in mind. He believes there is a future to be redeemed and cultivated. The ungodly eat and drink for the present because they have no hope for the future.

179

The present-oriented culture makes no future plans: "So I commended pleasure, for there is nothing good for a man under the sun except to eat and to drink and to be merry, and this will stand by him in his toils throughout the days of his life which God has given him under the sun" (Ecclesiastes 8:15). Jesus tells us to plan for the future, to count its costs so that we will be prepared for whatever might befall us (Luke 14:28-30). When the reality of time overcomes the indifferent, they often turn to the state for salvation (1 Samuel 8).

THE WAY TO GROW POOR. ✳ THE WAY TO GROW RICH.

The Christian is to avoid debt. The reason for the prohibition is clear: *The rich rules over the poor, and the borrower becomes the lender's slave* (Proverbs 22:7).

8. Those who seek present rewards are unaware of God's long-range purposes. The ungodly often do prosper, but in the long-term their riches will be transferred to the godly: "The wealth of the sinner is stored up for the righteous" (Proverbs 13:22b). When Israel entered the promised land, the productiveness of the Canaanites was transferred to Israel: "Then it shall come about when the LORD your God brings you into the land which He swore to your fathers, Abraham, Isaac, and Jacob, to give you, great and splendid cities which you did not build, and houses full of good things which you did not fill, and hewn cisterns which you did not dig, vineyards and olive trees which you did not plant, and you shall eat and be satisfied" (Deuteronomy 6:10, 11). "One prayer in the Psalms actually asks the Lord to bring material blessings to His enemies in order that they might be ensnared by the gifts [Psalm 69:22]. The wealth of the wicked, in the final analysis, is laid up for the use of the righteous [Proverbs 13:22; Ecclesiastes 2:26]" (Gary North, *An Introduction to Christian Economics*, p. 216).

God may also punish His people for their indifference and self-sufficiency. There is a connection between obedience to God's word and prosperity (Deuteronomy 8:1-10). Over time, a prosperous nation can forget the Source of its prosperity and fail to honor Him with its obedience: "Beware lest you forget the LORD your God by not keeping His commandments and His ordinances and His statutes . . ." (v. 11). The accumulation of wealth is then attributed to the creativity, wisdom, and might of men: "My power and the strength of my hand made me this wealth" (v. 17). God then raises up oppressors against the people so they once again will acknowledge the Source of their original wealth: "But you shall remember the LORD your God, for it is He who is giving you power to make wealth, that He may confirm His covenant which He swore to your fathers, as it is this day. And it shall come about if you ever forget the LORD your God, and go after other gods and serve them and worship them, I testify against you today that you shall surely perish. Like the nations that the LORD makes to perish before you, so you shall perish; because you would not listen to the voice of the LORD your God" (vv. 18-20).

9. Covetousness can blind the Christian to the real treasures of life. The covetous person sets his desires on the accumulation of "things" with little regard for their proper use. Covetousness is greed. William Hendriksen describes the effects of greed: "The Greek word for *greed* is very descriptive. Literally it means: the thirst for *having more*, always having more and more and still more. It is as if a man in order to quench his thirst takes a drink of salt water which happens to be the only water that is available. This makes him still more thirsty. So he drinks again and again, until his thirst kills him . . . Jesus tells these people — and is telling us today — not to become enslaved to this demon of greed, and he adds: *for a man's life* [the life that really matters] *does not consist in the abundance of his possessions*, his earthly goods" (*The New Testament Commentary: The Gospel of Luke*, p. 662).

The man who built larger barns cared only for wealth and not the potential economic benefit for God's kingdom and stewardship stored along with it. His wealth possessed him. While God gives us power to make wealth (Deuteronomy 8:18), He does not give that power so our barns will be filled for non-productive purposes. God calls each of us to kingdom activity — the work of dominion. The work of the kingdom takes money. It is a sin for a Christian to store his wealth while kingdom activities struggle because they lack adequate funding. Wealth for the covetous man creates inactivity, the very thing God despises: "Soul, you have many goods laid up for many years to come; take your ease, eat, drink and be merry" (Luke 12:19).

Article 1, Section 10 of the United States Constitution makes it clear that to coin money means *gold and silver Coin*.

The Bible's critique of inflation is as valid for our day as for Isaiah's: *Your silver has become dross, your drink diluted with water* (Isaiah 1:22).

The effects of war create conditions that bring on famines of great proportions. Here the king of Syria is being told that women were eating their own children in order to survive (2 Kings 6:24-31).

Lesson 9

The Causes
of Poverty

God requires His people to care for the poor. To call this untrue, one must deny the Bible: "Dispense true justice and practice kindness and compassion each to his brother" (Zechariah 7:9) and "He who oppresses the poor reproaches his Maker, but he who is gracious to the needy honors Him" (Proverbs 14:31). God directs Christians to offer relief for the oppressed, the hungry, prisoners, the blind, strangers, widows and orphans. Such help, however, is not to be indiscriminate. The Bible clearly states that there are many poverty-stricken because they failed to follow God's laws regarding work: "If anyone will not work, neither let him eat" (2 Thessalonians 3:10).

It is not enough to look at the poor and their condition without considering why they find themselves in the straits of poverty. Have they been debilitated because of illness? Has natural disaster wiped out a family's savings? Is a family poor because of debt? Do governmental policies inhibit the poor from being productive citizens? Has the poor man been oppressed because of his race or station in society? Does a nation's religious ideals prohibit economic growth?

Some would have us believe the Bible teaches a primitive communism. Did the early church practice a community of goods where individuals were mandated to turn their goods and land holdings over to the church leadership? "[T]he community of goods, described [in Acts 4:32-37], was not a social regulation or an article of primitive church polity, but the natural and necessary acting out of the principle of oneness, or identity of interest among the members of Christ's body, arising from their joint relation to himself" (J. A. Alexander, *The Acts of the Apostles*, Volume 1, p. 185). The actions of these early Christians were voluntary and not the edict of church or state.

185

Without a thorough understanding of the Bible, any attempt to answer these difficult issues ends in failure. Care for the poor must show itself in action that ultimately *helps* the poor and honors God. For example, the Christian is not helping the poor by merely feeding him. Obviously, taking care of an individual's *immediate* needs is mandatory (James 2:14-16), but how often do programs designed for the poor consider long-term results? Is it possible to aggravate the poor man's condition by not addressing the *real* causes of his poverty?

[T]he community of goods, described [in Acts 4:32-37], was not a social regulation or an article of primitive church polity, but the natural and necessary acting out of the principle of oneness, or identity of interest among the members of Christ's body, arising from their joint relation to himself.

–J. A. Alexander

All actions and results of actions have theological or *religious* starting points; therefore, the Bible must be our guide in determining the solution — not history, unaided reason, the will of the majority, a political party, the tactics of guilt manipulators, or the misinformed. Those with good intentions will not bring long-term relief to the really poor if they fail to realize that good intentions can in no way supplant the blueprint God has given to solve the condition of the poor. The solution to poverty must be answered in the light of what the Bible says about man's fallen condition and the *religious* factors which create the climate for poverty.

The Christian realizes we all live in a fallen world, and poverty, as well as sickness and death, results from man's first sin. Prior to the fall the earth gave its fruit freely, and Adam and Eve understood their responsibilities under God and realized the benefits of the tree of life (Genesis 2:15, 16). Adam and Eve's sinless state did not mean they were free from obligation to cultivate and keep the garden. Rather, the obligation to labor for their sustenance was interwoven with the creation mandate. Since the fall, however, the earth is stingy and man has become irresponsible in carrying out his dominion task: "Cursed is the ground because of you; in toil you shall eat of it all the days of your life. Both thorns and thistles it shall grow for you; and you shall eat the plants of the field; by the sweat of your face you shall eat bread" (3:17b-19). Some even go so far as to murder others in order to possess what does not belong to them (4:19, 23, 24).

The Bible, therefore, never deals with poverty outside the context of man's fall into sin. (Every subject must be considered in relation to the fall of mankind into sin. The subject of poverty is not unique in this regard.) Productive plant life has to compete with thorns and thistles. Sinful men and women often refuse to follow God's commandments which relate to productive work. Some murder or steal to gain prosperity rather than follow the commandments which relate to productive labor. Others have no conception of the consequences of their sinful inactivity and its relation to poverty: "Go to the ant, O sluggard, observe her ways and be wise, which, having no chief, officer or ruler, prepares her food in the summer, and gathers her provision in the harvest. How long will you lie down, O sluggard? When will you arise from your sleep? 'A little sleep, a little slumber, a little folding of the hands to rest' — and your poverty will come in like a vagabond, and your need like an armed man" (Proverbs 6:6-11). There is an additional element added to man's sinful condition — the scarcity of resources that exists due to the earth's limited resources. The struggle for these resources often leads to covetousness, envy, and war.

Each individual must shoulder personal responsibility for his activity or inactivity. In some cases, however, poverty results from other sinful men taking advantage of those who find themselves in a temporary destitute situation. If the lazy man should be rebuked for his disobedience, the unscrupulous opportunist should be held equally responsibile for his repudiation of God's law regarding the poor:

God's people are not to wrong or to oppress a stranger or afflict a widow or an orphan (Exod. 22:21-22; 23:9; Lev. 19:33-34). They must not pervert justice due to the sojourner, orphan or poor man. They are not to take a widow's garment in pledge, make false charges against the innocent, or take bribes and subvert the cause of those who are in

187

the right (Exod. 23:6-8; Deut. 10:18; 19:16-21). The man of God is to love, feed, and clothe orphans, widows, and sojourners (Deut. 10:18).

When a godly man lends money to a poor man, he is not to exact interest from him (Exod. 22:25-27; Deut. 23:19-20; Lev. 25:35-38), because the purpose of lending him money is to help relieve his poverty, not to increase it. If a poor man is unable to repay the debt in seven years, the lender is to release him from it (Deut. 15:1-2) (John T. Willis, "Old Testament Foundations for Social Justice," in *Christian Social Ethics*, ed. Perry C. Cothan, p. 33).

The poor as well as the prosperous have a responsibility to follow God's law. The poor man must determine what the law says regarding his condition. Is it possible he is poor due to his unwillingness to follow God's commandments in the area of productive work, savings, and long-term planning? Are there ways the prosperous can help the poor get out of their cycle of poverty? Can businessmen God has blessed with an abundance of resources train the unskilled and offer interest-free loans to those denied credit by lending institutions as "poor risks"? Can time be spent with those who have little or no knowledge in the area of management, so one day they can operate alone? The poor, over the long-haul, are not helped by making money available to them without needed biblical instruction in the area of management, stewardship, and planning.

The Christian's task in helping the poor is to add the compassion that goes with understanding. The poor man's condition includes more than lacking material possessions. He is a human being who needs to be treated as an image-bearer of God; therefore, care for the poor includes respect for his dignity. Present-day welfare programs cannot meet the demands of dignity. It is true that money is spent on poverty programs, but there is more to dignity than money. Dignity includes being what God intends each of us to be. True and lasting dignity comes from acknowledging our sin, repenting of our rebellion, and submitting to the freeing gospel of Jesus Christ. Nothing less will measure up: "By taking sin seriously we take man seriously. Evil may mar the divine image and cloud its brilliance, but it cannot destroy it. The image can be defaced, but it can never be erased. The most obscene symbol in human history is the cross; yet in its ugliness it remains the most eloquent testimony to human dignity" (R.C. Sproul, *In Search of Dignity*, p. 95).

Questions For Discussion

1. Why are some cultures poverty-stricken while others seem to reap the blessings of God? (Genesis 3:17-19; Leviticus 18:24-28; Deuteronomy 28; Isaiah 24)

2. What factors contribute to the condition of poverty?

a. Proverbs 10:2-4; 12:11, 24; 13:4, 11

b. Deuteronomy 23:12, 13; Mark 5:25-34

c. Luke 14:28-32; 15:11-32 [especially vv. 13, 14]

_____

_____

_____

_____

_____

_____

_____

d. Genesis 12:10, 11; 47:13-26; 2 Kings 6:24-31; Acts 11:27-30

_____

_____

_____

_____

_____

_____

_____

e. Judges 3:1-8, 17; 6:1-6, 11

_____

_____

_____

_____

_____

_____

f. 1 Samuel 8; 1 Kings 21

_____

_____

_____

_____

_____

_____

_____

g. Leviticus 19:13; Deuteronomy 24:14, 15; Amos 8:4-6

_____

_____

_____

_____

_____

3. How can poverty-stricken nations be relieved of their poverty? (Leviticus 26; Deuteronomy 8; 28; Proverbs 12:11; 14:1, 23; Matthew 28:18-20)

_____

_____

_____

_____

_____

_____

4. Does the Bible teach the goal of economic equality? Should civil governments enforce economic equality? (Proverbs 25:21; 2 Corinthians 8:13-15)

_____

_____

_____

_____

_____

5. Are there times in the Bible where the sharing of goods does happen? Are these examples the norm for all Christians to follow? (John 12:6; 13:29; Acts 2:44-46; 4:32-37)

_____

_____

_____

_____

_____

6. What place should the state play in caring for the poor? (Proverbs 11:1; Amos 8:4-6; Leviticus 19:15; cf. 2 Timothy 5:8; Luke 10:30-37; 1 Timothy 5:8)

Summary

"Evidence exists that welfare state policies do more than injure those from whom something is *taken*; they also injure those to whom something is *given* (by the state). Liberal housing programs did not make more low-cost housing available for the poor; the result has been much less available housing, at a cost of billions of dollars. Minimum wage legislation does not really help people at the bottom of the economic ladder; it ends up harming them by making them less employable, thus increasing unemployment among the very people the legislation is supposed to help. The short-sighted and politically expedient policy of paying for social welfare through deficit government spending has flooded the economy with billions of dollars of increasingly worthless money and ravaged the poor by subjecting them (and everyone else) to an inflation that continues to raise the prices of basic necessities beyond their reach. Regardless of where one looks, welfare state programs have failed. Liberal social policies have done the most harm in basic areas like food and clothing. The people who have been hurt the most have been those least able to afford it, the very people, the liberal assures us, he is trying to help" (Ronald H. Nash, *Social Justice and the Christian Church*, p. 60).

There are many people who are not able to work because of debilitating disease. The disease or injury and the money required for medical care can bring an individual to poverty.

Answers to Questions for Discussion

1. Man's rebellion against God resulted in His curse upon the created order. Prior to the fall, the Garden gave its fruit freely and work was a pleasure. Since the fall, however, the earth brings forth its fruit with great effort: "Cursed is the ground because of you; in toil you shall eat of it all the days of your life. Both thorns and thistles it shall grow for you; and you shall eat the plants of the field; by the sweat of your face you shall eat bread" (Genesis 3:17b-19). The curse of the ground can gradually be overcome, but not entirely removed, through reliance on the saving work of Jesus Christ and diligent obedience to the commandments of God. Many nations around the world lack sufficient food, proper sanitation, and adequate housing. Is there a reason for their condition? Is there a relationship between following the commandments of God and receiving the blessing of God in return? More-over, is there a resultant curse upon a people if they reject the gospel of Jesus Christ and fail to follow His commandments? The rise and fall of nations would indicate that there is.

The Bible makes it clear there is a direct correlation between obedience to the Christian faith and the virtual elimination of poverty. Material blessings are promised when those nations follow the commandments of God: an increase of herds, full food baskets and barns, productive lands, and enough money to lend to other nations (Deuteronomy 28:1-14). The curse is promised to those nations that fail to acknowledge God as the Lord: "The LORD will send upon you curse, confusion, and rebuke, in all you undertake to do, until you are destroyed and until you perish quickly, on account of the evil of your deeds, because you have forsaken Me" (v. 20; cf. vv. 15-68). "In terms of biblical law, a culture that engages in long-term rebellion against God's law will sink to the level of abject poverty and deprivation. The law promises that . . . . But if God is on His throne, His people will be blessed. He controls the environmental conditions, and He can cause the desert to blossom (Isaiah 35; 43:19-21). But He will not do it without the Spirit being poured forth in regeneration and sanctification: physical, material, economic blessings flow from cultural obedience (Isaiah 32:15-16)" (David Chilton, *Productive Christians in an Age of Guilt-Manipulators*, p. 116f.).

2. a. Laziness (Proverbs 10:4, 5; 12:24; 13:4, 11): The Bible makes it clear that hard work is necessary if poverty is to be replaced with prosperity. Man's original calling was to cultivate and keep the garden of Eden (Genesis 2:15). The fall made hard work even more necessary. The lazy individual will be overcome by "thorn and thistles": "Poor is he who works with a negligent hand, but the hand of the diligent makes rich" (Proverbs 10:4). There are governmental implications attached to those who are diligent in their labors: "The hand of the diligent will rule, but the slack hand will be put to forced labor" (12:24). Those who fail to obey God's laws concerning hard work will be reduced to slaves, living off the productivity of others: "The soul of the sluggard craves and gets nothing, but the soul of the diligent is made fat" (13·4) A welfare state creates a non-productive class that becomes dependent upon governmental agencies for care, and works "progressively" to impoverish the productive and diligent.

Poor is he who works with a negligent hand, but the hand of the diligent makes rich (Proverbs 10:4).

b. Illness (Mark 5:25-34; Deuteronomy 23:12-14): There are many people who are not able to work because of debilitating disease. The disease itself and the money required for medical care can bring an individual to poverty. This was the case of the woman who had a hemorrhage for twelve years. She "had spent all that she had and was not helped at all" (Mark 5:25-34). When an illness saps the working ability and resources of the people of God it is the duty of individual Christians, families, and the church at large to care for them (cf. Luke 10:30-37; Acts 6:1-6; 1 Timothy 5:8). Churches could establish a fund to pay for insurance policies for the elderly (the group most uninsurable and least able to afford medical costs). It is not sound economics to create an emergency medical fund when one debilitating disease could wipe out an accumulated fund of $100,000. Civil governments are not given the authority or responsibility to make provision for those unable to care for themselves through compulsory giving programs.

In some cases illness results from poor sanitation and personal hygiene. For example, in some parts of India manure is gathered in baskets, carried home, patted in thin disks, and plastered on walls and the ground to dry for fuel. There are open-air latrines. Such unsanitary conditions breed disease. Many cultures, because of pagan religious customs, are afflicted with diseases that have been virtually eradicated in Christian cultures. When the gospel is preached in these pagan cultures the laws dealing with sanitation and hygiene must be preached as well: "You shall also have a place outside the camp and go out there, and you shall have a spade among your tools, and it shall be when you sit down outside, you shall dig with it and shall turn to cover up your excrement" (Deuteronomy 23:12, 13). Disease can be curtailed and productivity will naturally increase if these laws are learned and obeyed.

c. Present-oriented living (Luke 14:28-32; 15:11-32): The accumulation of wealth can be only as good as its manager. The present-oriented individual will squander his wealth on present desires while ignoring future responsibilities and opportunities. Counting the cost of present expenditures is a must if wealth is to be maintained from generation to generation: "For which one of you, when he wants to build a tower, does not first sit down and calculate the cost, to see if he has enough to complete it?" (Luke 14:28). The prodigal (wasteful) son is the prime example of the results of present-oriented living: "The [prodigal] son gathered everything together and went on a journey into a distant country, and there he squandered his estate with loose living. Now when he had spent everything, a severe famine occurred in that country, and he began to be in need" (Luke 15:13, 14).

Many of the world's poor are poor precisely because of such present-orientedness. They have little or no concept of deferring the gratification of their desires in order to achieve increased material well-being at some future time; consequently, they squander their resources and remain poor. Government welfare programs, far from "solving the problem of poverty" or "eliminating the causes of poverty and crime," have but perpetuated the problems, since they do not get to the root of the matter - the world view of the people involved. Present-oriented living has infected other economic classes as well. The massive accumulation of debt by middle-income consumers indicates that present-oriented living is not restricted to any one economic class. Debt results in a slave mentality and condition: "The rich rules over the poor, and the borrower becomes the lender's slave" (Proverbs 22:7).

d. Famine (Genesis 12:10, 11; 47:13-26; 2 Kings 6:24-31; Acts 11:27-30): The Bible has much to say about famine and its effect on a culture's economic productivity. The Garden of Eden knew no famine nor even potential for famine. Man's rebellion, however, changed the productivity of the ground (Genesis 1:29, 30; 2:8, 9; 3:17-19), weather patterns (2:6), and man's desire to control his culture under God (3:22). While environmental factors *contribute* to famine, improper economic management or deliberate destruction of the environment is usually the *cause*. War, willful destruction of crops, communistic land control, government interference by regulation or taxation, and currency debasement (inflation) are the most typical causes (cf. 2 Kings 6:24-31); therefore, man playing God is the greatest famine-maker. Famine can also be attributed to the *direct* judgment of God (1 Kings 17:1ff.).

Famines are costly because they often force cultures to relocate: "Now there was a famine in the land; so Abram went down to Egypt to sojourn there, for the famine was severe in the land" (Genesis 12:10). Famines pressure families and nations to divert income-producing funds to survival funds. Famines can be so devastating that a slave state results: "For every Egyptian sold his field, because the famine was severe upon them. Thus the land became Pharaoh's" (Genesis 47:20). In the eyes of the people, Pharaoh was their savior: "You have saved our lives! Let us find favor in the sight of our lord, and we will be Pharaoh's slaves" (v. 25). In many countries famine is the rule rather than the exception. In order to rescue a culture from the effects of

197

famine, *temporary* relief must be given with instructions on why famine occurred and steps implemented to prevent future famines (Acts 11:27-30).

Christians often are generous in giving food, clothing, money, and other items to alleviate suffering of poor people overseas. Some even seek to teach these people how to use modern technology in their native lands. Hopefully, all Christian relief efforts stress the need for a saving knowledge of Jesus Christ on the part of the recipients of the Christian aid. But how many Christian relief organizations have taught the need — the absolute mandatory requirement — for Christians to order their societies in conformity with biblical precepts and laws? How many missionaries have followed the example of John Eliot, the great Puritan missionary to the Indians? Eliot sought not only to impart saving knowledge of Jesus Christ, but also, through preaching and example, taught them to reconstruct their society according to biblical principles. What converted Christians in foreign lands need most are missionaries who will bring the saving word of the Lord to them and the commandments that bring blessing, prosperity, and peace.

John Eliot, the great Puritan missionary to the Indians, sought not only to impart saving knowledge of Jesus Christ, but also, through preaching and example, taught the Indians to reconstruct their society according to biblical principles.

e. Judgment (Judges 3:1-8, 12; 6:1-6, 11; Daniel 1:1, 2): During the period of the Judges, the Israelites were beset by external, foreign oppression. Because the Israelites had forsaken God as their Ruler, God showed them that rejection of His lordship meant judgment: God "sold them into the hands" of Israel's enemies where tribute had to be paid to these foreign kings (Judges 3:8, 15). Instead of accumulating capital for building their culture, the Israelites had to use their wealth for paying tribute and fighting wars. During the time of Gideon, the Midianites acted as bandits, confiscating and destroying the means of production: "For it was when Israel had sown, that the Midianites would come up with the Amalekites and the sons of the east and go against them. So they would camp against them and destroy the produce of the earth . . ." (Judges 6:3, 4) Survival was the name of the game. Gideon had to hide his wheat in a wine press to save it from the Midianites, in order just to survive (v. 11).

f. State Intervention (1 Samuel 8; 1 Kings 21): Poverty comes on a nation when people vote for policies they think, in the long-run, will not be destructive. The people of Samuel's day desired a king who would confiscate their wealth and the means of production so they would be saved like all the other nations (1 Samuel 8:11-17). State intervention (tyranny) does not come automatically: it results from a nation's desiring promised prosperity and statist "salvation" of those seeking office. Intervention by the state in the financial resources of the nation is a means by which they can make their promises a temporary reality. State intervention is a slow process, but its end result is oppression. Tyranny was so prevalent in Israel under Ahab's reign that theft and murder were the order of things: "Arise, take possession of the vineyard of Naboth, the Jezreelite, which he refused to give you for money" (1 Kings 21:15).

g. Oppression (Leviticus 19:13; Deuteronomy 24:14, 15; Jeremiah 22:13-17): Those who contracted to work for an agreed upon wage should be paid promptly. "Wages are to be paid promptly, at the specified and contracted time. In antiquity, payment was by the day; this meant that payment had to be made at the end of the working day, not the next morning. Failure to pay at the required time was thus a criminal act: it was theft" (R.J. Rushdoony, *Institutes of Biblical Law*, p. 497). The poor often are most mistreated because they have little power to confront such criminal behavior on their own. According to the Bible, however, the poor can turn to civil authorities as a ministry of justice to force oppressive employers to meet their *contractual* obligations to those they hire.

God displays His disfavor to those who prosper because they oppress hired workers: "Woe to him who builds his house without righteousness and his upper rooms without justice, who uses his neighbor's services without pay and does not give him his wages" (Jeremiah 22:13). Those who do such things are "practicing oppression and extortion" (v. 17). The agreed upon work of an employee is a debt contracted by the employer. Failure to pay an employee is failure to honor contracted debt. If the ox is to be paid for his labor when contracted (Deuteronomy 25:4), then surely the workman should be granted at least equal treatment: "For the Scripture says, 'You shall not muzzle the ox while he is threshing,' and 'The laborer is worthy of his wages' " (1 Timothy 5:18; cf. Matthew 10:10; Luke 10:7).

The poor man's condition includes more than lacking material possessions. Present-day welfare programs do not help the poor over the long-term. The Bible commands us to work. Welfare policies that encourage individuals not to work will lead to a society of slaves.

3. Many in our day would say poverty is environmental or the result of exploitation by rich nations. The Bible, however, tells a different story. Poverty can be traced back to a nation's failure to keep the commandments of God (Leviticus 26 and Deuteronomy 28). This might sound simple, but it is true. The most prosperous countries of the world, until they began to follow socialistic policies, are the countries most affected by the Reformation's return to biblical principles in the area of economics. Socialistic economic practices remove most people's work incentives since the state owns the means of production and reaps benefits of the citizen's labor. Is there any wonder that socialistic countries must borrow from the United States and other countries that have remnants of a biblical economic base? (see Deuteronomy 28:12).

The answer for the elimination of poverty is not wealth redistribution by the state. Rather, the elimination of poverty can only come by the regeneration of individuals and biblical reconstruction in the economic sphere. *First,* entire nations must come under the preaching of the gospel of Jesus Christ. The command by Jesus to go into all the world and make disciples of all the nations should tell the Christian that the world's problem is ethical and not environmental. Pagan religions will bring about pagan economic policies: "Unless the LORD builds the house, they labor in vain who build it" (Psalm 127:1).

Second, a biblical education must follow the gospel. This is why Jesus told His disciples to teach the newly converted whatsoever He had taught them (Matthew 28:19, 20). New Christians do not know what to do instinctively; they must be taught what is wrong and be instructed in what is correct (cf. Ephesians 4:17-32). Through "practice they will have their senses trained to discern good and evil" (Hebrews 5:14).

Third, present-oriented cultures must be changed to future-oriented cultures. This means the concept of saving for the future and passing an inheritance down to future generations must be part of the thinking of all cultures (Proverbs 12:11; 14:1, 23): "This *present-orientedness* is a crucial factor in slum communities and in underdeveloped (backward, primitive) nations. In contrast are those who are distinctly *future-oriented.* Compared with backward cultures, future-oriented cultures place a high premium on future income . . . . Time is seen as an opportunity for future dominion" (Gary North, *The Dominion Covenant: Genesis,* p. 126f.).

Fourth, cultures must be warned about the consequences of turning away from the God of the Bible and His economic laws and choosing pragmatic (humanistic) ways to structure culture: "But you shall remember the LORD your God, for it is He who is giving you power to make wealth . . . And it shall come about if you ever forget the LORD your God, and go after other gods and serve them and worship them, I testify against you today that you shall surely perish" (Deuteronomy 8:18, 19).

Fifth, government interference in the marketplace must be eliminated except in areas of criminal activity. Producers and consumers must sell and buy freely without restrictions by government bureaucracies so long as they do not commit crimes. For example, the "free market" does not mean that prostitution and illicit drug trafficking can become legal. Men and women are not free to sell *everything* in the marketplace. Moreover, the free market assures the seller he will not be restricted by "fair price" or minimum wage legislation. The magistrate's duty is to protect the good and punish the evil doer (Romans 13:3, 4), not control free trade (Revelation 13:16, 17).

Sixth, the Christian community must speak up when the poor are mistreated by the state or by oppressive employers (cf. Leviticus 19:13; Amos 8:4-6).

4. God's word instructs us to care for the poor. Even our enemies are to be aided: "If your enemy is hungry, give him food to eat; and if he is thirsty, give him water to drink" (Proverbs 25:21; cf. Romans 12:20). Christians in need should be helped from our supply: "But whoever has the world's goods, and beholds his brother in need and closes his heart against him, how does the love of God abide in him?" (1 John 3:17; cf. James 2:14-17).

The question is, "Should Christian aid to the poor create equality in economic matters; i.e., should wealth be redistributed so that everybody has the same amount of usable capital?" The New Testament's use of "equality" has reference to what a person *needs*: "The 'equality' intended by Paul in II Corinthians [8:13-15] is simply that Christians should try to meet the *needs* of destitute members of the body of Christ, giving them 'what is necessary for their body' (James 2:16). Paul's mention of the gathering of manna by the migrant community of Israel does not constitute sumptuary legislation for all Christians for all time. The point of the quotation is to stress the ideal of even the poorest *members of the congregation* having sufficient food. The equality

202

refs to provision for actual needs. We must not confuse the modern socialist notion with Paul's statement. In the specific sense of the Greek term [for equality], a wealthy master and his slave are *equal* if they both have enough to eat [Colossians 4:1] — even though the actual possessions of the master may be vastly disproportionate to those of the slave. The Bible requires me to help those in need of food and clothing" (David Chilton, *Productive Christians in an Age of Guilt-Manipulators*, p. 180f.).

There are many who espouse a *forced* economic equality by governmental action. The Bible makes it clear that civil governments have a very limited responsibility and no authority to redistribute wealth from one segment of society (the rich) to another (the poor). Romans 13 tells us that the evil-doer should be punished. Unless being rich is evil, the civil authorities have no right to take from the rich to give to the poor. Social and economic equality does not justify theft by governmental action. The Bible does present a real equality, an equality before the law of God. Moreover, who will implement the system of wealth redistribution? What standard will be used? How will those who refuse to work be dealt with? Will they still be eligible for the redistributed funds even if they do not work? What incentive will the hard working individual have in continuing to work when he knows that his "excess" profits will be taken away from him and given to less prosperous individuals? Once all the wealth is redistributed, what then?

5. There are examples of the sharing of goods during the time of Jesus and the early church. But when the reader takes a closer look at the circumstances, the modern socialistic (mis)understanding of these incidents fades away. Jesus and His disciples shared a common money box kept by Judas (John 12:6; 13:29). It must be remembered, however, that the common purse was necessary because of their nomadic lifestyle. Much of the time they slept out of doors: "The foxes have holes, and the birds of the air have nests; but the Son of Man has nowhere to lay His head" (Matthew 8:20). While it was a common purse, it was still a *voluntary-giving purse*. No one was forcing the disciples to follow Jesus. Moreover, Judas acted as a treasurer, not a confiscating government official. Should this unusual example of special circumstances be established as the norm for all living situations? The circumstance is similar to the living conditions of a military campaign or an army on maneuvers, but when the war is over normal living habits return.

Ananias, why has Satan filled your heart to lie to the Holy Spirit, and to keep back some of the price of the land? While it remained unsold, did it not remain your own? And after it was sold, was it not under your control? (Acts 5:3, 4).

The second example is more well-known and greatly misunderstood. It has been proposed that the common sharing of the early church, often referred to as an "early experiment in communism," should be the church's example throughout history. Again, certain points are rarely considered: *First*, a great influx of new converts over-taxed the infant church: 3000 new believers were brought into the church (Acts 2:41) and shortly thereafter, 5000 more were converted (4:4).

Second, because discipleship must follow conversion, most, if not all of the new converts decided to stay in Jerusalem to receive instruction: "And they were continually devoting themselves to the apostles' teaching and to fellowship, to the breaking of bread and to prayer" (2:42). Provisions had been planned for the Pentecost feast, but nobody expected to stay beyond the end of the feast (cf 2:9-11; 6.1). Emergency measures had to be taken to care for the needs of the people.

Third, those who decided to liquidate their property did so *voluntarily*. No coercion by church leaders or state officials forced land owners to make their lands available for the needs of the saints. The basic tenet of socialism is the *forced* redistribution of wealth from one class to another. This early church incident has nothing to do with wealth redistribution. Rather, its purpose was to meet the temporary and immediate needs of thousands of individuals stranded in a foreign city (2:45).

Fourth, the land and its proceeds remained the private property of the land holders. Peter, speaking to Ananias, makes this point crystal clear: "While [the property] remained unsold, did it not remain your own? And after it was sold, was it not under your control?" (5:4). The sin of Ananias and Sapphira was not that they held back some of the proceeds of their sold property; rather, it was the *lie* they told about the sale of the land that brought judgment upon them.

Fifth, the aid was first given to the household of faith, not to the world at large. The Apostle Paul gives us the following injunction: "So then, while we have opportunity, let us do good to all men, and especially to those who are of the household of the faith" (Galatians 6:10).

Sixth, the action by the early church was a *temporary* measure not repeated in the biblical literature. If it was the intention of the early church to try an experiment in communistic living it was something of a failure. Some years later a need arose in Jerusalem for charity from the more prosperous Antioch church: "And in the proportion that any of the disciples had means, each of them determined to send a contribution for the relief of the brethren living in Judea" (Acts 11:29).

6. For many, the answer to man's problems is intervention by centralized political governments because they have the power to enforce legislation where the private citizen does not. It is true that civil governments are given authority by God, but as we have seen in other places, that authority is very limited. Gary North writes: "No one institution should be regarded as sovereign outside of its own legitimate, but strictly limited, sphere. Society in this perspective is a matrix of competing sovereignties, each with certain claims on men, but none with total claims in all areas" (*An Introduction to Christian Economics*, p. 226). Civil governments have the authority and the responsibility to *defend* the people against evil men and *punish* criminals. The standard for their judgments is the law of God.

In economic matters, civil governments are not to determine a "just" or "fair" price, but they should insure the poor, or anyone else of not being cheated through dishonest scales and other forms of theft: "A false balance is an abomination to the LORD, but a just weight is His delight" (Proverbs 11:1; cf. Amos 8:4-6). Civil governments are to maintain an orderly society so the free exchange of goods can take place among free citizens. The state has no authority to *force* the rich to care for the poor. Confiscation of wealth in order to meet the needs of the poor is also outside the authority of civil governments. The poor are not to be favored by the state when the law is in view: "You shall do no injustice in judgment; you shall not be partial to the poor nor defer to the great, but you are to judge your neighbor fairly" (Leviticus 19:15). In the last analysis, caring for the poor begins with the individual being diligent in all his economic affairs (2 Thessalonians 3:6-15) and giving when an opportunity arises (Luke 10:30-37). Families are to care for their own members (1 Timothy 5:8). The church community is under obligation to care for the truly needy, those who have no visible means of support (5:3-16). The state is to maintain a peaceful society by enforcing the law of God by punishing evil doers and promoting the good (2:1, 2; cf. Romans 13:3, 4).

For too long the church has neglected its role as proclaimer of the "whole purpose of God" (Acts 20:27). Instead of assuming responsibility for making known the biblical answers to poverty's questions, the church instead has retreated from the world and turned its responsibilities over to the state. We now see the burgeoning effects of this neglect. Federal aid has increased along with poverty.

Now when he had spent everything, a severe famine occurred in that country, and he began to be in need. And he went and attached himself to one of the citizens of that country, and he sent him into his fields to feed swine (Luke 15:14, 15).

Now when you reap the harvest of your land, you shall not reap to the very corners of your field, neither shall you gather the gleanings of your harvest (Leviticus 19:9).

Lesson 10

The Conquest
of Poverty

Wealth and poverty should not be discussed apart from a consideration of God's law. The law of God is the directive whereby an individual can release himself from poverty's grip. The individual who possesses wealth and fails to follow laws governing the use of wealth is sinning. In the same way, the poor man who fails to abide by the laws that govern his impoverished condition also is in rebellion against God. If God gives the rich man the power to make wealth, then God also gives the poor man power to get out of the poverty trap. The wealthy should not take advantage of the poor, and the poor should not envy the wealthy. Both should be governed by the law of God.

History shows that when the gospel of Jesus Christ enters a culture and is embraced by it, there is an immediate change in the people's understanding of their world. They no longer see their world in the grip of impersonal forces hostile to their attempts to make a living. Rather, they see their world and all it contains as a gift from God. These new converts also understand that God has made them stewards of His creation and as stewards it should be governed according to the standards of His word. The advance of Christianity changed the world. J.C. Ryle, writing almost a century ago, concluded it was the Christian religion that brought the world out of darkness:

The veriest infidel cannot deny the effect that [Christianity] produced on mankind. The world before and the world after the introduction of Christianity were as different worlds as light and darkness, night and day. It was Christianity that starved idolatry, and emptied the heathen temples, — that stopped gladiatorial combats, elevated the position of women, raised the whole tone of morality, and improved the condition of children and the poor. These are facts which we may safely challenge all the enemies of revealed religion to gainsay (*The Upper Room*, p. 60).

The people were no longer bound by superstition and idol worship. God was seen as a God of order. There was an understanding of cause and effect. Natural (creational) laws were seen as God's way of ordering the universe and man's way of reaping the benefits of the created order.

The world before and the world after the introduction of Christianity were as different worlds as light and darkness, night and day. It was Christianity that starved idolatry, and emptied the heathen temples, — that stopped gladatorial combats, elevated the position of women, raised the whole tone of morality, and improved the condition of children and the poor.

–J. C. Ryle

God established a law in Israel that would be a beacon to the nations: "So keep and do [the statutes and judgments], for that is your wisdom and your understanding in the sight of the peoples who will hear these statutes and say, 'Surely this great nation is a wise and understanding people.' For what great nation is there that has a god so near to it as is the LORD our God whenever we call on Him? Or what great nation is there that has statutes and judgments as righteous as this whole law which I am setting before you today" (Deuteronomy 4:6-8). Jesus continues this theme by exhorting His disciples to use His commandments as the standard for the nations. There will be no hope of societal change if the commandments of God are ignored. "All authority has been given to Me in heaven and on earth. Go therefore and make disciples of all the nations, baptizing them in the name of the Father and the Son and the Holy Spirit, teaching them to observe all that I commanded you, and lo, I am with you always, even to the end of the age" (Matthew 28:18-20).

Deuteronomy 28 informs us that obedience or disobedience to the covenant promises has certain inevitable economic results. Obedience brings about economic blessing: "Blessed shall be. . .the produce of your ground and the offspring of your beasts, the increase of your herd and the young of your flock. Blessed shall be your basket and your kneading bowl. . .And the LORD will make you abound in prosperity, in the offspring of your body and in the offspring of your beast and in the produce of your ground. . .The LORD will open for you His good storehouse, the heavens, to give rain to your land in its season and to bless all the work of your hand; and you shall lend to many nations, but you shall not borrow" (vv. 4, 5, 11, 12). Disobedience results in economic curses: "Cursed shall be your basket and your kneading bowl. Cursed shall be the offspring of your body and the produce of your ground, the increase of your herd and the young of your flock . . . And the heaven which is over your head shall be bronze, and the earth which is under you, iron. The LORD will make the rain of your land powder and dust; from heaven it shall come down on you until you are destroyed" (vv. 17, 18, 23, 24).

Moreover, sickness, wars, disease, crime, captivity by foreign powers, and even cannibalism will come on any nation that fails to acknowledge the covenant stipulations outlined in Scripture. The Psalmist says, "I have been young, and now I am old; yet I have not seen the righteous forsaken, or his descendants begging bread" (Psalm 37:25). It is not enough to teach people sound economic principles. Cultures are package deals. In order to change a culture so prosperity can prevail, that culture's religion and law structure must change. This can only happen by discipling the nations and teaching them to observe *everything* Jesus commanded. The Bible must be seen as more than a book on personal redemption from the final penalty for sin. The solution to man's earthly concerns are found on the pages of Scripture; therefore, when the Bible speaks on economics, the Christian has a duty to reconstruct economic matters according to those principles.

A future-orientation must be developed. The biblical presentation of history is linear, not a series of recurring historical cycles. The Christian should be future-oriented enough to consider his grandchildren when he makes economic decisions (cf. Psalm 78:1-8). The present-oriented individual consumes present-day capital with no regard for the future. He eats, drinks, and is merry *today* for tomorrow he dies (Ecclesiastes 8:15). Esau sold his future for a bowl of stew because he despised his birthright which promised *future* blessings: "Behold, I am about to die; so of what use then is the birthright to me" (Genesis 25:32). "What men *believe* has more relevance than the goods that men receive from messianic, humanistic civil governments. If time is seen as a burden, welfare funds can do little to lower the pressure of the perceived burden. And when time is seen as an opportunity for conquest, the funds of expansion will be generously provided by private loans from people who want to invest in productive cultures that are marked by future-oriented entrepreneurs. *Capital flows toward those who believe in the future, who accept the burdens of time as an opportunity for personal growth and personal profit*" (Gary North, *The Dominion Covenant: Genesis*, pp. 130-31).

The question is not, "Should the poor be helped?" Rather, it is "*How* should the poor be helped?" The Bible is very specific when it comes to prescribing remedies for man's problems. Paul tells us that "All Scripture is inspired by God and profitable for teaching, for reproof, for correction, for training in righteousness; that the man of God may be adequate, equipped for every good work" (2 Timothy 3:16, 17). To look for solutions outside Scripture is to deny that Scripture is adequate to equip the Christian *for every good work*. The answer to the problem of poverty is not to have civil government solve it through its many welfare programs. If history shows us anything, it is that governments increase the effects of poverty (cf. Genesis 47:13-19 and 1 Samuel 8). Civil governments continue to exact a greater portion of our incomes through taxation, to fund social programs that do not work over the long-run. God placed the responsibility to care for the really poor with each individual, family, church, and those institutions *voluntarily* supported by our tithes and gifts. The conquest of poverty will come when people are obedient to the commandments of God: "There shall be no poor among you, since the LORD will surely bless you in the land which the LORD your God is giving you as an inheritance to possess, *if only you listen obediently to the voice of the LORD your God, to observe carefully all this commandment which I am command-ing you today.* For the LORD your God shall bless you as He has promised you, and you will lend to many nations, but you will not borrow; and you will rule over many nations, but they will not rule over you. If there is a poor man with you, one of your brothers, in any of your towns in your land which the LORD your God is giving you, you shall not harden your heart, nor close your hand from your poor brother" (Deuteronomy 15:4, 5).

Questions For Discussion

1. What laws has God established to care for the poor?

a. Numbers 18:24; Deuteronomy 14:28, 29.

_____

_____

_____

_____

_____

b. Luke 10:30-37; Acts 4:32-37; 11:29.

_____

_____

_____

_____

c. Leviticus 19:9, 10; 23:22; Deuteronomy 23:24, 25; 24:19-21 and Exodus 23:10, 11; Matthew 12:1.

_____

_____

_____

_____

d. Exodus 22:25; Leviticus 25:35-37; Deuteronomy 15:1, 2, 9.

_____

_____

_____

_____

213

2. In addition to the general poor, who else is eligible to benefit from the poor laws? Explain.

a. (Exodus 22:21-24; Numbers 9:14; Leviticus 24:22; Deuteronomy 10:18, 19; Jeremiah 7:3-7; Zechariah 7:9-14).

_____

_____

_____

_____

_____

_____

_____

b. (Exodus 22:22-24; Deuteronomy 27:19; Isaiah 1:17; Matthew 15:4-6; 1 Timothy 5:3-16; James 1:27)

_____

_____

_____

_____

_____

_____

_____

3. How does envy affect the poor? (Genesis 26:12-15; Esther 5:11-13; Proverbs 14:30; 27:4)

_____

_____

_____

_____

_____

_____

_____

_____

4. What is the remedy for envy and how can the poor prosper? (Deuteronomy 8:18; Proverbs 24:30-34; Isaiah 48:17-19; Philippians 4:4-12, 19; 1 Thessalonians 4:11; 1 Timothy 6:6-8).

_____

_____

_____

_____

_____

_____

_____

_____

_____

_____

_____

The Jubilee Principle

There is renewed interest in the Jubilee Principle as a way of redistributing wealth and creating land reforms. Unfortunately, many well-intentioned Christians misunderstand the significance and application of the Jubilee Year (Leviticus 25). Since economic principles are being suggested on the basis of the Jubilee laws, it is necessary that a study be made of its intent and application for our day.

5. What is the significance of the Jubilee? (Leviticus 25)

_____

_____

_____

_____

_____

_____

_____

_____

_____

6. Is the Jubilee a way of redistributing wealth from one class of people to another? (Leviticus 25)

_____

_____

_____

_____

_____

_____

_____

_____

_____

Summary

"Ultimately, poverty has no future, except for the ungodly who are dispossessed. Ezekiel's vision of the kingdom's growth throughout the world (symbolized by the gradually rising stream flowing from the temple, Ezekiel 47:1-12) showed the blessings of God affecting virtually everything in life, bringing health and prosperity to the world. Even the salty Dead Sea, symbol of God's curse upon Sodom and Gomorrah, will become fresh — but some few places will be 'left for salt' (v. 8-11), still under the judgment of God. The Bible looks forward to the time when none of God's people will be poor, when by God's gracious providence the land will be distributed to all those who are obedient.

"This will never come about through ungodly acts of expropriation. It will never happen as long as the church continues to heed unbiblical philosophies which seek to turn her away from obedience to God's law. Institutional poverty will never be cured by socialism or statism. Ungodliness can only extend the Curse. The conquest of poverty is not really based on the issue of poverty at all. It is an issue of obedience, of godliness, of submission to the Lord Jesus Christ at all points" (David Chilton, _Productive Christians in an Age of Guilt-Manipulators_, p. 252).

A certain Samaritan, who was on a journey, came upon him; and when he saw him, he felt compassion, and he came to him and bandaged up his wounds, pouring oil and wine on them; and he put him on his own beast, and brought him to an inn, and took care of him (Luke 10:33, 34).

Answers to Questions for Discussion

1. God's word shows very definitely how the poor should be helped. Any attempt to help the poor without detailed application of the biblical laws that deal with poverty will ultimately fail.

a. *Tithes* (Numbers 18:24; Deuteronomy 14:28, 29): The tithe is a way of financing Christian reconstruction. In the Old Testament as in the New there are a variety of uses for the tithe. One of its uses was to provide for the poor. The tithe that was not left for the national Levites (Numbers 18:24) was returned to the local towns to be distributed by local leaders. This was to be done every third year to care for the Levite who had no inheritance, and "the orphan and the widow" (Deuteronomy 14:29). It was the function of the Levites (church leaders) to allocate the tithe. Local ecclesiastical authorities were responsible for the leadership (cf. Deuteronomy 22:15; 25:7). In the New Testament a national priesthood no longer exists (Hebrews 7:11-28; 1 Peter 2:9, 10) so the tithe is to be brought to the *faithful* elders of the local church to have them distribute a portion to those who are truly needy (cf. Acts 4:35; 1 Corinthians 16:2).

b. *Private giving* (Luke 10:30-37; Acts 4:32-37; 11:29): Private giving goes beyond the tithe and usually is reserved for emergencies. When individuals or families see a need among the people of God, it is their duty to try and meet it. When relief was needed for the saints in Judea, the brethren in Antioch met the need (Acts 11:29). The profits from the sale of additional land holdings by some of the more prosperous Christians in Jerusalem were used to meet the temporary needs of the infant church (Acts 4:32-37).

Probably the most well-known example of private giving to meet immediate needs is the story of the Good Samaritan (Luke 10:30-37). When the Samaritan traveller saw a need he immediately responded. Moreover, he did not seek assistance from any governmental agency. Private giving allows the giver the flexibility to help when the need arises. He does not have to go through bureaucratic red tape to accomplish his mission of mercy. Cotton Mather (1663-1728), in his *Essays to Do Good* (1710), "proposed that men and women, acting either as individuals or as members of voluntary associations, should engage in 'a perpetual endeavor to do good in the world' " (Robert H. Bremner, *American Philanthropy*, p. 12).

Cotton Mather (1663-1723), in his *Essays to do Good* (1710), proposed that men and women, acting either as individuals or as members of *voluntary associations, should engage in "a perpetual endeavor to do good in the world."*

c. *Gleaning* (Leviticus 19:9, 10; 23:22; Deuteronomy 23:24, 25; 24:19-21 and Exodus 23:10, 11; Matthew 12:1): The Old Testament gleaning laws are often a neglected set of laws that set standards to care for the poor. They rarely are mentioned today because of their agricultural setting, but contemporary application can be made. The gleaning laws were established for *regular* charity to the poor. The poor were permitted to gather what remained after the harvest: "Now when you reap the harvest of your land, you shall not reap to the very corners of your field, neither shall you gather the gleanings of your harvest. Nor shall you glean your vineyard, nor shall you gather the fallen fruit of your vineyard; you shall leave them for the needy and for the stranger. I am the LORD your God" (Leviticus 19:9, 10; cf. 23:22; Deuteronomy 24:19-21). During the Sabbatical year the land was to receive its rest.

Harvesting was not permitted, but the poor could glean during the Sabbatical year (Exodus 23:10, 11). "A similar law, not dealing with poverty as such, allowed anyone entering a neighbor's field to pick grapes or grain and eat his fill, as long as he did not carry food away from the premises (Deuteronomy 23:24-24; see Matthew 12:1)" (David Chilton, *Productive Christians in an Age of Guilt-Manipulators*, p. 84).

Three additional points need to be considered: *First*, landowners apparently had the right to prohibit some people from gleaning. Probably only the deserving poor were permitted to glean (Ruth 2:4-16); therefore, care for the poor was a local responsibility where landowners knew the condition and character of the poor. *Second*, gleaning was *hard work*. The landowner was not obligated to glean the fields for the poor. Rather, it was the responsibility of the poor to labor for their food. Gleaning was never intended to create a welfare state. Its main purpose was to meet temporary needs. An industrious gleaner might even be hired by the landowner for some future harvest. *Third*, "A point of importance with respect to gleaning is that, in the older form, it was agricultural; modern life is more urban. A significant attempt at urban gleaning began some years ago, the Goodwill Industries. By collecting discarded goods and items, and then repairing and selling them by using unemployed or handicapped persons, an income for many has been provided. The rise of welfarism has limited the growth of urban gleaning, but its potentialities are very real and deserving of greater development" (R.J. Rushdoony, *Institutes of Biblical Law*, p. 249).

Gleaning continues to be practiced across our country in spite of the fact that we no longer are exclusively an agrarian society. John Naisbitt, in a telling analysis of future trends, writes of the resurgence of gleaning: "Americans, especially senior citizens, are helping themselves by salvaging the vast food resources usually wasted in production and harvesting (about 20 percent of all food produced, according to the U.S. Agricultural Department). 'Gleaners' groups in Arizona, California, Michigan, Oregon, and Washington State go into the fields and find food passed over by the harvest, then distribute it to community groups. St. Mary's Food Bank in Phoenix, Arizona, which collects cast-aside and gleaned food, sent 2 million pounds of food to schools and social service groups and fed 48,000 emergency victims for three days during 1979. Now St. Mary's helps other groups all across the country to learn the self-help approach to cutting waste and feeding the poor.

In Portland, Oregon, Tri-County Community Council Food Bank sent 700,000 pounds of salvaged food to eighty social service agencies" (*Megatrends*, p. 153).

d. *Lending* (Exodus 22:25; cf. Leviticus 25:35-37; Deuteronomy 15:1, 2, 9): Lending laws to help the poor should be considered separate from business loans. There seems to be no biblical evidence that interest could not be charged to a fellow believer for a *business* loan (Matthew 25:27), but *charitable* loans were interest-free: "If you lend money to My people, to the poor among you, you are not to act as a creditor to him; you shall not charge him interest" (Exodus 22:25; cf. Leviticus 25:35-37). Moreover, in the seventh year all interest-free loans to the poor had to be cancelled by the lenders if the loan was not repaid: "At the end of every seven years you shall grant a remission of debts. And this is the manner of remission: every creditor shall release what he has loaned to his neighbor; he shall not exact it of his neighbor and his brother, because the LORD'S remission has been proclaimed" (Deuteronomy 15:1, 2).

So then, while we have opportunity, let us do good to all men, and especially to those who are of the household of faith (Galatians 6:10).

Even if the year of release was near, wealthy Israelites were not to withhold charity loans: "Beware, lest there be a base thought in your heart, saying, 'The seventh year, the year of remission is near,' and your eye is hostile toward your poor brother, and you give him nothing; then he may cry to the LORD against you, and it will be a sin in you" (15:9). "If the poor man was unable to repay the loan within the specified time, the creditor was to cross the debt off his books altogether, accepting the loss, strong in the faith that, since all events move in terms of God's law, he would receive God's blessings — not merely the warm feeling that 'virtue is its own reward,' but material, economic blessings" (David Chilton, *Productive Christians in an Age of Guilt-Manipulators*, p. 85).

Interest-free loans that would be cancelled during the seventh year were difficult to secure. Only the poorest of the poor could qualify and only for the barest necessities. The purpose of the loans was not to raise the economic status of the poor; rather, the loans were to insure that the poor individual and his family would have the basics for living — food, shelter, and clothing. The Christian is obligated to lend to those who are in desperate need with no other place to turn. The Christian is not obligated to subsidize the many wants of the poor, nor either voluntarily to redistribute his own wealth or coercively redistribute the wealth of others in order to achieve some undefined level of social and economic equality.

2. a. *Strangers* (Exodus 22:21-24; Numbers 9:14; Leviticus 24:22; Deuteronomy 10:18, 19; Jeremiah 7:3-7; Zechariah 7:9-14): The Bible tells us God loves the stranger: God "shows His love for the alien by giving him food and clothing. So show your love for the alien, for you were aliens in the land of Egypt" (Deuteronomy 10:18, 19). Aliens and strangers (immigrants) are usually without family ties and immediate job opportunities. While the Bible places basic economic responsibilities on families (1 Timothy 5:8), the alien usually cannot rely upon such resources. Christians then become the "family" for these immigrants, supplying their temporary needs.

God's expression of love results in action. True love is following the commandments of God. Jesus said, "If you love Me, you will keep My commandments" (John 14:15). To oppress the stranger will bring divine judgment: "If you afflict him [the stranger] at all, and if he does cry out to Me, I will surely hear his cry; and My anger will be kindled, and I will kill you with

222

the sword; and your wives shall become widows and your children fatherless" (Exodus 22:23, 24). Any nation that fails to care for an immigrant population will become an immigrant nation (cf. Jeremiah 22:3-5). Christians should be reminded that caring for strangers is an opportunity to present the gospel of Jesus Christ, the reality of His law-order, and their resultant blessings, both spiritual and material.

    b. *Widows and Orphans* (Exodus 22:22-24; Deuteronomy 27:19; Isaiah 1:17; Matthew 15:4-6; 1 Timothy 5:3-16; James 1:27): Scripture puts the widow and orphan in the same category with the stranger: "And you shall not wrong a stranger or oppress him . . . . You shall not afflict any widow or orphan," and "cursed is he who distorts the justice due an alien, orphan, and widow. And all the people shall say, 'Amen' " (Exodus 22:21, 22 and Deuteronomy 27:19). The family, as has been pointed out, is the *primary* provider. When, however, there are no family members to provide for the destitute, the church of Jesus Christ must assume the responsibility. The orphan is particularly in need of assistance. Since there are no parents to care for him, every opportunity should be made to find families willing to provide the needed care. If this cannot be done then adoption by a Christian family is a biblical alternative: "Seek justice, reprove the ruthless, defend the orphan, plead for the widow" (Isaiah 1:17).

    The widow often finds herself in a similar position of economic peril due to the death of her husband, most often the sole economic provider. But Paul makes a distinction between widows who can remarry and those "who are widows indeed," those without a family, too old to remarry, and thus unable to receive support from family members (1 Timothy 5:3-16). Paul, however, makes it clear that support for widows is first a family affair if there are family members: "If anyone does not provide for his own, and especially for those of his own household, he has denied the faith, and is worse than an unbeliever" (1 Timothy 5:8). Fathers must begin now to plan for the future of their family in the event of hard economic times, sickness, and an untimely death. This will mean a rigorous savings program, deferred gratification, and a life insurance policy that can supply an income on interest alone.

    Notice how difficult the Bible makes it for the widow to receive outside-the-family aid: A widow is to be placed on the list for aid only if she herself is engaged in charitable service, "having a reputation for good works; and if she has brought up children, if she has shown hospitality to strangers, if she has washed the saints' feet, if she has assisted those in distress, and if she has devoted herself to every good work" (1 Timothy 5:10). If such restrictions are put on widows, who are singled out for special care, then what restrictions should be placed on the able-bodied worker? If an individual will not work, considering that he is able to work, charity should not be given to him (2 Thessalonians 3:10; 1 Thessalonians 4:11).

If anyone does not provide for his own, and especially for those of his own household, he has denied the faith, and is worse than an unbeliever (1 Timothy 5:8).

3. A distinction must be made between covetousness and envy. *Covetousness* means to desire the possessions and privileges of others. Its effect upon an individual can lead him to theft or inactivity. *Envy*, however, is much more destructive: "Envy is the feeling that someone else's having something is to blame for the fact that you do not have it. The principal motive is thus not so much to *take*, but to *destroy*. The envier acts against the object of his envy, not to benefit himself, but to cut the other person down to his own level — or below" (David Chilton, *Productive Christians in an Age of Guilt-Manipulators*, p. 158).

Instead of attempting to follow godly patterns of prosperity as outlined in Scripture, the envious individual seeks to destroy the resources of the productive: "Now Isaac sowed in that land, and reaped in the same year a hundredfold. And the LORD blessed him, and the man became rich, and continued to grow richer until he became very wealthy; for he had possessions of flocks and herds and a great household, so that the Philistines envied him. Now all the wells of which his father's servants had dug in the days of Abraham his father, the Philistines stopped up by filling them with earth" (Genesis 26:12-15). Instead of learning what made Isaac wealthy, the Philistines *envied* his position of wealth and sought to *destroy* it. The envier says, "If I can't have what he has, then he can't have it either!"

Envy is with us today. The following story depicts the destructive nature of envy: "A missionary doctor of nearly half a century's experience in the Near East told a revealing story. When he returned on one occasion from home leave in the United States he brought back with him some Golden Bantam seed corn, which he gave to a friend of his, a Moslem farmer in a small village. When the doctor saw his friend several months later he asked him how the corn was doing. Then the farmer had to confess: You see, I didn't plant the corn, because if I did my neighbors would pull it up. If I gave some of the seed to my neighbors, the other villagers would destroy it. If the whole village were given seed for a new crop, the next village would burn the new-fangled and superior crop. And so I thought it best not to plant it at all, and thus avoid trouble" (Helmut Schoeck, "The Envy Barrier," in *Foreign Aid Reexamined*, p. 90).

Socialism and Communism work on the principle of envy. The rich are blamed for the plight of the poor. In order to remedy the situation the wealth of the rich is confiscated and divided among the masses. The long-term effects are non-productive workers, discouragement to work beyond job description requirements, lack of thrift and wise investment, social and economic non-cooperation, increased "class" hostility, crimes of envy, and hostility against those of superior ability, socio-economic status, and education: "A sound heart is the life of the flesh: but envy the rottenness of the bones" (Proverbs 14:30, KJV). The question remains, "When the wealth has been redistributed and invariably destroyed, who will then care for the new poor?"

4. *First,* the poor must understand that being wealthy is not evil in itself. God gives His people the "power to make wealth" (Deuteronomy 8:18; cf. Genesis 26:12, 13). The poor must never seek to blame others for their condition unless theft and corruption have placed them in such a position (cf. Amos 8:4-6).

Second, the poor must be evangelized like every other segment of society. No individual can fully understand the implications of the word of God on family life, work, the elimination of debt, responsibility, thrift, and savings without a new mind.

Third, the poor must be instructed in what the Bible says about diligent work. The Bible tells us we are to labor "six days" (Exodus 20:9-11). The lazy man or woman will be overcome by more productive people: "I passed by the field of the sluggard, and by the vineyard of the man lacking sense; and behold, it was completely overgrown with thistles, its surface was covered with nettles, and its stone wall was broken down. When I saw, I reflected upon it; I looked, and received instruction. 'A little sleep, a little slumber, a little folding of the hands to rest,' Then your poverty will come as a robber, and your want like an armed man" (Proverbs 24:30-34).

Fourth, Scripture instructs us that "each one shall bear his own load" (Galatians 6:5). Every individual must realize he is responsible for his own actions. The poor should only consider charitable gifts as a way of relieving a temporary burden (cf. Galatians 6:2).

Fifth, God promises that "the wealth of the sinner is stored up for the righteous" (Proverbs 13:22). The Bible tells us not to envy the wicked even though it seems they are favored by God (Proverbs 23:17; 24:19 Psalm 37; Psalm 73:3-9). Godly living is a prerequisite for the abolition of poverty.

Sixth, Scripture tells us we must be content with what we have and not covet what we do not have: "And if we have food and covering, with these we shall be content" (1 Timothy 6:8). This does not mean the poor should not work hard to secure for themselves the material blessings of God. Rather, the content person can be thankful in his present condition while at the same time trying to better his spiritual and material position.

Seventh, the poor must be made aware that in a godly society in which godly economic principles are followed by individuals and civil governments, the blessings of God in the form of Christian economic liberty will allow for both the best possible provision for the poor and the greatest probability of advancement for oneself and one's children. The basically free traditional American economy, which remained basically (but not perfectly) free as long as America retained a fundamental allegiance to Christian principles and the authority of God's word, provides the greatest modern example of this truth. The countless millions of immigrants to these shores and their descendants who have achieved increased material well-being by diligent work in our economy are proof that a free economy based upon the absolutes of God's word bring about great economic productivity.

The Jubilee Principle

5. The nation of Israel operated in seven-year cycles. At the end of each cycle the land was to receive rest and debts were to be cancelled. At the end of seven cycles of seven years (49 years), the 50th year became the year of Jubilee. The most significant aspect of the Jubilee was that all lands sold during the previous fifty years must be restored to the original owners. Debts may have forced landowners to lease their land during some period of the forty nine years, but when the Jubilee year arrived the property had to return to its original owner. Was this God's plan of "wealth redistribution"? Should the Jubilee concept be a model for present-day welfare reform?

The laws pertaining to the Jubilee year were tied to the land and people of Israel. (God by divine decree made Israel the original owners and dispossessed the Canaanites, Hivites, Jebusites, Hittites, etc.). *Since the people of God (the church) now include Gentiles and the land now includes the world* (Matthew 28:19; Acts 1:8), *there is no way that the Jubilee laws can be made to apply today.* Moreover, the Jubilee was designed to be temporary because of the fulfillment it was to have in the work of Jesus Christ. Like many of the laws of the Old Testament the Jubilee laws were *typological*. The fulfillment of the Jubilee is to possess Jesus Christ. The promise of the land was originally given to Abraham: "For all the land which you see, I will give it to you and to your descendants [seed] forever" (Genesis 13:15; cf. 17:8). Paul applies this land promise to Jesus Christ: "Now the promises were spoken to Abraham and to his seed. He does not say, 'AND TO SEEDS,' as referring to many, but rather to one, 'AND TO YOUR SEED,' that is, Christ" (Galatians 3:16). Therefore, those who are Christ's receive the promises made to Abraham: "And if you belong to Christ, then you are Abraham's offspring, heirs according to the promise" (3:29). The promise was "for an everlasting possession" where Jehovah "will be their God" (Genesis 17:8).

The perpetual possession of the original inheritance signified the relationship a believer has with Jesus Christ; therefore, to possess the land was to possess Jesus Christ. "In terms of this, the Jubilee required that the land could not be permanently alienated from godly heirs. This was a symbol that God would never leave or forsake His people — that, by His grace, His people would remain in the land, instead of getting kicked out as Adam and Eve were, and as were the previous heathen inhabitants of the land, who were spewed out of the earth (Leviticus 18:24:29)" (David Chilton, *Productive Christians in an Age of Guilt-Manipulators*, p. 173). Jesus points to the typological nature of the Jubilee principle when He applies its fulfillment to His sacrificial work: "THE SPIRIT OF THE LORD IS UPON ME, BECAUSE HE ANOINTED ME TO PREACH THE GOSPEL TO THE POOR. HE HAS SENT ME TO PROCLAIM RELEASE TO THE CAPTIVES, AND RECOVERY OF SIGHT TO THE BLIND, TO SET FREE THOSE WHO ARE DOWNTRODDEN, TO PROCLAIM THE FAVORABLE YEAR OF THE LORD . . . Today this scripture has been fulfilled in your hearing" (Luke 4:18, 19, 21; cf. Isaiah 61:1, 2). True liberty and security can only come through the atonement of Jesus Christ (see Leviticus 25:9).

6. Those who contend that the Jubilee laws were a way of wealth redistribution in order to create economic equality have not considered the following: *First*, the reason an individual had to sell his land during those years probably was due to his ineffective use of the land. In order to get out of debt he had to lease his land to another more productive land user. While the land may have returned during the Jubilee year, this was no guarantee the original owner could or would make it produce after its return.

Second, the individual leasing land from the debtor would, in fact, be able to plant and sell the produce of the land up to the time of the Jubilee. While the land had to revert back to the original owner at Jubilee time, the profits from the years of the lease still remained with the man leasing the land.

Third, the land laws were inheritance laws. There was no indiscriminant redistribution. During the Jubilee the land returned to the *family* of the original owner. There was no provision to divide up the land among those who were in need of additional wealth.

Fourth, immigrants, usually the poorest class of people, did not benefit by the Jubilee and their interest-bearing debts were not cancelled. Only the Israelite was affected by the land laws during the Jubilee year.

Fifth, non-Israelites (nations surrounding Israel) could not participate in the Jubilee celebration and benefit from the year of release. "The Jubilee, for a limited time and in a limited area, called for *restoration* not 'redistribution' or 'equalization' — of specified, non-income producing, ancestral lands to deserving heirs [cf. Proverbs 13:22; 17:2; Revelation 21:7]. It cannot be applied outside Israel. It cannot be applied after the resurrection of Christ. And it cannot legitimately be used as a smokescreen for socialism" (David Chilton, *Productive Christians in an Age of Guilt-Manipulators*, p. 175).

Sixth, only lands *outside* walled cities were included in the Jubilee restoration. Homes, tools, boats, and family possessions, including monetary assets, were not transferred. "Sold property within walled cities could be redeemed within a year. After the passage of a year, the exchange was regarded as permanent and immune to the changes otherwise affected by the Jubilee (Lev. 25:29-30)" (Ronald Nash, *Social Justice and the Christian Church*, p. 78).

While the Bible places basic economic responsibilities on families (1 Timothy 5:8), the alien usually cannot rely upon such resources. Christians then become the *family* for these immigrants, supplying their temporary needs.

Books for Further Reading and Study

The purpose of the *God and Government* workbook series is to give Christians an overview of what the Bible says about government, particularly civil government. *God and Government: Issues in Biblical Perspective*, the second volume in the three-volume series, was not designed to answer all the questions raised regarding the development of a biblical world view, exercising dominion under God, or developing an economic system consistent with the Word of God. In order to take the student further in his or her study, a list of books and newsletters has been provided covering a variety of topics relating to this study. A number of these books are out of print. I have included a list of out-of-print book services that can assist you in locating them for your library.

I. Developing a Biblical World View

Blamires, Harry. *The Christian Mind*. Ann Arbor, MI: Servant Books, (1963) 1980. Blamires develops the thesis that Christians have surrendered their minds to secular explanations of reality. In addition, he examines the presuppositions that are needed to develop a Christian mind. The author's conclusion is that there will be an inevitable collision between the Christian mind and the secular mind.

Clark, Gordon H. *A Christian View of Men and Things*. Grand Rapids, MI: Eerdmans, 1952. The author responds to a variety of naturalistic philosophies by developing a Christian view of man and his world: history, politics, ethics, science, religion, and epistemology are considered.

DeMar, Gary. *Surviving College Successfully: A Complete Manual for the Rigors of Academic Combat*. Brentwood, TN: Wolgemuth & Hyatt, 1988. This book serves a number of purposes not solely related to a college education. While Part II deals with study skills, Part I explains the essential elements that make up a person's world view. In addition, the Christian world view is contrasted with the rationalistic and materialistic world view that drives much of our society.

Geisler, Norman L. and William D. Watkins. *Worlds Apart: A Handbook on World Views*, 2nd ed. Grand Rapids, MI: Baker Book House, (1984) 1989. This helpful book is a compendium and Christian analysis of a number of major world views that are now circulating in our culture. The authors introduce the meaning and function of a world view and then explore seven major world views of our day — theism, atheism, pantheism, panentheism, deism, finite godism, and polytheism.

Hoffecker, W. Andrew, ed. *Building a Christian World View*, Vol. 1, *God, Man, and Knowledge*. Phillipsburg, NJ: Presbyterian and Reformed, 1986. Traces the main currents of the biblical and classical world views and the attempts at synthesis. In the second part, the authors develop a Christian theory of knowledge and compare it with rationalism, empiricism, positivism, existentialism, and pragmatism.

_____. *Building a Christian World View*, Vol. 2, *The Universe, Society, and Ethics*. Phillipsburg, NJ: Presbyterian and Reformed, 1988. In this sequel to the first volume in *Building a Christian Worldview*, the authors show what happens when world views are implemented at the personal and societal levels.

Holmes, Arthur F. *Contours of a World View*. Grand Rapids, MI: Eerdmans, 1983. "Holmes discusses the nature of world views, both secular and Christian, and the overall contours of a distinctively Christian world view in relationship to the history of ideas as well as to the contemporary mind, outlining a Christian view of things as a live alternative to the naturalistic humanism prevalent today." This book is not for the beginner, nor will it satisfy those who want practical ways to develop and implement a biblical world view.

North, Gary, ed. *Foundations of Christian Scholarship*. Vallecito, CA: Ross House Books, 1976. Beginning with the presupposition that the Bible is the word of God, inerrant and infallible, the authors present a biblical perspective on psychology, history, economics, education, political science, sociology, mathematics, apologetics, philosophy, and theology.

North, Gary, ed. *The Biblical Blueprint Series*, 10 vols. (Ft. Worth, TX: Dominion Press, 1987). These ten books set forth a basic understanding of a biblical world view. They include such topics as government, poverty, economics, education, family, and political action.

Schaeffer, Francis. *The Works of Francis Schaeffer*. Westchester, IL: Crossway Books, 1982. A newly-revised and formatted edition of all 22 books written by Francis Schaeffer (except his booklet on baptism published in 1973). This fine series attempts to develop the needed theological and philosophical framework that goes into the construction of a Christian world view.

Schlossberg, Herbert and Marvin Olasky. *Turning Point: A Christian Worldview Declaration*. Westchester, IL: Crossway books, 1987. A good introductory volume on world view concerns. Examines basic world view components and shows how they have been worked out in history. While there seems to be a revival of world view issues, this short volume shows that the church has a long history of world view activism.

Sire, James. *How to Read Slowly*. Downers Grove, IL: InterVarsity Press, 1978. This is a sequel to *The Universe Next Door*. When a Christian reads fiction, nonfiction, poetry, history, and background material for any subject he should be aware of what lies behind what an author writes. By reading "slowly" (reflectively) the reader can best understand the world view of an author. A very good book for high school and college students.

_____. *The Universe Next Door*. Downers Grove, IL: InterVarsity Press, (1977) 1988. A catalog of world views. Develops the basic presuppositions that make up the Christian world view and then evaluates non-Christian ideologies: deism, naturalism, nihilism, existentialism, eastern pantheistic monism, and the New Age movement. In this updated and expanded edition, you will also find an analysis of Marxism, a world view (actually an outgrowth of naturalism) that has had a major impact around the world but is no in the throes of disintegration.

Van Til, Henry. *The Calvinistic Concept of Culture*. Grand Rapids, MI: Baker Book House, 1959. Explains the relationship between Christians and their culture from a calvinistic (Reformed) perspective. Develops a concept of culture where every aspect of the Christian's life must be evaluated in terms of the biblical faith. Van Til's thesis is that "culture is religion externalized," therefore, we can determine a nation's religion by studying its culture.

II. Humanism

Blamires, Harry. *The Secularist Heresy*. Ann Arbor, MI: Servant Books, (1956) 1980. This book is a re-issue of *The Faith and Modern Error*, first published in 1956. Because the book spans previous decades when the signs of secularism were making a frontal attack on all Christian institutions, the reader is confronted with the truism that ideas have consequences. Blamires reminds us that when we attempt to do battle with the onslaught of humanism that we must not "forget to be Christian."

Geisler, Normal L. *Is Man the Measure?* Grand Rapids, MI: Baker Book House, 1983. Geisler shows that humanism wears many masks. If we are going to be able to confront the effects of humanism we must be aware of its many types: evolutionary, behavioral, existential, pragmatic, Marxist, egocentric, and cultural. While this book contains many helpful insights there is one significant flaw. In the chapter, "The Helpful Emphases of Secular Humanism," the author fails to see humanism's subtle subversion of Christianity.

Guinness, Os. *The Dust of Death*. Downers Grove, IL: InterVarsity Press, 1973. A brilliant exposition of contemporary humanism and its roots. Guinness shows that a rejection of Christianity leads to despair and the rise of counter cultures that have no future. Must reading for every thinking Christian.

Hitchcock, James. *What is Secular Humanism?* Ann Arbor, MI: Servant Books, 1982. This book probes the origins of humanism, "its momentum through history, its present impact on Western civilization, and its probable future course." Hitchcock's remedy for the steady "secularization" of man is to remind him that all of life must be evaluated from God's perspective and that man is ultimately dependent upon God for all things.

Schlossberg, Herbert. *Idols for Destruction.* Nashville, TN: Thomas Nelson Publishers, 1983. The author asserts that humanism is nothing more than sophisticated idol worship. The idols of history, humanity, mammon, nature, power, and religion are scrutinized in exacting detail. "Idolatry in its larger meaning is properly understood as any substitution of what is created for the creator. People may worship nature, money, mankind, power, history, or social and political systems instead of the God who created them all."

III. Dominion and Ownership

DeMar, Gary and Peter J. Leithart. *The Reduction of Christianity: A Biblical Response to Dave Hunt* (Atlanta, GA: American Vision, 1988). A great deal of controversy has been generated over the issue of "dominion." This book is a comprehensive answer to critics who denounce the very concept of dominion. *Reduction* also includes a biblical and historical study of the kingdom. New Age humanism is also evaluated. Includes a comprehensive annotated bibliography.

Lee, Francis Nigel. *The Central Significance of Culture.* Nutley, NJ: Presbyterian and Reformed, 1976. The author analyzes the Christian's comprehensive responsibility under God to cultivate the world over which God has made us stewards. Religion and culture are inextricably bound together. For the Christian, to function in the area of culture or society is only the outworking of his religious duty under God.

Robertson, Pat. *The Secret Kingdom.* Nashville, TN: Thomas Nelson Publishers, 1982. A popularly written book dealing with the "laws of the kingdom." Robertson maintains that the heart of Jesus' work is the kingdom of God; therefore, Christians are living in the midst of the kingdom and under the lordship of King Jesus. Kingdom living expresses itself in the Christian taking dominion in every area of life.

Rushdoony, Rousas J. *The Institutes of Biblical Law.* Nutley, NJ: The Craig Press, 1972. "The *Institutes* is a detailed study of the Ten Commandments, with the other laws of the Bible catalogued under one or more of the Ten Commandments." Christians must know what to do when the command to have dominion is followed. The law of God is the "blueprint" for our dominion task.

_____. *Law and Society.* Vallecito, CA: Ross House Books, 1982. The purpose of *Law and Society,* the second of a projected three volume set, is to show how God's law applies to every aspect of our lives and world. God's Word describes consequences, curses and blessings, for disobedience and obedience. We cannot understand history apart from this fact.

_____. *Politics of Guilt and Pity.* Fairfax, VA: Thoburn Press, (1970) 1978. Rushdoony explains that psychosomatic sickness, gambling, alcoholism, drug addiction, the wave of do-good-ism, and the condoning of crimes and lawlessness can be attributed to sinful man's attempt to justify himself through self-atonement. Too often the state is looked upon as the "savior" for mankind. When this happens dominion is then transferred from the many institutions to the one state. The chapters on "The Purposes of Law," "The Meaning of Justice," "Liberty and Property," "The Priestly State," "The Royal State," "Eminent Domain," and the "Biblical Doctrine of Government" are especially helpful.

IV. Economics

It is not possible to include all the books that relate to economics. The following list contains books that are decidedly Christian in their perspective. Each author attempts to build an economic system based upon the principles found in the Bible. Some are more successful than others. There are, however, a number of good books not written from a biblical perspective that are very sound. These are not include. A number of the books listed below contain bibliographies that will prove helpful.

Beisner, Calvin E. *Prosperity and Poverty: The Compassionate Use of Resources in a World of Scarcity.* Westchester, IL: Crossway Books, 1988. Discusses a wide range of topics: stewardship, justice, the relationship of civil government and the economic sphere, and the nature and causes of poverty. A very helpful book.

Chilton, David. *Productive Christians in an Age of Guilt-Manipulators.* Tyler, TX: Institute for Christian Economics, 1981 (third edition, revised, July 1982). A biblical treatment of the so-called "Christian Socialism" movement espoused by a number of prominent Christians. Chilton's thesis is that the Bible presents a "blueprint" for helping the poor — personal charity rather than economic policies that concentrate power in the state. Cultures are "package deals." Every aspect of a culture must be transformed before long-term prosperity can be realized. This transformation must begin with the change of a culture's religion. This edition includes a response to Ronald Sider's revised *Rich Christians in an Age of Hunger.* An extensive bibliography is included.

Clouse, Robert G., ed. *Wealth and Poverty: Four Christian Views of Economics*. Downers Grove, IL: InterVarsity Press, 1984. Since three of the authors claim that there is no economic system which is inherently Christian in nature, the title of this book is somewhat misleading. Each author presents his position while the other authors respond. This volume shows how much secular thinking has become a part of Christian scholarship and social criticism.

Davis, John Jefferson. *Your Wealth in God's World: Does the Bible Support the Free Market?* Phillipsburg, NJ: Presbyterian and Reformed, 1984. A helpful primer on economic theory and practice using the Bible as the standard. Beginning with a biblical view of creation, work, and individual creativity, the author shows clearly that a free enterprise system is rooted in the principles of Scripture and backed by the lessons of history.

Grant, George. *Bringing in the Sheaves: Transforming Poverty into Productivity*. Brentwood, TN: Wolgemuth & Hyatt, (1985) 1988. What is the best way to help the poor? Increased government programs have done little to relieve the poor, and in actuality, poverty has increased since the Great Society programs of the 1960s. Condemning the State's policies is not enough, however. There must be biblical and workable solutions. This books outlines a program for change that is both workable and just.

_____. *The Dispossessed: Homelessness in America*. Westchester, IL: Crossway Books, 1986. Following his line of arguments that he made in *Bringing in the Sheaves*, George Grant offers solutions to the homeless problem in America. Homelessness has its causes, the Bible sets forth a cure.

Hodge, Ian. *Baptized Inflation: A Critique of "Christian" Keynesianism*. Tyler, TX: Institute for Christian Economics, 1986. John Maynard Keynes' economic influence has been felt in our nation's social policies since the mid-1930s. Their failed results were reduced to rubble by the mid-1960s. But old tales die hard. While the secular world finally rejected Keynes, a number of Christians picked up the broken pieces in an attempt to develop a "Christian" economic theory. Hodge dismantles Keynes and his disciples.

Nash, Ronald H. *Social Justice and the Christian Church*. Milford, MI: Mott Media, 1983. There is a deep concern among Christians today to help the poor. But what method should be followed? Many who seek to help with greater government intervention may in fact subject the poor to greater poverty. The author addresses his subject by dealing with the usually undefined term "justice" and its relationship to poverty. Contrary economic ideologies are also evaluated.

_____. *Poverty and Wealth: The Christian Debate over Capitalism*. Westchester, IL: Crossway Books, 1986. A readable summary of economic concepts comparing free market economics with a planned state-driven economy. Dr. Nash interacts with a number of Bible texts that socialist theorists use to justify their radical economic ideology.

North, Gary. *The Dominion Covenant: Genesis*. Tyler, TX: Institute for Christian Economics, (1981) 1987. The first volume in a multi-volume study of the Bible from an economic point of view. North confronts the religious presuppositions used in the construction of economic theories. He maintains the only workable and lasting economic system is biblical economics. An up-to-date bibliography is included. Additional volumes in the series include (at this date) three volumes on Exodus: *Moses and Pharaoh*, *The Sinai Strategy*, and *Tools of Dominion*.

_____. *An Introduction to Christian Economics*. Nutley, NJ: The Craig Press, 1973. A series of articles dealing with contemporary economic issues. A handy short-course in economics for those unfamiliar with economic theory or who had economic courses in college and came away believing economics is a dry subject. A very helpful bibliography of older economic works is included.

_____. ed. *Journal of Christian Reconstruction*. Symposium on Economics, Vol. II, No. I, Summer, 1975 and Symposium on Inflation, Vol. VIII, No. 1, Summer 1980 (Chalcedon, P.O. Box 158, Vallecito, CA 95251). Two very helpful volumes that deal with the basics of economic principles and the problems relating to governmental policies that lead to inflation.

_____. *Puritan Economic Experiments*. Tyler, TX: Institute for Christian Economics, 1989. A brief study of the failure of Puritan economics relating to common ownership, price controls, and sumptuary legislation. Dr. North's conclusion is forceful: Any attempt to add to the laws relating to economic principles as outlined in Scripture will meet with failure, no matter how good the intentions.

Richardson, John R. *Christian Economics: The Christian Message to the Market Place*. Houston, TX: St. Thomas Press, 1966. A very readable and practical guide to economic questions. Uses the law of God as a basis for demolishing the specious arguments of collectivism in its many forms.

Rose, Tom. *Economics: The American Economy from a Christian Perspective*. Mercer, PA: American Enterprise Publications, 1985. Roses' first volume, *Economics: Principles and Policy from a Christian Perspective* (see below), deals primarily with microeconomic topics, while this volume deals primarily with macroeconomics, although it is virtually impossible to separate the two.

_____. *Economics: Principles and Policy From a Christian Perspective*. Milford, MI: Mott Media, 1977. Presents the biblical rationale for economics. The book is written in textbook format, so it is easily adaptable to Christian schools, Sunday School classes, and personal study. A teacher's guide is also available.

Rushdoony, Rousas, John. *The Roots of Inflation*. Vallecito, CA: Ross House Books, 1982. This book maintains that "inflation is only in part an economic problem. It is at heart a religious and moral problem." Rushdoony encourages us to return to Scripture as our sure guide in all matters, including monetary policy.

Taylor, E. L. Hebden. *Economics, Money, and Banking*. Nutley, NJ: The Craig Press, 1978. Dr. Taylor follows six general principles of biblical economics: scarcity of materials, hard and honest work, faithful stewardship, honest money, the duty of compassion, and a limited state.

V. The Tithe

Kendall, R.T. *Tithing: A Call to Serious, Biblical Giving*. Grand Rapids, MI: Zondervan Publishing House, 1983. Kendall believes that Christians are commanded to tithe. "If every Christian would tithe the church would begin to make an impact on the world that could change it. The church instead is paralyzed." A section is included where the author responds to twenty objections to tithing.

Landsdell, Henry. *The Tithe in Scripture*. Grand Rapids, MI: Baker Book House, (1908) 1963. This reprint is an abridgment of the author's larger work, *The Sacred Tenth*. Landsdell presents the history of the tithe from Cain and Abel to the Apostle Paul's teaching and personal example. The author concludes that the tithe is a divine mandate for our day.

Jordan, James B. "Thesis on Tithing," in *The Law and the Covenant*. Tyler, TX: Institute for Christian Economics, 1985. A series of numbered propositions dealing with the tithe.

VI. The Myth of Neutrality

Jordan, James B., ed. *Christianity and Civilization: Failure of the American Baptist Culture*. Tyler TX: Geneva Divinity School, 1982. The authors maintain that any attempt to accommodate the Christian faith to prevailing ideologies to gain an audience by the humanists is doomed to fail. Since there is no neutrality, it is necessary to confront the issues on the basis of religious presuppositions.

Morey, Robert A. *A Christian Handbook for Defending the Faith*. Phillipsburg, NJ: Presbyterian and Reformed 1979. An introduction to the basics of defending the faith simple enough for high school and college students to understand. Familiarity with philosophical terminology is not needed. Dr. Morey begins his methodology with an analysis of the basic presuppositions that give meaning to differing world views.

Pratt, Richard L. *Every Thought Captive: A Study Manual for the Defense of Christian Truth*. Phillipsburg, NJ: Presbyterian and Reformed, 1979. A training manual of Christian apologetics written for the high school student, but profound enough so all can benefit. Teaches the Christian how he can deal adequately with the questions of unbelievers from the position of the adequacy of Christian theism and not from some ineffective neutral starting point.

Rushdoony, Rousas J. *The Mythology of Science*. Nutley, NJ: The Craig Press, 1967. Using science as the basis for this work, Rushdoony shows the impossibility of neutrality. Facts, scientific or otherwise, are not neutral. Interpretation of the facts rest on certain "religious" presuppositions. The chapter "Paradigms and Facts" is especially helpful.

_____. *The Word of Flux*. Fairfax, VA: Thoburn Press, 1975. This book deals with the question of how we know. Is man the interpreter of all reality or is man's knowledge dependent upon God's independent and comprehensive knowledge of all things?

_____. *Infallibility: An Inescapable Concept*. Vallecito, CA: Ross House Books, 1978. This small book establishes the case that every system of thought claims for itself infallibility. The Christian as well as the humanist looks to an absolute standard of authority.

Schaeffer, Franky. *A Time for Anger: The Myth of Neutrality*. Westchester, IL: Crossway Books, 1982. Schaeffer analyzes secular world views and how their presuppositions color the interpretation of the facts. The author "shows how our supposedly neutral society ridicules, ignores and rejects the Christian point of view about morality, truth, science and almost every other area of life."

Van Til, Cornelius. *The Defense of the Faith*. Philadelphia, PA: Presbyterian and Reformed, 1963. Dr. Van Til shows that the only way to confront the unbeliever is to attack the underlying presuppositions that support his system. Any attempt to be "neutral" immediately defeats the Christian's defense.

The three-volume GOD AND GOVERNMENT series is just one of the many superb Christian educational products available from American Vision.

American Vision is a non-profit Christian educational organization that is a unique presence in today's Christian culture. American Vision believes and proclaims the message that God's Word is the standard for all of life. The Bible is the ultimate authority for questions concerning government, law, business, economics, family, ethics, the arts, science, and every other area of life.

American Vision presents its message through books, audio and video tapes, seminars, radio and television media, a monthly magazine, and personal presentations.

Products that complement this series are:
    America's Christian History: The Untold Story by Gary DeMar: $8.95*
    America's Christian History: The Untold Story, the award-winning audio drama: $6.95*
    Biblical Worldview monthly magazine: one-year subscription for a purchase of any American Vision product or a donation of any amount ($20/year suggested donation). Please call for a free sample.

* please add 12% postage and handling with orders.

To order any of these fine products, or to find out more about the work of American Vision, contact:

American Vision
10 Perimeter Way, Suite B-175
Atlanta, GA 30339
(404) 988-0555

Telephone orders: 1-800-628-9460. We accept either Visa or MasterCard.

Bibliography

Alexander, Archibald. *Evidences of the Authenticity, Inspiration and Canonical Authority of the Holy Scriptures.* Philadelphia, PA: Presbyterian Board of Publication, 1836.

Alexander, J. A. *A Commentary on the Acts of the Apostles.* Carlisle, PA: The Banner of Truth Trust, (1857) 1980.

Bavinck, Herman. *The Doctrine of God,* trans. William Hendriksen. Carlisle, PA: The Banner of Truth Trust, (1951) 1977.

Bremner, Robert H. *American Philanthropy.* Chicago, IL: The University of Chicago Press, (1960) 1982.

Bruce, Robert V. *Alexander Graham Bell and the Conquest of Solitude.* Boston, MA: Little Brown and Company, 1973.

Calvin, John. *Commentary on a Harmony of the Evangelists, Matthew, Mark, and Luke,* Vol 3. Grand Rapids, MI: Baker Book House, reprinted 1990.

_____. *Institutes of the Christian Religion.* John T. McNeill, ed. Philadelphia, PA: Westminster Press, 1960.

Combs, Harry. *Kill Devil Hill.* Boston, MA: Houghton Mifflin Company, 1979.

DeJong, Norman. *Christianity and Democracy.* Nutley, NJ: The Craig Press, 1978.

Harper, Norman E. *Making Disciples.* Memphis, TN: Christian Studies Center, 1981.

Hendriksen, William. *New Testament Commentary: Exposition of the Gospel of Luke.* Grand Rapids, MI: Baker Book House, 1979.

Hodge, Archibald A. *Evangelical Theology.* Carlisle, PA: The Banner of Truth Trust, (1873) 1977.

Hodge, Charles. *A Commentary on 1 and 2 Corinthians.* Carlisle, PA: The Banner of Truth Trust, (1857, 1859) 1974.

Holt, Rackham. *George Washington Carver: An American Biography.* Garden City, NY: Doubleday, Doran and Company, Inc., 1943.

Humanist Manifesto I and II. Buffalo, NY: Prometheus Books, 1973.

McWhorter, Thomas O. *Res Publica.* Nutley, NJ: The Craig Press, 1966.

Moore, Thomas V. *A Commentary on Zechariah.* London, England: The Banner of Truth Trust, [1856] 1968.

Murray, John. *The Sovereignty of God.* Philadelphia, PA: Great Commission Publications [1943] 1977.

Naisbitt, John. *Megatrends.* New York, NY: Warner Books, 1982.

North, Gary. *Government by Emergency.* Ft. Worth, TX: American Bureau of Economic Research, 1983.

_____. *Unconditional Surrender.* Tyler, TX: Geneva Press, 1981.

Norton, Thomas James. *The Constitution of the United States its Sources and its Applications.* New York, NY: The World Publishing Co., 1941.

Pink, Arthur W. *The Sovereignty of God.* London: The Banner of Truth Trust, [1928] 1968.

Pit, Jan. *Persecution: It Will Never Happen Here?* Orange, CA: Open Doors with Brother Andrew International, 1981.

Rand, Howard R. *Digest of the Divine Law.* Merrimac, MA: Destiny Publishers, 1943.

Rice, N.L. "The Moral Effects of Christianity." *Lectures on the Evidences of Christianity.* ed. William S. Plumer. New York, NY: Robert Carter Brothers, 1852.

Rose, Thomas G. and Robert M. Metcalf. *The Coming Victory.* Memphis, TN: Christian Studies Center, 1980.

Rushdoony, Rousas John. *Law and Liberty.* Fairfax, VA: Thoburn Press, 1971.

_____. *The Nature of the American System.* Fairfax, VA: Thoburn Press, [1965] 1978.

_____. *The Philosophy of the Christian School Curriculum.* Vallecito, CA: Ross House Books, 1981.

_____. *Revolt Against Maturity.* Fairfax, VA: Thoburn Press 1977.

Ryle, John Charles. *The Upper Room.* London, England: The Banner of Truth Trust, [1888] 1970.

Saunders, John. "Christian Based Communications," *The Journal of Christian Reconstruction,* ed. Douglas Kelly. Vallecito, CA: Chalcedon, Vol. X, No. 1, 1983.

Schaeffer, Francis. "The Secular Humanist World View Versus the Christian World View and Biblical Perspectives on Military Preparedness," in *Who Is For Peace?* Nashville, TN: Thomas Nelson, 1983.

Schoeck, Helmut. "The Envy Barrier," *Foreign Aid Reexamined.* ed. James W. Wiggins and Helmut Schoeck. Washington, DC: Public Affairs Press, 1958.

Sproul, R. C. *In Search of Dignity.* Ventura, CA: Regal Books, 1983.

Singer, C. Gregg. *From Rationalism to Irrationality.* Phillipsburg, NJ: Presbyterian and Reformed, 1979.

Sowell, Thomas. *Knowledge and Decisions.* New York, NY: Basic Books, 1979.

Tenney, Merrill C. *New Testament Times.* Grand Rapids MI: Eerdmans, 1965.

Whitehead, John W. *The New Tyranny.* Ft. Lauderdale, FL: Coral Ridge Presbyterian Church, 1982.

Willis, John T. "Old Testament Foundations of Social Justice," *Christian Social Issues,* ed. Perry C. Cothan. Grand Rapids, MI: Baker Book House, 1979.

Picture Credits

Lesson 2

Lesson 3

Lesson 4

Lesson 10

Answers to Questions for Discussion

Lesson _____   Question _____

_____
_____
_____
_____
_____
_____
_____
_____
_____
_____
_____
_____
_____
_____
_____
_____
_____
_____
_____
_____
_____
_____
_____
_____
_____
_____
_____
_____
_____

Answers to Questions for Discussion

Lesson _____ Question _____

_____

_____

_____

_____

_____

_____

_____

_____

_____

_____

_____

_____

_____

_____

_____

_____

_____

_____

_____

_____

_____

_____

_____

_____

_____

_____

_____

_____

Answers to Questions for Discussion

Lesson _____   Question _____

_____

_____

_____

_____

_____

_____

_____

_____

_____

_____

_____

_____

_____

_____

_____

_____

_____

_____

_____

_____

_____

_____

_____

_____

_____

_____

_____

_____

_____

_____

_____

Answers to Questions for Discussion

Lesson _____   Question _____

_____

_____

_____

_____

_____

_____

_____

_____

_____

_____

_____

_____

_____

_____

_____

_____

_____

_____

_____

_____

_____

_____

_____

_____

_____

_____

_____

_____

_____

_____

_____

_____

_____

Notes

Notes

Notes